Index Fund Management

"This is a wonderfully accessible and relevant book. Whether you are coming to the subject for the first time or wanting an update on the latest thinking, Fadi's book will educate and entertain. His understanding of the importance of human behaviour alongside financial theory is refreshing."
—Sarah Aitken, *Head of Distribution EMEA, Member of LGIM's Executive Team*

"Comprehensive, insightful and immediately useful for investors! Fadi brings an enormous wealth of knowledge and experience on both theory and practice to the reader in an easy, accessible style. He provides a unique overview of the different types of factors and alternative risk premia, their rationale and how to implement them efficiently in a portfolio. This is the new reference book in this field, a must read for all practitioners and people considering using factors and alternative risk premia in their investment strategy."
—Emiel van den Heiligenberg, *Head of Asset Allocation at Legal & General Investment Management*

"The book is a great introduction into the world of factor investing and alternative indexation. Accessible, yet very comprehensive. Read the book—and learn from one of the best in the field."
—Vitali Kalesnik PhD, *Partner, Director of Research for Europe at Research Affiliates*

"The discussion of active and passive money management is needlessly polarised. This timely book, written by a practitioner, explains clearly and comprehensively some of the increasingly-popular strategies that might help investors find a middle way."
—Kevin Gardiner, *Former Chief Investment Officer (Europe), Barclays Wealth & Investment Management*

Fadi Zaher

Index Fund Management

A Practical Guide to Smart Beta, Factor Investing, and Risk Premia

Fadi Zaher
Index Solutions & Investment Specialists
London, UK

ISBN 978-3-030-19399-7   ISBN 978-3-030-19400-0 (eBook)
https://doi.org/10.1007/978-3-030-19400-0

© The Editor(s) (if applicable) and The Author(s), under exclusive licence to Springer Nature Switzerland AG 2019
This work is subject to copyright. All rights are solely and exclusively licensed by the Publisher, whether the whole or part of the material is concerned, specifically the rights of translation, reprinting, reuse of illustrations, recitation, broadcasting, reproduction on microfilms or in any other physical way, and transmission or information storage and retrieval, electronic adaptation, computer software, or by similar or dissimilar methodology now known or hereafter developed.
The use of general descriptive names, registered names, trademarks, service marks, etc. in this publication does not imply, even in the absence of a specific statement, that such names are exempt from the relevant protective laws and regulations and therefore free for general use.
The publisher, the authors and the editors are safe to assume that the advice and information in this book are believed to be true and accurate at the date of publication. Neither the publisher nor the authors or the editors give a warranty, express or implied, with respect to the material contained herein or for any errors or omissions that may have been made. The publisher remains neutral with regard to jurisdictional claims in published maps and institutional affiliations.

Cover illustration: GettyImages / aleksandarvelasevic
Cover design by eStudio Calamar

This Palgrave Macmillan imprint is published by the registered company Springer Nature Switzerland AG
The registered company address is: Gewerbestrasse 11, 6330 Cham, Switzerland

To Leila, Jamil and Rose

Acknowledgements

The seeds of this book were planted few years ago, during my time at Barclays Wealth and Investment Management and grew along the journey at Kleinwort Benson and Legal & General Investment Management (LGIM). I benefited intellectually and practically from discussion with colleagues, clients and friends on financial markets and factor investing. Today, factor investing is among the fastest growing areas in the financial industry, and this book aims to bring a consolidated views and central debates on the topic from a professional and academic points of view.

I owe many people for the discussions and feedback on the topic over the years. I would like to express my gratitude to colleagues and friends (in approximate chronological order): Anup Prasad, Dayu Ren, Helene Oger-Zaher, Keyvan Andersson, Dominik Bekkewold, Carlos Andersson, Kevin Gardiner, William Hobbs, Amie Stow, Petr Krpata, Tanya Joyce, Greg B. Davies, Christian Theis, Wei Yang, Aaron Gurwitz, Michael Dicks, Einar Holstad, Mark Cooke, David Head, Ying Xu, Thomas Fekete, Adrian Biesty, Anthony Skitini, Michael Rath, Mouhammed Choukeir, Mohamed Ellouze, Alexander Mirtchev, Delyth Richards, Gene Salerno, Andrew Thompson, Fahad Kamal, Geoffrey Boullanger, Daria Kuzina, Karl Sawaya, Denis Nagy, Roman Joukovski, Mike Bayley, Emiel van den Heiligenberg, John Roe, Chad Rakvin, Colm O'Brien, David Barron, Greg Behar, Aniket Das, Shaun Murphy, Aaron Meder, Adam Willis, Aimee Bowkett, Roger Bartley, Anna Walsh, Anne-Marie Morris, Dan Attwood, David Chapman, Howie Li, Joseph Firth, Lee Collins, Nelson Nery, Sebastien Monfort, Tasos Kontos, Ciera Radia, Mathew Webb, Mehdi Guissi, Graham Moles, Paul So, Sarah Peasey, Panagiotis Berdos, Silvio Corgiat Mecio, Simon Hynes, Max Julius, Eliza Grimond, Lucy Johnstone, Johannes Davis, Vitali Kalesnik, Christina

Alexi, Jennifer Steding, Amjed Younis, Timo Pfeiffer, and many members of LGIM's Index and Multi-Asset teams.

Special thanks to Joseph Johnson and Tula Weis at Palgrave Macmillan, Andrzej Pioch, Daria Kuzina, Kevin Gardiner, Vitali Kalesnik, Wei Yang, David Barron, Julia Alpar and James Zucker for reading the manuscript and for their reviews and valuable input. All views expressed in this book are mine. Peer reviewers, colleagues and various employers are not responsible for the views or the content.

Lastly, I would like to extend my appreciations to Kenneth R. French, Solactive, Bloomberg and others for permission to use their data to construct many of the examples in the book.

Contents

1	**Introduction: What We Talk About in Factor Investing**	**1**
Part I	**Evolution of Factor Investing and Index Fund Management**	**7**
2	**Stepping Up to Factor Investing**	**9**
2.1	History of Significant Advances in Indices and Indexed Funds	12
2.2	Growth and Adaptation of Factor Strategies	14
2.3	The Taxonomy of Risks and Returns	16
2.4	Factor Investing Versus Traditional Index and Active Fund Management	18
2.5	The Misconception of Factor Investing in the Press	19
2.6	Consideration When Looking at Factor Investing	20
2.7	Concluding Remarks	21
3	**Architecture and Art of Indexation**	**23**
3.1	Why Index Architecture Matters	24
3.2	Representativeness of the Index Strategy	26
3.3	Modularity of an Index	27
3.4	Availability: The Amount of Stocks and Bonds Outstanding	29
3.5	Stock and Bond Weightings	30
	3.5.1 Market Value Weighting	32
	3.5.2 Equal Weighting	33

ix

x   Contents

		3.5.3	Price Weighting	34
		3.5.4	Outcome-Oriented Weighting: Tilting and Optimisation	34
	3.6	Index Maintenance and Operations		35
	3.7	Replication and Management of Index Funds		37
		3.7.1	Trading Strategies	38
		3.7.2	Securities Lending	39
		3.7.3	Cash Management	40
	3.8	Crowding Risk of Index Funds		40
	3.9	The Capacity of Index Funds		42
	3.10	Concluding Remarks		43

Part II Equity Factor Investing   45

4 Equity Factor Investing: Value Stocks   47
   4.1   Schools of Value Investing   49
   4.2   The Value and Growth Debate   51
   4.3   Intrinsic Value   54
   4.4   Systematic Screening Approaches   56
       4.4.1   Benjamin Graham Screen   58
       4.4.2   Price-to-Book (P/B) Screen   60
       4.4.3   Price-to-Earnings (P/E) Screen   62
       4.4.4   Price-to-Sales (P/S) Ratio   64
       4.4.5   Comparison and Combination of Screens   65
       4.4.6   What Constitutes Good Screen Criteria?   68
   4.5   Behavioural Drivers of Value Factor   69
   4.6   Market Structure and Reward for Risk   71
   4.7   Considerations for Value Investing   72
   4.8   Concluding Remarks   74

5 Equity Factor Investing: Quality   77
   5.1   Investment Horizon for Quality   79
   5.2   Quality Factor Screens   80
       5.2.1   Profitability Screen   81
       5.2.2   Asset Growth and Investment Screen   83
       5.2.3   Leverage Screen   85
       5.2.4   Earning Accruals Screen   87
       5.2.5   Corporate Governance Screen   88
       5.2.6   Combined Quality Screens Among Practitioners   90

	5.3	Drivers of the Quality Premium	93
	5.4	Quality and Valuation of Stocks	95
	5.5	Consideration for Quality Strategies	96
	5.6	Concluding Remarks	98
6	**Equity Factor Investing: Low Risk**	**99**
	6.1	Why Considering Low Volatility Factor Investing?	101
	6.2	Low Risk Factor Approaches and Construction	102
	6.3	Common Low Volatility Factor Indices	105
	6.4	Behavioural Drivers of the Factor Premium	107
	6.5	Market Structures Driving the Factor Premium	109
	6.6	Considerations When Implementing Low Volatility Strategies	110
	6.7	Low Volatility in Asset Allocation	114
	6.8	Concluding Remarks	115
7	**Equity Factor Investing: Momentum**	**117**
	7.1	Evolution of Momentum Investing	118
	7.2	Rules-Based Momentum Index Strategies	121
		7.2.1 Cross-sectional Momentum Strategies	121
		7.2.2 Time Series Momentum Strategies	123
	7.3	Market-Based Index Strategies	125
	7.4	Behavioural Drivers of Momentum Premium	127
		7.4.1 Herding Behaviour	127
		7.4.2 Representativeness and Confirmation Bias	129
	7.5	The Reward for Risk and Market Structures	130
	7.6	Consideration for Momentum Strategies	132
	7.7	Concluding Remarks	133
8	**Equity Factor Investing: Size**	**135**
	8.1	Defining the Size Factor	137
	8.2	Construction of Size-Based Index Strategy	138
	8.3	The Existence of the Size Premium	139
	8.4	Risk-Based Explanation of the Size Premium	141
	8.5	Non-Risk Based Explanation	142
		8.5.1 The January Effect	143
		8.5.2 Inefficient Pricing	143
		8.5.3 Attention, Coverage and Transparency	144
		8.5.4 Behavioural Drivers of the Size Factor	145

	8.6	Criticism of the Size Premium	146
	8.7	Considerations When Investing in Small Size	147
	8.8	Concluding Remarks	149
9	**Equity Multi-Factor Investing**		**151**
	9.1	Factor Cyclicality and Diversification	153
	9.2	Blending the Factors into Multi-Factor Strategy	155
		9.2.1 The Top-Down Approach	155
		9.2.2 The Bottom-Up Approach	157
	9.3	So Which Approach Is Best?	159
	9.4	Multi-Factor Indices in the Market	160
	9.5	Timing the Factors	160
		9.5.1 Factor Sensitivities and Factor Dynamics	162
	9.6	Considerations When Timing the Factors	164
	9.7	Multi-Factor Portfolio Analysis	165
		9.7.1 Portfolio Return-Based Style Analysis	166
		9.7.2 Security-Based Style Analysis	168
	9.8	Concluding Remarks	168

Part III   Fixed Income and Multi-Asset Factor Investing   **171**

10	**Fixed Income Factor Investing**		**173**
	10.1	Why Factor Investing in Fixed Income?	174
	10.2	Drivers of Bond Risk and Return	175
	10.3	Misconception When Thinking of Bond Factors	178
	10.4	What Are the Factors in Bonds?	180
	10.5	Government Bond Style Factors	181
		10.5.1 Size Factor for Government Bonds	182
		10.5.2 Quality Factor for Government Bonds	185
		10.5.3 Value Factor for Government Bonds	188
		10.5.4 Momentum Factor for Government Bonds	189
		10.5.5 Low Volatility Factor for Government Bonds	190
	10.6	Corporate Bond Style Factors	191
		10.6.1 Quality Factor for Corporate Bonds	192
		10.6.2 Value Factor for Corporate Bonds	196
		10.6.3 Momentum Factor for Corporate Bonds	199
		10.6.4 Size Factor in Corporate Bonds	200
		10.6.5 Low Volatility Factor for Corporate Bonds	201
	10.7	Multi-Factors Strategies For Bonds	202

			Contents	xiii
	10.8	Considerations When Building Bond Factors		202
	10.9	Concluding Remarks		203
11	**Multi-Asset: Alternative Risk Premia**			**205**
	11.1	Why Are We Thinking of ARP?		207
	11.2	Fund Manager Types in ARP		209
	11.3	Taxonomy of ARP Strategies		210
	11.4	Carry Premia Across Assets		213
		11.4.1	Currency Carry Premium	213
		11.4.2	The Commodity Carry Premium	216
		11.4.3	The Bond Carry Premium	219
		11.4.4	Other Carry Premia	221
	11.5	Value ARP Strategies		222
		11.5.1	Currency Value Premium	222
		11.5.2	Commodities Value Premium	224
		11.5.3	Fixed Income and Equities ARP Value Premia	226
	11.6	Momentum and Trend-Following Strategies		227
	11.7	Portfolio Construction of ARP Strategies		229
	11.8	Access to ARP Strategies		231
	11.9	A Consideration When Selecting ARP		232
	11.10	Concluding Remarks		233

Bibliography 235

Index 241

List of Figures

Fig. 1.1	Factor drivers and nutrients analogy. Source: Author, based on John Cochrane and Andrew Ang anology. Note: For illustrative purposes only	2
Fig. 2.1	Equity factor investing timelines. Source: Author, academic publications	10
Fig. 2.2	Key index fund timelines. Source: Author, fund launch dates and historical announcements	13
Fig. 2.3	Growth of dedicated factor investing (assets under management, USD, Billions). Source: Author's compilation from Morningstar, Bloomberg and ETFG	15
Fig. 2.4	Sources of risk-return and evolution. Source: Author	17
Fig. 3.1	Geographical revenue of largest 100 listed stocks in the U.K. Source: Author's calculations, income statements and Bloomberg. Note: The revenues (year-end) are weighted based on the market value of each stock	25
Fig. 3.2	Weighting comparison of market value, equal and price weighting. Note: Author's construction and calculations of free float-adjusted market capitalisation index based on 1000 listed stocks on U.S. Exchanges with a minimum free float of 80% as at 8th October 2018. The data source used for the construction is Bloomberg. Top 10 stocks constitute 14% of the index	32
Fig. 3.3	Benchmark returns versus full and 'smart' replication of index funds. Source: Author. Note: For illustrative purpose only	38
Fig. 4.1	Value U.S. listed ETFs. Source: Bloomberg, Dec. 2008–Dec. 2017	49

Fig. 4.2	Value versus growth performance. Source: Author's calculations, Kenneth French database, Jul. 1963–Dec. 2017 for the U.S. Note: The figure represents the difference in total returns of low value ("value") and high value ("growth") using combined screens of top 30th and bottom 30th percentile of price-to-book, price-to-earnings and price-to-cash flow. The performance difference between value and growth is calculated as the rolling 12-month total returns. Historical returns are not a leading indicator of future performance	52
Fig. 4.3	Intrinsic value and margin of safety. Source: Author, Bloomberg data between Aug. 2005–Dec. 2017. Note: For illustrative purpose only	55
Fig. 4.4	Berkshire Hathaway share price versus S&P 500. Source: Bloomberg, Dec. 1987–Dec. 2017	58
Fig. 4.5	P/B portfolios for the U.S. versus the market capitalisation. Source: Author's calculations, Kenneth French database, Jul. 1963–Dec. 2017 for the U.S. Note: The time series are logged and rebased to Jul. 1963. The high P/B is top 30th percentile, the average P/B is 40–70th percentile, and low P/B is the bottom 30th percentile. The stocks are market value weighted within each percentile bucket	61
Fig. 4.6	P/E portfolios for the U.S. versus the market capitalization index. Source: Author's calculations, Kenneth French database, Jul. 1963–Dec. 2017 for the U.S. Note: The time series are logged and rebased to Jul. 1963. The high P/E is top 30th percentile, the average P/E is 40–70th percentile, and low P/E is the bottom 30th percentile. The stocks are market value weighted within each percentile bucket	63
Fig. 4.7	Optimist and pessimist price targets for the largest U.S. 500 stocks. Source: Bloomberg, analyst reports, Dec. 2004–Dec. 2017. Note: The optimist and pessimist price targets are based on the median estimate of market analysts. The sample of analysts includes at least five price targets per company	73
Fig. 5.1	Global quality relative to market capitalisation over holding periods. Source: Author's calculation, Kenneth French database, Jan. 1990–Dec. 2017 for global equities. Note: The construction of the quality factor is equal weighting of high profitability measures, low investment and low earnings variability portfolios. Historical returns are not a leading indicator of future performance	80
Fig. 5.2	The link between the balance sheet, cash flow and income statement. Source: Author. Note: For illustrative purposes only	81
Fig. 5.3	Structure of profit measures. Source: Author. Note: For illustrative purposes only	82

Fig. 5.4	Operating Profit-to-Book Value (OP/BV) screen and market capitalisation strategies. Source: Author's calculations, Kenneth French database, Jul. 1963–Dec. 2017 for the U.S. Note: The time series are logged and rebased to July 1963. The high OP/BV is 30th percentile of the companies with highest OP/BV, the Mid OP/BV is 40–70th percentile, and low OP/BV is the bottom 30th percentile. The portfolios are market value-weighted based on each stock's market capitalisation. Market Cap is the market capitalisation portfolio. Historical returns are not a leading indicator of future performance	84
Fig. 5.5	Low, average, high investment and market capitalisation portfolio. Source: Author's calculations. Kenneth French database, Jul. 1963–Dec. 2017 for the U.S. Note: The time series are logged and rebased to July 1963. The high Inv. is 30th percentile of the companies with the highest investment, the Mid Inv. is 40–70th percentile, and low Inv. is the bottom 30th percentile. The portfolio is market value weighted based on each stock's market capitalisation. Market Cap is the market capitalisation portfolio. Historical returns are not a leading indicator of future performance	85
Fig. 5.6	Accrual portfolios versus market capitalisation. Source: Author's calculations. Kenneth French database, Jul. 1963–Dec. 2017 for the U.S. Note: The time series are logged and rebased to July 1963. The high accruals is 30th percentile of the companies with the highest accrual, the Mid accruals is 40–70th percentile and low accruals is the bottom 30th percentile. The portfolio is market value weighted based on each stock's market capitalisation. Market Cap is the market capitalisation portfolio. Market Cap denotes the market capitalisation portfolio. Historical returns are not a leading indicator of future performance	89
Fig. 5.7	Correlation between quality and value premia. Source: Author's calculation, Kenneth French database, Jul. 1963–Dec. 2017 for the U.S. Note: The quality premium is defined as the difference between the quality portfolio and the market capitalisation index total returns. Quality is defined as an equally weighted portfolio with high profitability, low asset growth and low accruals	96
Fig. 6.1	The low volatility premium for the U.S. and portfolios with different risks. Source: Author's calculations, Kenneth French database, Jul. 1963–Dec. 2017 for the U.S. Note: The time series are logged and rebased to July 1963. The low beta portfolio is the bottom 30th percentile, the medium beta is 40–70th percentile and the high beta is the top 30th percentile. The portfolios are market value weighted based on each stock's market capitalisation. Market Cap is the market capitalisation portfolio. Historical returns are not a leading indicator of the future performance	100

Fig. 6.2	The risk-return relationship and the market. Source: Author. Note: The market capitalisation index is typically the representation of the broad market portfolio. The risk-free rate is often short-dated Treasury bill	101
Fig. 6.3	The drawdown of low and high risk factor versus the general market. Source: Author's calculation, Kenneth French database, Jul. 1963–Dec. 2017 for the U.S. Note: The low beta portfolio is the bottom 30th percentile and the high beta is the top 30th percentile. The figure is based on rolling 12-month cumulative drawdown	102
Fig. 6.4	Relative sector allocation: low volatility factor and market capitalisation index. Source: Author's construction of global low volatility index and market capitalisation index and Solactive, Jan. 2012–Jan. 2017. Note: The 100 stocks are narrowed from the largest 1000 stocks in the U.S. with free-float of 80%	112
Fig. 6.5	Correlation of volatility strategies and short-term interest rates. Source: Author's calculations, Federal Reserve of St. Louis, Kenneth French database, Jul. 1963–Dec. 2017 for the U.S. Note: The short-term interest rate is the 3-month Treasury bill rate, the factor premium is the difference between volatility and market capitalisation returns on a monthly basis. The definition of 'high' and 'low' interest is based on Z-score of short term interest rates	113
Fig. 6.6	Balanced asset allocation with factors. Source: Author's construction. Note: The asset allocation is a compilation of typical "balanced" portfolio allocation (base asset allocation) of Wealth Managers in the United Kingdom in 2017	114
Fig. 6.7	Integration of factors into the asset allocation. Source: Wealth Management Association Asset Allocation, Solactive and Bloomberg-Barclays bond indices. Note: AA denotes Asset Allocation. GBP hedged returns, Jul. 2005–Dec. 2017. Regional allocation is kept similar in the overall asset allocation. This example is for illustrative purposes only	115
Fig. 7.1	Newton's momentum trade of South Sea Company. Source: Author's creation, stock price data from Frehen et al. in 2013	119
Fig. 7.2	Momentum portfolio and market capitalisation historically. Source: Author's calculations. Kenneth French database between Jul. 1962–Dec. 2017 for the U.S. Note: The portfolios as market value-weighted (market capitalisation weighted) portfolios. Low Mom is the bottom 30th percentile, and High Mom is top 30th percentile, Mid Mom is the 30–70% percentile. The price returns are monthly prior (2–12) return. For illustrative purposes only. Historical returns are not a leading indicator of future performance	120
Fig. 7.3	Cross-sectional momentum. Note: For illustrative purposes only	122

List of Figures

Fig. 7.4	Comparison of the number of securities between strategies. Source: Author's calculations. Stock prices from Bloomberg between Dec. 2003–Sep. 2018. Note: The lookback period and rebalancing period is six months, similar to the example in Table 7.1	125
Fig. 7.5	High and low momentum relative risk to the U.S. market capitalisation. Source: Author's calculations. Kenneth French database, between Jul. 1963–Dec. 2017 for the U.S. Note: For illustrative purposes only	131
Fig. 8.1	Company profile by size factor index. Source: Author, Bloomberg. Note: M denotes million and B denotes billion in USD, EUR or GBP. The shaded area is the target segment of the size factor. *Market capitalisation in USD is as at 19 December 2018	136
Fig. 9.1	The business, market cycle and factors. Note: For illustrative purposes only	153
Fig. 9.2	Historical factor performance and multi-factor. Source: Author's calculations, Kenneth French database Jul. 1963–Dec. 2017 for the US. Note: The time series are logged and rebased to July 1963. The stocks are market capitalisation weighted after screening for the top 30th percentile for each factor. Factor definitions used are: value as high book-to-market (or low price-to-book), high quality as a combined definition of low investment and high operating profitability, size as the smallest 30% by market capitalisation in the stock universe, low volatility as the low beta definition as a proxy for low risk, and momentum as the monthly prior (2–12) returns. The multi-factor is just simply the average of the various building blocks for illustrative purposes. Historical returns are not a leading indicator of future performance	154
Fig. 9.3	Example of building blocks and equal weighted allocation. Note: For illustrative purposes only. This chart assumes that the single-factor sleeves are equally weighted. Each block—quality, value, low volatility and other factors—are filled with stocks that score the highest on each of the factors to create the multi-factor strategy	156
Fig. 9.4	Bottom-up approach illustration. Note: The scores are between −1 and +1 derived on the stock-specific characteristics described in previous chapters. The best score is +1, and the worst score is −1. For illustrative purposes only	157
Fig. 9.5	Comparison between the top-down and bottom-up approach. Source: Author's recreation of Bender and Wang (2016), Exhibit 8, Jan. 1993–Mar. 2015. Note: Results are based on a historical simulation of an equally-weighted combination of value, volatility, quality, and momentum factor for developed markets.	

	The excess return and tracking error is against a broad developed market capitalisation index	159
Fig. 9.6	Multi-factor risk and return attribution. Note: For illustrative purposes only	166
Fig. 10.1	Bond risk premia. Note: For illustrative purposes only	176
Fig. 10.2	U.S. interest rates, credit spread and recession. Source: The U.S. Federal Reserve Bank of St. Louis, BofAML for U.S. Corporate Index from 1996, NBER, and Author's compilation of historical credit spreads between 1973–1996, Full time period Jan. 1973–Apr. 2018. Note: The 3-month T-bill is a proxy to illustrate the short-term interest rate and the 10-year is a proxy for long-term interest rate in the U.S.	177
Fig. 10.3	Performance of bond indices in various interest rate environments. Source: Author's calculation, U.S. Federal Reserve, Bloomberg, Bloomberg-Barclays Indices, Mar. 2003–Dec. 2017. Note: The global aggregate, treasury and short duration (1–3 years) are based on Bloomberg-Barclays indices' total returns	179
Fig. 10.4	GDP versus debt-weighted global treasuries. Source: Author's calculations, Bloomberg-Barclays index, Dec. 2008–Dec. 2017	183
Fig. 10.5	Regional difference between GDP and debt-weighted index. Source: Bloomberg-Barclays as at Dec. 2017	184
Fig. 10.6	Fiscal strength versus debt-weighted index. Source: Author's calculations, Bloomberg-Barclays index, Dec. 2008–Dec. 2017. Note: The strategies are adjusted for USD market value and duration basis	186
Fig. 10.7	RAFI-HY US versus Bloomberg Barclays U.S. high yield. Source: FTSE-RAFI, Bloomberg-Barclays. The RAFI index focuses on bonds with up to 10-year maturities	194
Fig. 10.8	Distance-to-default approach. Note: For illustrative purposes only, Default point is often defined as a combination of short term and long term liabilities (e.g. the total value of short term and half the long term liabilities)	195
Fig. 10.9	Corporate bond value factor versus debt-weighted bonds. Source: Author's reading from Li et al. (2012), Aug. 1999–Feb. 2012	196
Fig. 10.10	Fallen angel performance relative to investment grade. Source: King and Zaher (2017), LGIM, Markit, iBoxx, Bloomberg, Jan. 2012–Feb. 2012. Note: Price changes are calculated based on the average of all prices for 64 GBP fallen angels that entered the index during the sample period	198
Fig. 10.11	High yield asset growth and performance 1981–2017. Source: NYU Salomon Center estimates, Credit Suisse, Citi Bank, Barclays data, 1981–2017	200

Fig. 10.12	Size factor for investment grade and high yield between 1994–2015. Source: Houweling and Zundert in 2017, Table 3 in the research paper, Jan. 1994–Jun. 2015. Note: The excess return is the size factor return over duration-matched Treasury bonds	201
Fig. 11.1	The commonality of risk premia. Note: For illustrative purposes only	206
Fig. 11.2	Branches of ARP strategies. Note: For illustrative purposes only	211
Fig. 11.3	Contango and backwardation. Source: Author's construction and Bloomberg, Dec. 2017. For illustrative purposes only	217
Fig. 11.4	Shapes of the yield curve in some developed markets. Source: Author's construction and Bloomberg, Dec. 2017. For illustrative purposes only	220
Fig. 11.5	Mean-reversion of spot rates versus USD of few G10 currencies. Source: Author's calculation and Bloomberg, Oct. 1985–Dec. 2017. For illustrative purposes only. Historical returns are not a leading indicator of future performance	223
Fig. 11.6	Relative value trade example between soybean and corn futures. Source: Author's construction. Bloomberg, Dec. 1986–Dec. 2017. Note: +1/−1 std. dev. stands for one standard deviation of the price ratio. The ratio is based on the shortest maturity futures contracts. For illustrative purposes only. Historical returns are not a leading indicator of future performance	225
Fig. 11.7	Rules-based value strategy for rates. Source: Author's calculations. IMF database, Bloomberg, Dec. 2010–Dec. 2017. For illustrative purposes only. Notes: The overvalued and undervalued rate is defined based on the difference between nominal GDP (g) growth and 10-year interest rates (r) for each economy. If the g > r, then the 10-year bond is overvalued and vice versa. Historical returns are not a leading indicator of future performance	227
Fig. 11.8	60/40 portfolios and ARP strategies. Source: Author's calculations, Bloomberg, Barclays, Kenneth French database, Deutsche bank, Jan. 2001–Dec. 2017. Note: The base asset allocation (Base AA_60/40) of 60% equity and 40% bonds is based on a representative market cap and Bloomberg-Barclays Global Aggregate. FX denotes currency ARP for (carry, momentum and value) with the percentage allocation of ARP in a modified 60/40 asset allocation, Com. denotes commodities with similar factors to currencies; Multi-ARP is equally weighted ARP strategies across asset classes and styles	231

List of Tables

Table 2.1	Comparison between passive, smart beta/factors and active investment	19
Table 3.1	Example of building blocks and portfolio fit for indices	28
Table 3.2	Impact of free-float adjustment on stock weighting	30
Table 3.3	Classes of weighting methods	31
Table 4.1	Schools of value investing	50
Table 4.2	Comparison of value characteristics	66
Table 4.3	Comparison of commercial value indices	68
Table 5.1	Market indices for quality	93
Table 5.2	Example bankruptcy filings	97
Table 6.1	Common low risk factor approaches	103
Table 6.2	Example of low volatility and variance indices	106
Table 7.1	Cross-sectional momentum with various rebalancing and lookback periods	124
Table 7.2	Commercial momentum factor strategies	126
Table 8.1	Titling approach example with a blend of large, mid and small-caps	139
Table 8.2	Small-, mid-, large-cap and market cap for the U.S.	140
Table 8.3	Small and mid-cap outperformance versus large and market cap during January	143
Table 8.4	Analyst coverage by size	145
Table 9.1	Correlation (%) between various factor premia	154
Table 9.2	Bottom-up scores based on characteristics	157
Table 9.3	Comparison of various multi-factor indices	161
Table 9.4	Factor premia in various market and economic conditions	163
Table 10.1	Typical styles strategies in fixed income	181
Table 11.1	Correlation between various ARP strategies	208
Table 11.2	Comparison of various ARP strategies	230

1

Introduction: What We Talk About in Factor Investing

We do not often read about the important decision faced by investors in picking passive strategies—whether to invest in traditional index or factor investing strategies. The growth of passive investing accelerated sharply after the global financial crisis in 2008/2009. The same index strategy from various providers can have materially different outcomes. Investors considering factor strategies would benefit from some valuable lessons about the choices they are able to make and how these choices impact their investment outcomes—both positively and negatively.

This book is an attempt to write this down and focus on what matters in the hope that readers derive some comfort and confidence with factor investing. Conversations with many investors since 2008 have convinced me that there is a readership for it—including a large group of investors seeking a counterweight to the view that factor investing is doomed, and that capacity, overcrowding and the risks far outstrip the benefits.

Factor investing has grown in popularity on the back of the limitations of the traditional index strategies. Factor strategies adopt classic investment styles ranging from company fundamentals and security price behaviours, implemented through a rules-based index. The terms "smart beta", "risk factors" or "factors" are now common and frequent in the financial press in the past few years. When the investment industry uses terms like smart beta, factor-based investing, alternative beta most of the time these terms are mainly referring to the same thing.

These factors can be described as characteristics of securities that drive the risk and reward and they exist across different asset classes. Factors are like nutrients in a diet. An asset (stock or bond) acts as a food ingredient and a portfolio is the actual meal.[1] For example, chicken, salmon or broccoli are sources of protein, but contain other nutrients such as vitamins, fibre and carbohydrates that are important for a human body to function—Fig. 1.1 illustrates this analogy with factors. Similarly, a stock can contain quality, value and other characteristics based on the financial profile of the company and price behaviours.

The debate on the sources of risk and reward of factor investing and the broader context within the market debate is often blurred—some are spuriously precise and unconvincing. The dominant thought in Modern Portfolio Theory since the 1950s has been that markets are efficient. The idea is that the investor is not going to be able to collect information better than the consensus—the information everybody else already has. We know today that financial markets are not always efficient—people are complex, with emotions. Empirical evidence suggested that market data or investors' behaviour does not always support financial economic theories. If markets were fully efficient, there would be no bargains to profit from. The market's structure—the way it is organised and trades—and collective behaviour of the marketplace make today the new era of Modern Portfolio Theory.

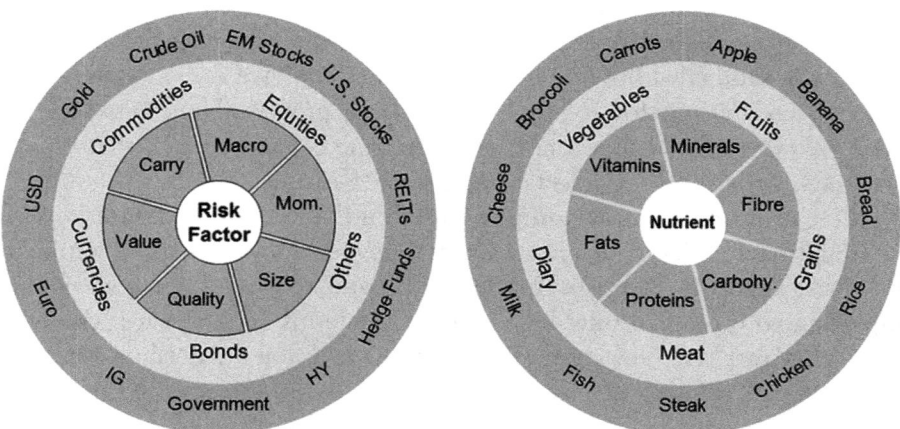

Fig. 1.1 Factor drivers and nutrients analogy. Source: Author, based on John Cochrane and Andrew Ang anology. Note: For illustrative purposes only

---

[1] This analogy has been used by two prominent academics John Cochrane and Andrew Ang.

Over the past decade, factor investing has emerged with new funds and growing assets under management. It is among the most innovative areas of global index fund management and it continues to grow. According to Morningstar, in June 2017 there were 1320 factor-based exchange traded funds globally with total assets under management of USD 999 billion. With the sizeable institutional inflows, the factor-based assets exceed USD 1 trillion today.

There are only a few factors in the world that matter today. For factor strategies to qualify as "true factors", they require persistent performance through time and economic rationale. The chances of discovering a new factor that is persistent has decreased in the past decade. There are limits as to what investors can do with the balance sheet and market price data. In the digital age, it is easy to data mine and come up with all sorts of factors as the cost of data mining has decreased with more publically available data technology. Before the availability of mass data and technology, people spent years gathering data and extensive programming to speed up calculations. At that time, only factor strategies based on economic principles were tested. Research on factor discoveries has revealed many of the factors as illusions. Today there are over 250 published factors with the majority being considered false factor discoveries. The decay of performance is more than 50% after the identification and publication of a factor.

Following periods of complexity in the financial markets, we often experience a back to basics mentality—a recent example is the simplification and increasing transparency of complex derivatives products such as collateralised debt obligations since the global financial crisis in 2008. The products are far simpler and more transparent today than back in 2007. However, when it comes to quantitative investment strategies, it would be foolish to deny the current complexity, abundance of investment strategies and jargon. Factor investing is different from a pure quantitative strategy. Factor investing is not necessarily a complex topic or a "black box" or deserves the complex quantitative techniques inflicted on it. The simplicity, transparency and accessibility of the main factor strategies will be discussed in various chapters.

The tendency for the public debate is often to focus on two camps—disaster or triumph—and to overlook the possibility of understanding how factor investing can help investors achieve their objective. The dissonance between academics, index machines, practitioners (the fanatics and sceptics), and media has passed to some extent unnoticed. On one side, warnings against over-optimism in passive and factor investing are commonplace: we are alerted to new passive bubbles on a weekly basis by the routine pessimists—an overdone fear. On the flip side, advocates of factor investing promise an ultimate guaranteed success—a false statement. Capital flow into strategies is a luxury problem for the fund manager, but also a curse if the underlying reason and common sense are absent from the investment thesis.

The lesson from the routine pessimists and eternal optimists is that received wisdom often creates confusion about what factor investing is, and can lead investors and decision-makers astray. One of the main messages in this book is contrary to the two camps. The main drivers for the growth in passive and factor investing is not that they are more complex nor is the money flowing in for the innovation of new factors. The main drivers are that people want to see what the simplicity and common sense of factor investing can bring to investment portfolios. With this in mind, the prospects for continued adaptation may be brighter than feared.

If we accept too easily the popular explanation for why we should invest in or avoid factor investing, without consideration of its purpose, then we may miss opportunities in achieving and understanding specific outcomes in portfolios—potential reward and risk or diversification objectives. This book aims to bring simplicity and allows embracing the topic with an open mind. It offers some perspective in the way in which the public debate is conducted, and how financial knowledge is formed and disseminated. It is human nature to complicate a topic that can have an abundance of variation when it comes to construction and outcomes. Sometimes we try too hard and end up making the wrong sort of sense of factor investing, or we infer meaning and causality where there is none. For example, trading illiquid securities to harvest a premium requires sophisticated trading capabilities or relying only on backtests to invest in a newly discovered factor. An index replication approach is unlikely to be successful in capturing this reward efficiently. The book will help readers guard against making these mistakes. It blends some of the insight of behavioural drivers, market structures and compensation for the risk that drive some of the factor returns.

There is no single definition of factor investing, evaluation tool or statistical technique that will help readers to implement this book's central message. Instead, this book requires approaching factor investing with an open mind, and being willing to ask what it is and by whom we are being told it, and why? It also requires that readers think carefully about what they want from factor investing. This book will show how such an approach can be cultivated and will illustrate clearly its simplicity and purpose in portfolios. It will also suggest what can reasonably be expected from a typical balanced factor portfolio; what it cannot do; and the sources of factor risk-returns that make it worthwhile.

I follow and have followed my advice as an active fund manager and researcher in the topic by helping to shape the investment policy and solution for client portfolios. The aim here is to try to make sense of why a particular factor strategy is deployed and how it is constructed for a specific purpose of outcome through passive implementation. The focus is on the potential risk-reward of investment strategies that have been persistent rather than temporary without any financial economic foundations. Performance is uncertain, and fees are not. However, higher-cost active investment solutions could be the right fund choice for many investors. This choice can be the case if investors decide to delegate the investment decisions, factor selections and implementation to someone else to worry for them.

This is a practitioner's sample of the successes and issues encountered in analysing and advising on factor investing and index strategies. My experience in asset management suggests that it will appeal to many trustees, advisors and individual savers who are interested in knowing whether factors are right for them, which factors to choose and how to implement them in the face of all that pessimism. I hope it will also be useful to many students, teachers and finance professionals as well as a wider readership. I have tried to reduce the jargon, complex equations and have tried to aim for simple and clear language in discussing the topic. References are limited to flagship research work and include those that mattered for the evolution of factor investing. Finally, I have tried to make each part and chapter of the book as self-contained as possible. The user of this book may find it useful to review and look into specific chapters, sections or read it straight through from the beginning to the end.

The ideas in this book are grounded solidly in finance and economics, but the most valuable insights are those I gained from my PhD studies at Lund University, the European Central Bank, as an investment strategist and fund manager at various financial institutions.

Part I of the book presents the case for factor investing and brings to life the good practice in building these strategies. It offers some guidance on how to take the broader perspectives that help unearth the opportunities, and are often missing from the narrower, two-camp views. It goes back to its origin, what it is and what it is not. Finally, it offers the basics of factor and index construction and illustrates exactly how the architecture of these strategies can look good. Part I also looks at efficient implementations for portfolios.

Part II sets out the main equity factor investing strategies or factors that matter and concludes with how to combine them. The main focus is on traditional factor investing strategies that have been in existence among active managers and that have made it into systematic rules-based index strategies. Among these strategies are value, momentum, quality, low volatility and small to the middle sized company investing. The aim is to provide a view of how to make sense of them, construct them and understand their limitations. Finally, Part II suggests how these can be combined and what is required for short to medium term investors and how to target long-term balanced exposure to the various factors.

Part III extends factor investing into fixed income, alternative asset classes and other financial instruments. Although potential factors in fixed income and other asset classes are not necessarily identical to equities, the principle is still to be rewarded for risk-taking and to explore market inefficiencies. The reasons why factor strategies have not taken off in asset classes other than equities are due to lack of research, historical data for bonds, liquidity, the appetite for index investment vehicles and evidence to justify a systematic approach. It is one of the most significant growth areas in risk premia strategies. This part will offer a practical and straightforward way of thinking in bonds and alternative risk premia in currencies and commodities as well.

The conclusion argues that it is worth considering factor investing. Factor portfolios should be constructed with a purpose and so avoid the potential damage of choosing a random strategy among the many options in the market, particularly within equities. The fact that many prominent academics, practitioners and investors have applied their skills to factor investing is a testament to the fascination and the interest in the subject. The discussions and debates are likely to continue in the finance industry, in academia and at cocktail parties.

Part I

Evolution of Factor Investing and Index Fund Management

This part provides an insight into the construction approach of an index strategy, why it matters, what to consider and what questions to ask when looking at a strategy implemented through indices. It explores some of the investment styles and approaches to building portfolios for equities and bonds. The aim is to provide readers with an insight into the implications of the investment style choice to help an investor with due diligence when selecting factor based mutual funds, exchange traded funds and other investment vehicles. Chapter 2 provides an introduction to factor investing and Chap. 3 provides an overview of index construction approaches.

2

Stepping Up to Factor Investing

The terms "smart beta" and "factor" are now common and have frequently been in the spotlight of the financial press in the past few years as well as at the forefront of investors' minds considering adopting its approach. Many may ask if it is just a passing trend or is it something that is likely to stay and form part of the traditional fund investment strategies of financial institutions in the decades to come. The answer lies in the origin of factor investing and how it emerged.

Factor investing is a systematic investment approach that targets specific attributes of securities, increasingly implemented through one-stop index-driven strategies. Leading academic studies from the 1970s onwards demonstrate that value, momentum, small stocks and low risk stocks outperformed the market on a risk-adjusted basis. These strategies are no different from traditional investment styles based on company fundamentals and price behaviours implemented through an index or active investment approach. A fundamental principle of value investing goes back to Benjamin Graham in the 1930s—the "Godfather" of value investing.

In the 1970s, academics started to challenge the wisdom of the traditional modern finance theory: the assumption of an efficient market and rational investors, and the linear relationship between risk and return (Fig. 2.1). It made sense then, due to limited financial data, the computational power available and financial theory, as knowledge could not be acquired from extensive empirical research.

The evolving landscape of financial markets and the new digital age have made it possible to innovate and serve a new range of investment strategies backed by empirical research. It also led to many academics and practitioners gaining a better understanding of security price behaviour and performance drivers.

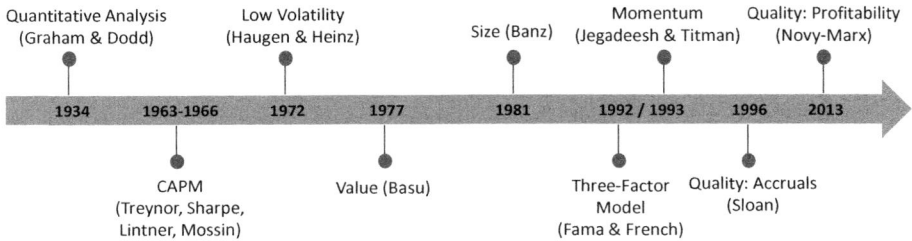

Fig. 2.1 Equity factor investing timelines. Source: Author, academic publications

In 1972, for instance, Robert Haugen and James Heinz famously showed that the relationship between risk and return was not linear and that low risk stocks outperformed higher risk stocks on a risk-adjusted basis—it was controversial wisdom back then. Decades later Eugene Fama, the Nobel Prize laureate and his colleague, Kenneth French, showed in the 1990s that small and value stocks performed markedly better than the traditional finance theory suggested. They also showed that stock performance was not solely explained by market risk, but also by other factors. Jegadeesh and Titman continued the journey by showing that better-performing stocks were likely to be future winners—this phenomenon is known as momentum. The specific story of each factor will be discussed in more depth throughout the book.

Despite the increasing academic and empirical evidence on factor investing, the investment community was slow to adopt these strategies in an index. This is due to the lack of one-stop packaging of such an approach into ready-made strategies by index providers. For example, the industry routinely saw growth and size as important in the 1990s, but implementation tools were fewer.

The Norwegian Government Pension Fund (NGPF) showed the importance of considering and understanding factor exposures in portfolios for large volumes of assets under management post-global financial crisis in 2008/2009. This prominent case helped bring attention to factor investing among a broader range of investors. Indeed, after the fund lost 23% of its value during the market panic while assuming that it was well diversified, the Ministry of Finance in Norway commissioned thorough research, with the assistance of academics, to help inform the debate into the future direction of the fund. Academic studies concluded that a big part of the excess returns (fund return over a benchmark, also known as active return) could be replicated by constructing portfolios designed to mimic the behaviour of factors, which also included exposures to equity market, credit spreads, interest rate risk (duration) and currency trading strategies—see Andrew Ang 2014 for discussion of the NGPF case. Some of the findings concluded that 70% of equity excess return could be explained by exposures to a handful of systematic factors up to 2008—overweight to small-cap stocks, underweight to worst-performing blue-chip stocks among others. During the market turmoil, the fixed income excess returns were driven mainly by factors such as liquidity and low volatility.

An additional boost to the take-up of factor investing by the industry emerged when the practitioners and investors questioned the traditional indexation approach of market capitalisation (indices based on the market value of stocks or debt)—that defined the convention of market returns until then. Looking at this approach through the lens of factor investing, the limitations of traditional indices became more apparent, and in particular, their concentration and exposure to the largest stocks or debt issuers at all times. Investing in large companies is not a problem if investors are seeking high liquidity and low transaction costs. However, the problem of market capitalisation indices, for example, is that weights of companies are proportional to their prices. The higher the price the more the allocation to the company. This feature could result in allocation to stocks with growth bias, or overweight overpriced securities and underweighting undervalued securities—see Arnott et al. in 2013 for discussion on the subject. This limitation, among others, led to the thinking of alternative ways of gaining exposure to financial markets and paved the way for accessing and using factor strategies.

With the increasing ability to create index funds of various investment styles, factor investing gained popularity among many asset owners and managers. However, most indices tracked by the asset manager are long-only (i.e. buys a portfolio of stocks either through direct holdings or derivatives contracts). This does not necessarily mirror the academic literature perfectly. Many of the published factors investing strategies in academia analyse the net performance from long and short exposures to the factors, which are not always transferable to cost-effective investable index funds. The long-only preference has an entirely different risk profile than a simultaneously long and short one, which is more market neutral. Also, the cost of short selling may be high or restricted in some segments of the market (e.g. emerging markets and small capitalisation stocks).

Most investors appreciate the transparency, scalability, ease of implementation into funds and the track record of such strategies. To some, it is also known as "evidence-based" investing, which combines investment styles backed by robust research foundations. This chapter provides an overview of factor investing and the philosophy of the various leading strategies. It focuses on the evolution, the sources of returns, misconceptions and criticisms of factor investing.

2.1 History of Significant Advances in Indices and Indexed Funds

Little did Charles Dow, Edward Jones and Charles Bergstresser know how their work would shape the financial industry for generations to come. These three journalists, who in 1882 founded Dow Jones and Company in and in 1883 first published a two-page summary on the financial news under the name "The customers' afternoon letter". They presented stock price movements together with unprecedented analysis. They aimed to bring information to the public and to provide readers with a clear picture of market performance.

This sort of information was particularly valuable back then since data about the stock market was inconsistent and only accessible to the privileged few. In 1896, Charles Dow created the stock index with the 12 largest companies of the U.S. stock market, known as the Dow Jones Industrial Average to give an idea of the direction and representation of "the market". Today, the index contains 30 constituents and remains one of the most followed indices in the market and serves as a "PR machine" for the U.S. stock market.

The concept of market representation was well received on paper but less so when it came to actual fund implementation of indices. It was too radically different and difficult. Decades later, Edward Renshaw and Paul Feldstein, two Chicago students, proposed the first theoretical model for an index fund, tracking market capitalisation index in 1960. Although this academic idea found little support, it did inspire Wells Fargo and American National Bank in Chicago to create the first institutional equity index fund in 1973. Wells Fargo and Illinois Bell pension funds seeded the strategy with USD 10 million. Then in 1975, John Bogle, founder of Vanguard, started the First Index Investment Trust. During that time, it was heavily criticised by competitors as being "un-American", and the fund was seen as "Bogle's folly". Vanguard added to this space with the first index bond fund in 1986 (see Fig. 2.2).

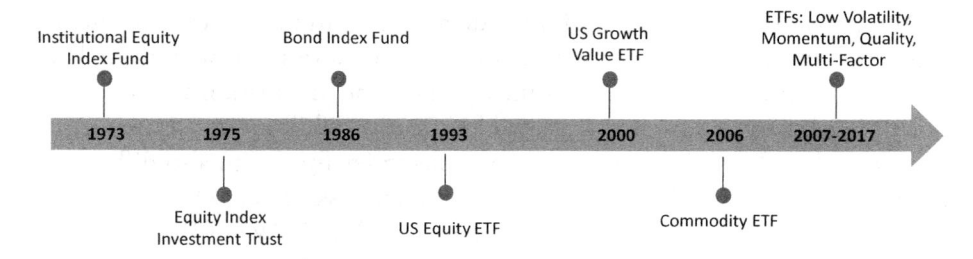

Fig. 2.2 Key index fund timelines. Source: Author, fund launch dates and historical announcements

Fixed income indices have a very different origin compared to equities. Historically they were developed for a single purpose and user, rather than as a general market benchmark. Investment banks developed their bond indices using proprietary methodologies and in-house prices. Many bond indices were designed by banks to create benchmarks for their products and for assessing performance. Today, this is increasingly changing to index and data providers.

The digital revolution, availability of data, the establishment of an intellectual portfolio construction foundation by academics transformed investors' options for investing. With academic support and research, the indexation of investment strategies enabled the extension of traditional market indices into factor investing.

An index-tracking fund automatically limits a manager's investment discretion of how the fund is managed and does not involve any market views outside the set rules of the index. Some look at the mechanics of which securities may enter or exit an index, but that is not necessarily a market view. The sole objective is to deliver the market returns, although an index manager can provide value through effective implementation and operations to perform in-line with or marginally outperform their benchmark.

A major evolution in pooled funds (investment vehicles with a group of investors) was the Exchange Traded Funds (ETFs), which emerged after the market crash in 1987 with the idea to bring more liquid index strategies to the market. State Street and American Stock Exchange launched the first ETF in 1993 to track the S&P 500. The growth of the ETF has been remarkable over the years. According to Ernest and Young 2017 "ETF survey", the AUM of ETFs reached USD 4.4 trillion with a cumulative average growth rate of 21% since 2005.

Alternative vehicles to an ETF include a mutual fund and an investment trust. The index tracker funds have many commonalities, but with some key differences. An ETF and a mutual fund are open-ended (creation and redemption of fund share classes can be created frequently), while an investment trust is close-ended. The pricing method of various index funds can also differ. An ETF, for example has visible dual pricing (bid and ask price), while a mutual fund has a single-price linked to the Net Asset Value (NAV) of the fund. An investment trust can differ from the NAV and is driven by the market demand for the underlying fund. In addition, an ETF discloses the underlying holding more frequently (e.g. daily) compared to a mutual fund and an investment trust that may disclose the holding on a monthly or quarterly basis.

With this proliferation of products come many of the new concepts. Among the most prominent strategies are those that are fundamentally weighted. These were developed by Robert Arnott at Research Affiliates. These strategies rank stocks by book value, dividends, sales, and cash flow instead of market value. Today there is a range of fundamentally weighted strategies and many competitors are lining up to differentiate themselves in this space.

Factor investing will continue to evolve and is unlikely to stop here. To rephrase the wisdom of Charles Darwin—it is not the best performing strategies, nor the most intelligent that survive. It is the strategies that are most adaptable to change in the context of continually evolving financial markets and investor appetite.

2.2 Growth and Adaptation of Factor Strategies

The assets under management in factor investing have been multiplying in the past years and are likely to continue to do so with the increasing number of accessible funds. Indeed, Morningstar states that there are more than 1300 registered ETFs. The same source also reports that the assets under management for factor and smart beta strategies grew from USD 280 billion in 2012 to USD 999 billion at the end of 2017—a compounding annual growth rate of 29% (see Fig. 2.3). The number is expected to reach close to USD 1.5 trillion by 2021 according to Citi Bank and Morningstar. These figures include all public mutual funds and ETFs for the institutional and retail markets. The overall number in the industry is probably higher as none of the statistics includes private and exclusive portfolios, which are often not disclosed by asset managers.

It is not a surprise that the FTSE-Russell Global Smart Beta survey in 2018 showed that investors were warming up to adopting factor-based strategies. Smart beta or factor adoption rates reached 48% among the survey participants. Factors have had more traction with European asset owners compared to North

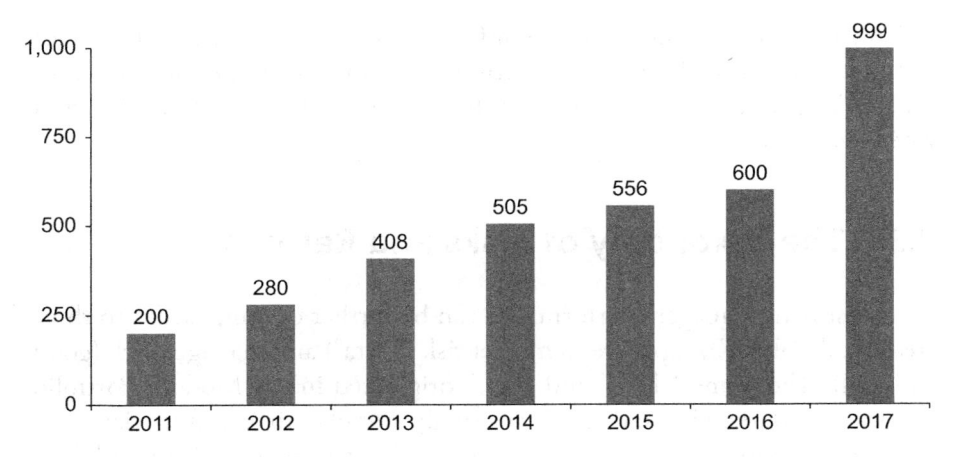

Fig. 2.3 Growth of dedicated factor investing (assets under management, USD, Billions). Source: Author's compilation from Morningstar, Bloomberg and ETFG

America. In Europe, 61% of asset owners use factors versus just 42% of North America, but adoption in the U.S. is increasing at a faster rate.

Factor investing is common in equities, but growing in other asset classes such as fixed income and other asset classes. At this stage, fixed income factor strategies have not taken off due to the lack of research and evidence for a systematic approach, and the consequent lack of available funds. This is one of the expected growth areas in the factor and alternatively-weighted index space in the coming years. The growth is likely to emerge with the increasing availability of historical bond data to understand the dynamics of the fixed income factors, which is currently limited compared to equities.

Future evolution is likely to continue with the integration of Environmental, Social and Governance (ESG) features into index and factor strategies. This integration is at a ramp-up stage—based on the FTSE-Russell 40% of global asset owners are expected to consider ESG with factor strategies in the future.[1] The speed of the integration is likely to be supported by less reliance on exclusionary ESG screening and instead with recent thinking of tilting toward companies with the strongest ESG foundations. Simple exclusion approach for ESG often involves removing companies based on pre-defined criteria (e.g. target carbon emission or ESG ratings). Demand for ESG strategies is likely to see healthy growth in the coming years as investment choice becomes more accessible. It will help investors deploy capital in line with their beliefs and ESG standards. This simply illustrates another dimension of portfolio choice within indexing.

---

[1] ESG consideration is more popular among the European asset owners compared to North America—55% versus 25%, respectively.

Now that we have looked at the history and investors' appetite for factor and index investing, the aim is to continue the evolutionary journey as to how the thinking around risks and rewards has evolved to form an integral part of where we are today.

2.3 The Taxonomy of Risks and Returns

An investment manager's performance can be further decomposed into three areas: skill ("alpha"), exposure to market risk ("beta") and manager luck (good and bad). The terms "alpha" and "beta" originated in the Modern Portfolio Theory by Markowitz and are increasingly popular in the financial press and in conversations about risk and return with investment advisors and fund managers. Today many people hear these terms without necessarily knowing what they mean. Most investors consider risks to decide which investment strategy to follow, and all investors consider a potential return.

Beta is a measure of volatility and co-behaviour relative to a particular market index. It can be seen as the amount of volatility that cannot be reduced by diversification. For example, to assess if a portfolio of large capitalised U.S. stocks is more or less volatile than a market capitalisation benchmark index like the S&P 500, the investor would typically look at the beta. If the beta is higher than one, then that means the portfolio is usually more volatile than the S&P 500, and if it is less than one, then it could be less volatile than the S&P 500. Beta magnifies the good and the bad as a measurement. An investor just buying the market portfolio effectively has a beta of one.

On the other side, alpha is a way to see if a manager is adding value relative to the amount of risk taken and the performance achieved from the market. It can be seen as the amount of volatility that can be reduced by diversification. Managing a portfolio that has the same amount of volatility as the stock market but that is producing a rate of return that is 2–3% better than the index, is often referred to as alpha generation.

Factor investing is neither a pure alpha nor beta, but a mix of the two. It aims to provide improved risk-return characteristics through a variety of investment styles. It is designed to take systematic deviations from a market capitalisation weighted index to harvest risk premium (also known as factor premium). A factor premium is often defined as the excess return of the factor over the broad market, while the traditional equity and bond risk premium (i.e. the market risk premium) is defined as the excess return of the market over a risk-free rate (e.g. cash or short-dated treasury bills).

The sources of risk and return and the way we understand them today have evolved in the past decades. Figure 2.4 describes these sources of return. The

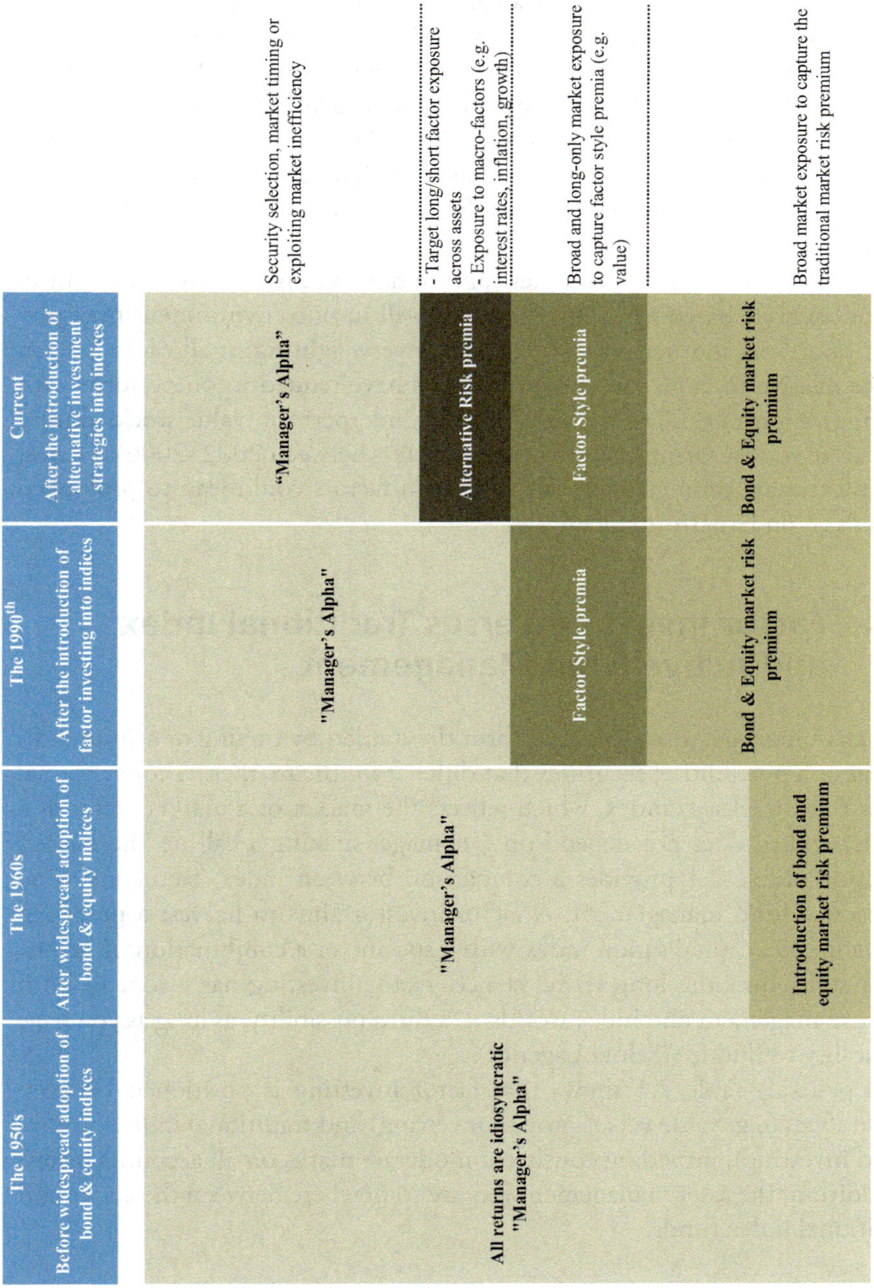

2 Stepping Up to Factor Investing 17

	The 1950s	The 1960s	The 1990th	Current
	Before widespread adoption of bond & equity indices	After widespread adoption of bond & equity indices	After the introduction of factor investing into indices	After the introduction of alternative investment strategies into indices
	All returns are idiosyncratic "Manager's Alpha"	"Manager's Alpha"	"Manager's Alpha"	"Manager's Alpha" — Security selection, market timing or exploiting market inefficiency
				Alternative Risk premia — - Target long/short factor exposure across assets; - Exposure to macro-factors (e.g. interest rates, inflation, growth)
			Factor Style premia	Factor Style premia — Broad and long-only market exposure to capture factor style premia (e.g. value)
		Introduction of bond and equity market risk premium	Bond & Equity market risk premium	Bond & Equity market risk premium — Broad market exposure to capture the traditional market risk premium

Fig. 2.4 Sources of risk-return and evolution. Source: Author

classification of returns has developed with the increasing adaptation and availability of systematic factor strategies in the past decades.

The quest for factor investing has expanded beyond equities and into fixed income, currencies and commodities. Although potential factors in fixed income and other asset classes are not necessarily identical to stocks, the objective is still to harvest premia from several risk factors. It can also be to move away from traditional market capitalisation weighted indices by alternatively weighting securities to enhance diversification. This will be discussed in depth in the next few chapters.

In general, economic and market conditions drive investment performance. Factor- or style based investing that does well in one environment may perform poorly in another one. Historically, overweighting small capitalisation stocks relative to large capitalisation stocks have tended to outperform with falling interest rates. Growth stocks could underperform value stocks during periods of robust earnings growth (e.g. quarters between 2002–2006). Hence, an unfortunate timing to allocate to certain factors could lead to prolonged periods of underperformance.

2.4 Factor Investing Versus Traditional Index and Active Fund Management

An active manager aims to outperform the market by buying or selling individual or a portfolio of securities that differ from the market. A conventional index fund tracks an index, which reflects the market or a market sector as a whole, and so does not depend on a manager making a call on the market direction. Table 2.1 provides a comparison between index, factor investing and active fund management. A factor investor aims to harvest a premium over a market capitalisation index with a specific or a combination of investment styles over the long term. Hence, factor investing has a foot in both active management and index worlds—"a third possibility, as long as you have the ability to find it" (Selma Lagerlöf).

In general, Table 2.1 shows that factor investing is positioned between active styles (e.g. value versus growth investing) and traditional indices (rules-based investing), providing consistent moderate marks on all accounts below. In addition, the asset management fees are somewhere between the active and traditional index funds.

Table 2.1 Comparison between passive, smart beta/factors and active investment

	Traditional index	Factor investing	Traditional active
Diversification	High	Moderate to high	Low to moderate
Management fee	Low	Moderate	High
Turnover	Low	Moderate to high	High
Transparency	High	High to moderate	Low to moderate
Manager discretion	Low	Moderate	High
Investment Capacity	High	Low to High	Low to high

Source: Author
Note: Some fixed income strategies and sector-specific factor strategies may have low investment capacity. Market capitalisation indices have low turnover in percentage terms, but significant capital amounts due to its scale

Investors may not see these benefits as being very advantageous if they believe that a particular market is not efficient. In this case, an active fund manager may be a better choice to exploit any inefficiency in specific markets and take responsibility for the investment risk on your behalf.

2.5 The Misconception of Factor Investing in the Press

In recent years, factor investing solutions have been bestsellers. Factor investing success is not a foregone conclusion, and there are plenty of exaggerations and misprints in the literature. In general, there are many ways to implement and define factor strategies. How index providers target factors varies in complexity and transparency. Some are based on publicly-available academic definitions while others are more proprietary. Investors need to weigh the trade-off between the potential of higher returns from more complex approaches against the level of transparency and the additional governance controls.

Factor-driven funds can underperform market capitalisation strategies, although that is not the long-term expadectation among investors. Typically, equity factor funds tend to own fewer of the largest stocks compared to market capitalisation benchmarks. If the higher weighted-stocks outperform in the broader market, the factor-based strategy will likely underperform a market cap strategy. An example of this is the largest U.S. technology stocks (e.g. Apple and Amazon), which are dominant in the U.S. and any global market capitalisation index. Many factor strategies tend to diversify away from this large sector, which can result in relative underperformance for factor investing strategies versus market capitalisation benchmarks.

It is essential to remember that factor-based strategies target factors that the investor believes will be rewarded over the long-term. An investment decision based on this conviction can outweigh sales and academic research statements to the effect that factors will guarantee superior performance in the future. While we can never be sure as to which factor may outperform, some factor strategies take less equity market risk than market capitalisation indices (i.e. low beta) and aim to improve risk-adjusted returns rather than beating the broad market over the long term.

Moreover, it is important to remember that past performance is not an accurate and reliable estimate of future performance. Certain factors have historically outperformed market capitalisation indices. However, investors who do not wish to be the authors of their misfortune should not view these factors' as the "holy grail", and likely to beat the broad market at all times. It is essential to understand if new individual factor strategies are influenced by hindsight as future returns. In this case, the returns will likely be lower than any backtest suggests.

It is human nature to hang on to certainties. It is one of the reasons why ex-post (historical) returns from backtests are often central to investors' decision making, while ex-ante (future) returns may be at least as good predictor of what may happen. Sometimes it is more of a risk to focus on the certainty (what has happened) than the uncertainty (what may happen).

While factors have historically done well, it is also important to recognise that factors have and can help investors to organise their portfolio and manage their risk objective—the Norwegian lesson mentioned at the beginning of the chapter is one prominent case amongst many. Equally, it is essential to listen and acknowledge the criticisms of factor investing.

2.6 Consideration When Looking at Factor Investing

The "factor zoo" is a common label for the main criticism of factor investing. The factor zoo refers to the over-reliance on historical backtest and the increasing number of factors that have emerged in the past few years—so far there are more than 250 factors that have been identified, ranging from the simple size and value factors cited earlier to GDP growth news and 52-week high strategies. This book focuses only on five of them. The existing academic literature and publications by investment practitioners all too often focus on historical backtests, searching for the evidence of the outperformance versus a conventional index weighted according to the market capitalisation of the underlying stocks.

These successful backtests often suffer from numerous biases and are strongly influenced by the researcher's methodology and the subjective choice of parameters that happen to work well in sample (i.e. the historical data points in the analysis). Over a long period the performance of the factors may look good, the returns are still prone to sharp drawdowns and prolonged periods of underperformance. Hence, the benefits of diversification can often be overstated—see Kalesnik and Linnainmaa in 2018 for discussion about historical performance and diversification debate.

Like any emerging investment trend, some professionals worry that it will spiral out of control at some point. While factor investors advocate that investors should diversify and hold on to their investment for a long time, some sceptics argue that in practice investors jump from factor to factor to chase the hot investment. Others sceptics believe that some factor strategies are only artificially doing well due to the new money flowing into them pushing up their prices—often referred to as overcrowding. Typically, more diversified strategies with a comfortable rebalancing time-window (i.e. periodic adjustment of a portfolio based on the index rules) tend to mitigate the issue. Fund managers can also spread out the trading strategy around the allocation of capital to various securities.

Some also argue that there is a natural capacity constraint, a maximum amount that can be invested in a given strategy that could limit the potential performance benefit of investing in factors in the long term. That is true for any investment that has a capacity limit, and factor strategies are no different. Typically, a fund manager concerned with capacity would close their book to new capital as the assets under management reach a certain level. However, in rules-based or index factor strategies, closing down a fund may not be an option as indices are publically available. This may result in performance deterioration and liquidity concerns.

2.7 Concluding Remarks

We have introduced the evolution and concept of factor investing in this chapter. Factor investing targets return and risk characteristics available through exposure to a variety of investment attributes and styles by taking systematic deviations from a broad market index to harvest a risk premium. The sources of risk and return and the way we understand them has evolved in the past decades. In the core of this book, we focus on five well-established factors in the academic literature which have been widely adopted among professionals in bonds and equities. The extension of factor investing to other asset classes and variations of the factor premium strategies is covered at the end of the book.

The assets under management have been increasing for factor-based strategies and alternative risk premia. This trend is likely to continue as more funds are becoming accessible to retail and institutional investors. The next chapter provides insight into index construction strategies and offers further consideration of issues and concerns around index and factor investing strategies.

3

Architecture and Art of Indexation

This chapter aims to provide insight into the architecture of traditional indices in equities, bonds, commodities, currencies as well as factor-based strategies. With a background on the process and critical considerations for index construction, the reader will hopefully be able to evaluate and question index strategies. We will also discuss crowding risk and capacity—reasons cited by the media for believing that index investing is doomed.

The simplest definition of an index is a group of stocks, bonds, commodities or currencies chosen to represent a market or an asset class. In other words, it is kind of a surrogate for gauging the performance of capital markets or investment strategies. Common equity indices, as we know them, are the likes of the S&P 500 for the U.S. and the FTSE 100 for the U.K. Examples of representation of global bond markets include Bloomberg-Barclays Global aggregate or J.P. Morgan Government Bond Index. Commodities indices aim to represent the global commodities (futures) market such as Thomson Reuters/Core Commodity CRB Index or the Goldman Sachs Commodity Index. The benefit of indices across asset classes is the transparency, representation of the market and the rules-based investment principles that often appeal to many people. These indices continue to evolve as they expand to represent different corners of the globe and specific segments of businesses.

Nevertheless, this evolution brought fragmentation and new layers of complex financial engineering. There are over 3 million market indices calculated globally every day—some target the wider markets while others focus on its subsets. The most significant insight is that many index strategies aim to do the same thing but end up with different outcomes due to different methodology.

To make sense of the increasing complexity and to help navigate the index fund choices investors could look at the way indices are designed and their alignment to overall investment objectives. The architecture behind an index is key to its risk and return profile. It reveals many of the investment biases—both intended and unintended. The S&P 500, for example, favours large and often growth oriented stocks, as the index is weighted according to each constituent's market value (i.e. the number of shares times the price). Those constituents are only 500 stocks out of an opportunity set of thousands in the U.S. The largest members of the index reflect previous strong performance over different market cycles. Only a small subset of the companies in this index drives its performance as a result. In general, when grouping securities into an index, we need to know how important each is to the representation being sought: they need to be weighted in some suitable way—according to their shares of total market value, perhaps, or their shares of total market revenue, or profits.

Similarly, traditional bond indices often represent issuers with the highest debt. A typical corporate Investment Grade (IG) index, for example, will have a consistently higher allocation to financial institutions as they tend to issue more debt than others in the corporate sector. Furthermore, commodity indices are weighted based on production and end up with high concentration to specific commodities such as energy. Currency indices follow the trend as well and are based on trade value in the currency and tend to end up with concentration to the U.S. dollar or Euro, which are the two largest reserves and traded currencies in the world. We will discuss the relevant features of index construction, the issues and how to evaluate them in the next sections.

3.1 Why Index Architecture Matters

Not all indices are created equally. Some are more transparent than others and security universes (targeted, narrow or broad) and allocation methods to constituent tend to differ. A key question is what objective or subjective inputs go into the strategy and how transparent it is. Everything we do has a degree of subjectivity, but the idea is to understand at which stage of the design process it stops and where rules-based calculations of the index kick in.

In general, the objective of transparent indices is to provide greater certainty to investors about their exposures and make it easy to evaluate and track performance. By contrast, indices based on a subjective approach are less predictable and could be harder to track. Using indices constructed with a more objective and transparent approach helps to eliminate additional uncertainties.

Uncertainties can further be reduced by understanding the index objectives and architecture, especially when faced with so many choices of similar strategies in the market. The aim should be to evaluate the methodology and the ingredients of the index to conclude whether it is delivering on its promises. It can help managing portfolio exposures over time and potentially avoid inadvertent exposures as well as unintended outcomes.

As a basic example, investing in the largest 100 stocks by market value in the U.K. in 2017 may not be a good way of gaining exposure to the U.K. economy. For the issuers representing constituents of this index, the majority of the revenues are from outside Europe such as North America and Asia (Fig. 3.1). Only about 45% of the stocks weighted by market value are from the U.K. and continental Europe.

This difference among various indices is also visible in the fixed income space. Given the more complex ecosystem of the bond market, there is even bigger room for a difference between indices. For the U.S. investment grade indices, for example, by Bloomberg-Barclays or Bank or Bank of America-Merrill Lynch have different inclusion and exclusion criteria of bonds and reinvestment criteria of coupons. A more extreme case is the difference

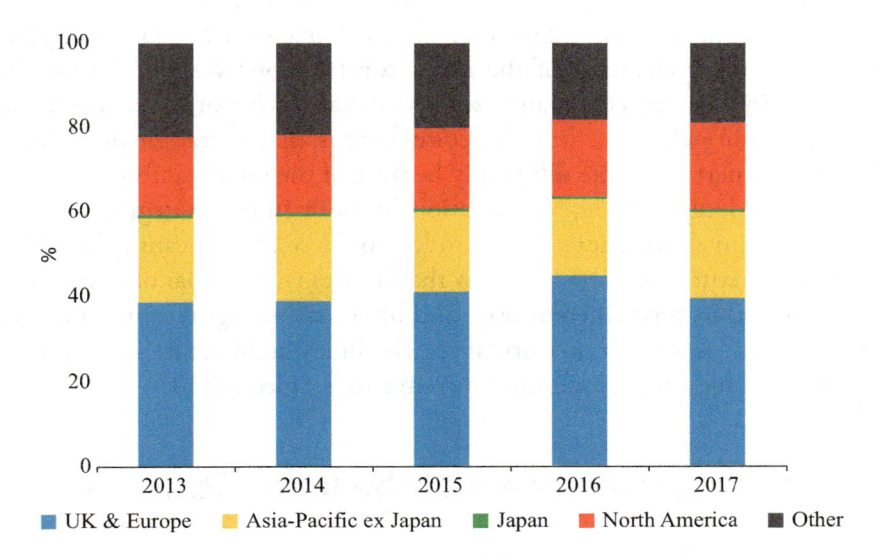

Fig. 3.1 Geographical revenue of largest 100 listed stocks in the U.K. Source: Author's calculations, income statements and Bloomberg. Note: The revenues (year-end) are weighted based on the market value of each stock

between the Dow Jones U.S. IG, which is equally weighted with a fixed and small number of bonds compared to the other three index provider equivalents. In general, the differences between these indices can vary materially and naturally lead to varying performance over time.

Moreover, traditional commodity indices can differ vastly between each other despite offering a similar diversified exposure. Some may have high allocation based on the world production of a specific segment of the commodities market. Some indices such as the S&P-Goldman Sachs Commodity Index may include over 50% to energy commodities, while another such as Bloomberg Commodity Index may have a more balanced exposure to various commodities. This variation could lead to different outcomes as commodities are not homogenous—oil and gas are materially different from gold, coffee and cotton. Hence, commodity prices are unlikely to go up and down at the same time in nominal price terms, unless we experience high global consumer price inflation. If an investor has already little or too much exposure to a specific sector in the asset allocation, it makes sense to look into what the index contains for exposure.

Within the factor space, a good observation is that value investing is commonly seen as underperforming in recent years. There is a significant dispersion of returns among 15 popular value indices—despite their correlation of 97% for over a decade. Some of these indices have declined by 28%, while others have risen by 20% between 2002–2017. The differences are driven by various weighting of constituents, value factor characteristics, rebalancing frequency and other elements of the index construction. We will discuss the weightings in the next section and examples of various factor characteristics in the forthcoming chapters, but the point here is that these self-proclaimed value indices perform quite differently because of the construction.

Despite a deceptively high correlation between index strategies in many asset classes, investors' choice of the index could create a meaningful difference in their returns. By now we know that indices with similar objectives can be constructed in very different ways and often lead to significantly different exposures and, as a result, performance. The index architecture is, therefore, core to delivering solutions in line with investor's expectations.

3.2 Representativeness of the Index Strategy

In the art world, the work by an artist can be classified into a representational (representative) and non-representation (abstract) category. Representational refers to something objective, figurative and naturalistic, something that viewers can recognise, for example, a tree, a person or a house. Non-representational art, on the contrary, is about non-recognisable objects, abstract shapes and forms. Like art, a well-constructed index should represent the investment universe and stated objectives. But in this case, representativeness can mean different things to index providers and index architects.

In general, a representative index can be broad or narrow. The aim is to allow the investor to view, track and understand the intended exposures either for a specific market in an asset class or a particular sector or segment. Representativeness can vary depending on the index objective such as simply market value exposure or factor based strategy. Market value based (e.g. market capitalisation) indices aim to represent the market exposure for a region, country, high or low-quality debt and currency. At the same time, factor indices in equities and bonds represent alternative weighting to traditional weighting based on the market value of securities. It is based on factor characteristics that target a specific or multiple exposures (e.g. value or momentum).

Moreover, the most common broad commodity indices by Bloomberg, Deutsche Bank, Goldman Sachs, CRB, Dow-Jones AIG typically represent 14 to 24 of the most traded and produced commodities. The indices buy commodities at a future date using derivative instruments (often futures contracts) trading on global exchanges, rather than the physical commodities. The opportunity set of traded commodities futures exceeds 45 commodities within energy, agricultural, metals and others. The representation of the index is often based on the production value and/or the liquidity of the constituents. That representation differs among the index providers.

It is critical to understand whether the final index is representative of the underlying market and investment strategy. It involves asking whether the factor or a risk premium index represents the desired exposure, target investment style and outcomes. Once it is established that the opportunity and exposure set for various asset classes is representative, it is crucial to understand where the index can be sliced and diced into multiple segments, which comes down to the modularity of an index.

3.3 Modularity of an Index

The great thing about a modular IKEA sofa is that consumers can create a preferred combination to get what they want. The sofa can be adapted in size, styles and covers, to represent the desired preference and fit into a living room. Having a broad and global index security universe and an approach that allows slicing the exposure can help to create efficient building blocks to fit in a portfolio of an asset allocator.

The idea of the building blocks fitted together without significant gaps and overlap refers to the modularity of an index. Modularity is about taking part in an index and then breaking it down into segments such as regions, countries, sectors or factor characteristics. Well-constructed indices are modular and can help to design the desired market and factor indices. Table 3.1 provides an example of modular indices.

Table 3.1 Example of building blocks and portfolio fit for indices

Equities

Regions	Countries/blocks	Sectors	Size	Factors
North America	U.S.	Financials	Large	Value
U.K.	U.K	Utilities	Medium	Quality
Europe ex. UK	Germany	Industrials	Small	Momentum
Emerging markets	BRICs	...	Micro-cap	Low volatility
Frontier markets		Staples		Size

Bonds

Segments	Currency	Regions/country	Size	Factors	Rating buckets	Maturity buckets (years)
Government bonds	USD	U.S.	Bond amount	Value	AAA	1–5
Agencies & Supras	EUR	Europe		Quality	AA	5–10
IG	GBP	Asia		Momentum	A	10+
HY	JPY	EM		Low-risk	BBB	
EM local currency	Local			Size	BB	
EM local currency	Hard				B	

Commodities

Segments	Components	Size
Energy	Crude/Brent crude oil	Production based
Industrial metals	Natural gas	
Precious metals	Gold	
Grains and softs	Silver	

Currencies

Country groups	Base currency	Size
G10	USD, EUR, GBP	Reserves held by the central banks
Emerging markets	BRL, INR, RUB, KRW	

Source: Author
Note: For illustrative purpose only. IG denotes Investment Grade, HY denotes High Yield

The regional building blocks can be broken down into the size of companies in the equity security universe and similarly in fixed income and commodities as shown in Table 3.1. It enables an asset allocator to avoid overlap between companies' characteristics, sector or size (a clear delineation or breakpoint between the small and large companies as an example).

The bottom line is that the market capitalisation benchmarks and factor strategies in the portfolio form an important part of the overall risk and return budget. Less modular indices can result in gaps, overlaps in an investor's portfolio, and can create unintended consequences in the longer term.

3.4 Availability: The Amount of Stocks and Bonds Outstanding

Now that we established the importance of the security universe, modularity and portfolio fit, it is time to move to the availability of the security universe to investors. It is an integral part of creating an efficient and investable index.

Stocks and bonds might be locked up as part of an Initial Price Offering (IPO) or restricted through a private placement (an exclusive agreement between borrowers and lenders). Hence, part or all of the outstanding securities within an index for an issuer could be held in large private holdings and not publicly available for trading. For equities, the number of shares available for sale and purchase by investors is different from the total number of shares that the firm has issued. This is referred to as a free-float adjustment in stocks and can impact weights within an index. An efficient index would capture this in the index construction approach to represent the "true opportunity" set for investors. The equivalent term for fixed income is private placement.

As an example, Table 3.2 shows the impact of free-float adjustment in a market capitalisation index. Companies like American Express change rank from 59 to 70 after adjusting the market value for availability in this way. The market value adjustment often happens before the security allocation takes place (this is the topic for the next section). When it comes to bonds, some government bond indices adjust for what the central bank purchase at auctions (e.g. System Open Market Account Holdings).

The majority of commodities are traded on exchanges via futures contracts or other derivatives, instead of physically. Availability in the context of commodities futures is referring to liquidity or the open interest of the commodity

Table 3.2 Impact of free-float adjustment on stock weighting

Company	Free float (%)	Market cap (USD, billion)	Rank (market value based)	Adjusted market value (USD, billion)	Rank adjusted for free float
Apple inc	88	1100	1	968	1
Amazon.com inc	84	912	2	766	4
American Express	82	92	59	75	70
General Motors c	89	46	119	41	132
Kellogg co	80	24	213	19	259
American Airline	89	15	316	13	342

Source: Author's calculations, Bloomberg
Note: The calculations of the free float-adjusted market capitalisation index is based on 1000 stocks listed on U.S. Exchanges with a minimum free float of 80% in Oct. 2018. The adjusted market value is the representative value of what can be traded in the market

in the market. Gold, the most traded precious metal, is often traded through derivatives while rhodium (a platinum type of metal) mostly trades in the physical market. In the energy sector, crude oil futures have higher liquidity than coal. Hence, two futures contract on commodities in the same segment can have different availability for trading and inclusion in an index.

3.5 Stock and Bond Weightings

This section continues the debate on the pillars of index construction and aims to provide an overview of various weighting schemes and their application. The weighting schemes define the allocation of securities in an index. Two indices, for example, can hold the same stock but differ in how they are weighted. Consequently, this leads to the sector- and stock-specific biases and also affects the risk and return profile of the indices. Academics and market practitioners have not been shy in developing new ways of weighting a portfolio. Table 3.3 provides an overview of some of the weighting schemes used in portfolio construction.

Every index irrespective of weighting has some degree of factor exposure. However, alternatively-weighted indices based on risk-based weighting schemes in Table 3.3 do not necessarily constitute factor investing indices on their own. A risk-based weighting may provide a portfolio with different weights than a simple index with stocks of lowest volatility in the universe. Some weighting schemes target the low risk factor, but may not capture other factors such as value or momentum. In general, a factor index targets characteristics of individual stocks that drive index risk-return, which in turn can be weighted with one or a combination of the weighting schemes.

Table 3.3 Classes of weighting methods

Weighting methods	Description	Pros	Cons
General weightings			
Value-weighting/ Market capitalisation	Allocation according to the size of the company's value of a security or value of debt	Allocates more capital to largest securities by market value to represent the market	Concentration to largest stocks or bonds
Price weighting	Allocate to securities based on their price levels	Simple	Tend to over-allocate to securities with the highest price
Equal weighting	Allocate equally across securities	Increase weight diversification compared to the market value-weighted index	A bias to small and mid-sized securities Higher turnover than market capitalisation
Fundamental-based weighting			
Fundamental weighting	Weight securities to target accounting and fundamental characteristics (e.g. book value, cash flows)	Captures company strength and breaks the link to security price and returns Can increase the capacity of a strategy due to a higher allocation to larger companies/securities	Accounting figures can be noisy
Risk-based weighting schemes			
Risk weighting	Allocate higher weights to securities with low risk and less to high risk	Simple Low volatility securities receive the lowest weight and vice versa	Bias to specific sectors or segments of the market if unconstrained Higher turnover
Equal risk contribution	Weights are determined based on each securities risk contribution to the final portfolio	Could increase risk diversification	Requires optimisation Does not necessarily reduce risk in the index
Maximum Sharpe ratio	Allocate to securities that provide the optimal Sharpe ratio of the final portfolio	Maximise the risk-adjusted returns in an index	Requires optimisation techniques Higher turnover
Minimum volatility/variance	Allocate to securities that generates the lowest volatility	Minimise the risk level in an index subject to target objectives	Requires optimisation techniques Can be concentrated (security, sector) without constraints

Source: Author
Note: Sharpe ratio is defined as the excess return of the investment over the risk-free interest rate per unit of risk (standard deviation)

Moreover, fundamentally-weighted indices tend to target specific factor characteristics and weight the index constituents accordingly. Two stocks with identical gross profitability of USD 100 million, for example, might be weighted 50% each with fundamental weighting, but by 70% and 30% if the weighting is based on market capitalisation. The fundamental characteristics and weighting will be discussed in the value and quality chapters.

3.5.1 Market Value Weighting

As we discussed, market value weighting is the most common index weighting method, known as market capitalisation weighting in equities and debt weighting in fixed income. It can be defined as price times the total number of listed shares for equities and price times the outstanding principal amount borrowed for fixed income. In general, market capitalisation weighted indices do not need regular rebalancing. Market value weighting adjusts along with prices in the market—the weight of the security increases as the price rises and vice versa. It leads to a lower turnover in an index compared to other weighting schemes mentioned in this section.

Market capitalisation and debt weighting are usually a more reliable assessment of market value than the price alone. It reflects the way markets behave. Large stocks or debt issuers have a significant impact on a market value weighted index than smaller ones. Figure 3.2 illustrates the cumulative weight of the equities by market capitalisation for the largest 1000 stocks in the U.S.

Similar to equities, fixed income indices tend to have a high concentration in the largest debt issuers. For example, a market-value weighted corporate IG index (e.g. Bloomberg-Barclays US Corporates) in USD has about 50% of

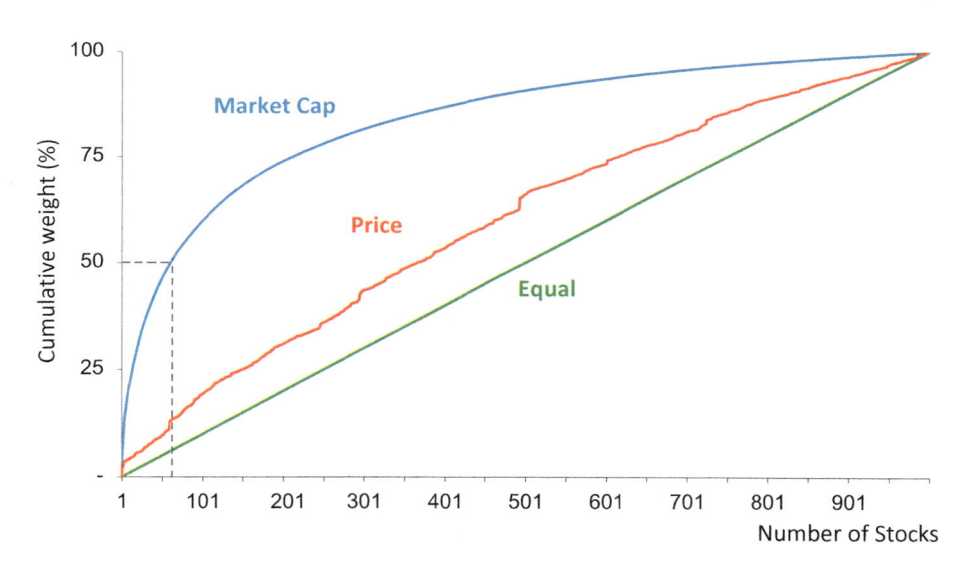

Fig. 3.2 Weighting comparison of market value, equal and price weighting. Note: Author's construction and calculations of free float-adjusted market capitalisation index based on 1000 listed stocks on U.S. Exchanges with a minimum free float of 80% as at 8th October 2018. The data source used for the construction is Bloomberg. Top 10 stocks constitute 14% of the index

the weight concentrated into about 60 borrowers, with a majority of them in the financial sector at the end of 2018. The Top 10 issuers constitute 16% of the index, mainly driven by banks.

As discussed, commodity indices can represent either a target, or a narrow or broad part of the market. When it comes to commodities, the closest approach to market value-weighting is world-production weighting. An example is the S&P-Goldman Sachs flagship commodities index. It is weighted by five-year averages of annual world production volumes. This approach is sometimes contested as a fundamental approach rather than a representation of commodities market capitalisation as for equities.

Currency indices aim to represent a basket of currencies against a base currency. These indices are often used to gauge the changes of a specific currency (base currency) against a basket of currencies. The Bloomberg Dollar Spot Index, for example, is a commonly referenced currency index of the USD against a basket of developed and emerging market currencies. Another version of this index, include other base currencies such as Euro and GBP. The typical weighting for currency indices that resemble market capitalisation weighted equities is trade- and liquidity weighting between two currencies.

Value weighted indices are still a dominant choice for investors and represent the opportunity set in a particular market aiming to earn the traditional risk premium (the compensation for taking risk) with low turnover. Nevertheless, the market capitalisation approach is not the only way to represent a market segment or weight securities. The next subsections provide further detail of alternative weighting schemes described in Table 3.3.

3.5.2 Equal Weighting

Equal weighting is the most straightforward weighting scheme to apply as each security has the same importance in an index. The constituent weights are simply calculated as: *1/(Total number of securities)*. Equal weighting can be applied in various ways to manage inadvertent sector biases for diversification of exposures. Figure 3.2 shows how an equal weighting can differ when applied to an entire index versus equal weighting within a sector (i.e. sector-neutral basis without taking active sector bets). Furthermore, equal weighting is also applied to commodities and other asset classes. For example, the CRB Commodity Index is an equal-weight index across various traded commodities in the futures market.

3.5.3 Price Weighting

Price weighting is often specific to equities and is one of the oldest methods for stock indices, illustrated in Fig. 3.2. A price-weighted index holds an equal number of shares for each security, but investors pay the price of the underlying shares to buy the index. The value of the index is the sum of all its securities prices divided by the total number of stocks. The more a stock price rises, the more it drives up the index's overall value. For example, assume two securities—Security A is priced at USD 10, and Security B is priced at USD 90. In this case, security A would weigh 10% while security B would have 90% weight. Hence, a small company may have a high price while a large company may have a low one. Under this weighting scheme based on the largest 1000 U.S. stocks, Booking Holdings stock with a market value of about USD 83 billion would be weighted 1.8% compared to Apple of about 860 billion in the market value would be weighted 0.2% at the end of 2017.

However, it is still used in some parts of the market. The Dow Jones Industrial Average and Nikkei 225 Stock Average are among the most popular price-weighted stock market benchmarks. The problem with this weighting scheme is that the price alone might not explain the total importance of a security to investors. That is why most indices are capitalisation-weighted and alternatively-weighted and why few professional investors track the Dow Jones Index.

3.5.4 Outcome-Oriented Weighting: Tilting and Optimisation

When it comes to portfolio construction, two conventional approaches for achieving a specific objective involve tilting or optimisation. These two approaches aim to improve or reduce exposure to chosen security attributes. For example, an outcome could include higher exposure to cheap stocks and fewer growth stocks or more ESG friendly companies. These approaches can use a pre-defined stock and bond universe that is representative of the target exposure.

Tilting is often used in factor and ESG index strategies and starts with a set of weights defined by a parent index. The initial weights can increase, stay unchanged or decrease. The tilt approach itself can vary depending on design and investment objectives. It can be expressed either through a security score (−1 to 1) or just as a percentage (e.g. deciles or quintiles) based on stock characteristics. For illustrative purpose, a score of 0.5 for a stock with 2% weight could mean a 1% increase in tilted weight, calculated as: (1 + 0.50) × 2%. A score of −0.5 could imply a reduction of 1% with a new security weight of 1%. Often tilting requires re-basing the portfolio or the index for all the constituent weights to ensure a sum of 100% is maintained.

Generally, the advantage of tilting is transparency and simplicity. It is quite straightforward to analyse up and down weights between the initial and tilted index. However, there are instances where the tilting approach becomes iterative and suffers from a lack of transparency, particularly in cases with too many constraints or when factors are involved. This is typically an "enhanced" tilting approach, which involves a semi-optimisation technique to meet the constraints and relevant risk management characteristics, such as concentration limits and investment risk parameters (sectors and stock-specific risks).

Optimisation techniques, sometimes associated with "black box", are widely used in portfolio management and index construction and go back to Harry Markowitz in the 1950s. Construction of the portfolio can involve minimisation of portfolio risk while aiming to achieve an expected return objective, the strength of factor exposures and possibly satisfying other constraints (diversification, liquidity among others). Once the investment and risk objectives are defined, the optimisation framework aims to generate a portfolio or an index. It is a less transparent construction approach as it can be hard to see what is happening under the bonnet.

On the positive side, if a solution to the problem exists optimisation can provide it and generate a portfolio in one go to solve and meet the many set constraints for a portfolio. As described in Table 3.3, several weightings such as Equal Risk Contribution, Maximum Sharpe ratio weighting are optimisation led methods. However, the optimisation approach is not only applicable to risk-based factor strategies. It can apply to fundamentally-weighted indices as well. For example, it is possible to create a portfolio focused on high quality or undervalued securities by using a specific definition of factor characteristics. Having discussed security universes and weighting methodologies, we move on to index maintenance, which is essential for continuity and a more consistent profile of an index.

3.6 Index Maintenance and Operations

Maintenance of an index is the stepping stone into managing and measuring index performance. Once the index methodology and initial construction are complete, maintenance of an index requires technology and data feeds. This allows the capturing of periodic adjustments of securities before the information gets published on major platforms or websites. We will focus on three areas of maintenance in this section: liquidity together with tradability, rebalancing and reconstitution, as well as managing corporate actions.

Firstly, liquidity and tradeable securities are vital attributes of an efficient and implementable index. Most equity indices contain stocks that trade on exchanges and can be easily bought and sold, yet some areas of the market are less liquid (e.g. smaller companies). Bond index constituents often trade over the counter (OTC)—in other words between the fund managers and brokers, without an official exchange. For this reason, when exchange traded fund providers started to look at fixed income products about 10 years ago, they mainly used specially designed "liquid" or "compact" indices.

The other parts of the maintenance are rebalancing and reconstitution of an index—two terms that are often thrown around in the market. Distinguishing between them is essential. Rebalancing brings the index back into its targeted market value based on market capitalisation or factor style objectives. To make sure index composition remains accurate over time, index managers typically rebalance on a monthly, quarterly, semi-annual or annual basis. Market capitalisation weighted indices, for example, need less rebalancing compared to alternatively-weighted indices such as fundamentally or risk-weighted. Fixed income indices lead the way in rebalancing frequency, which can be monthly due to new and expiring bonds in the index.

Similarly, the rebalancing of derivative-based (e.g. futures contracts) indices in commodities, for example, requires further consideration. As a future's contract expires, it is rolled into a longer-dated contract. On the one hand, the more the index is rebalanced the higher is the turnover. On the other hand, this higher rebalancing frequency is often necessary to maintain consistent exposure over time and is not necessarily a bad thing. The simple message is that it is essential to be aware of the rebalancing frequency and its potential implications.

Reconstitution, in contrast with rebalancing, completely rebuilds an index from the beginning. The process reviews the broad global investment universe to represent the relevant individual constituents in an index. As part of the process, constituents are assigned to the appropriate company size bucket, credit rating, sector, country, region, factor style to ensure consistency over time. This process typically happens annually or over a more extended period.

Finally, daily changes for securities traded in the market can be linked to business activities of issuers—referred to as corporate actions. The list is long and typically includes mergers and acquisitions, initial public and secondary offerings, new bond issuance or buybacks, issuers calling back their callable bonds, or spin-offs among others. These can have a material effect on performance and the index strategy. It is critical to understand whether the index uses an objective and transparent process for regularly incorporating these actions. A subjective process can be used but could lead to more uncertainty about the exposures of the index.

3.7 Replication and Management of Index Funds

After defining the index, most fund selectors spend significant time and recourse in the due diligence process. They aim to understand the manager's philosophy, process, people and performance—these are also known as the four Ps. Index fund management and the underlying index evaluation are no different in this regard and subject to the "four P rule". For an index fund, the philosophy is often linked to how the index benchmark is replicated. The process involves pre-trade and post-trade analysis and how decisions are made. People is about the team and the institution that manages the strategy. Finally, performance is a question of the fund manager's ability to replicate the index and if the strategy is providing the intended exposure.

Index fund management requires a little bit more than a decent computer program to track the index. In some areas, a machine could track the main market capitalisation indices such as the Dow Jones Industrial Average, the S&P 500 or FTSE 100. Unlike active management, no stock picking is involved in index management. However, an index-tracking fund that just buys all the constituents to replicate an index is likely to underperform its benchmark as illustrated in Fig. 3.3. For example, a bond index fund manager who buys the entire bond universe in an index, especially the global ones with over 10,000 bonds is likely to underperform the benchmark. The trading spread alone may send the portfolio off track from its benchmark, the index it is trying to track. This applies broadly to any index in any asset class.

Typically, factor index strategies can be managed with flexibility while tracking the underlying index. This can be achieved through efficient implementation: avoiding forced buying or selling and participating in the new issue market (i.e. new debt offering by issuers). In general, bond funds incur transaction costs from trading to match their reference benchmarks, but these are not excessive if managed within a tracking error budget. In general, government bond index funds have a turnover of about 15–25% per annum with monthly rebalance—corporate bonds tend to exceed this turnover rate.

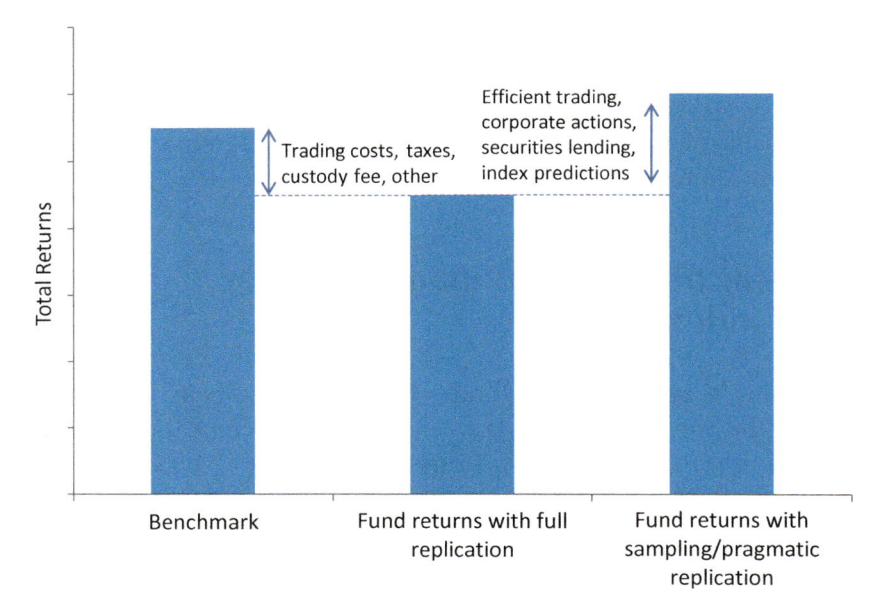

Fig. 3.3 Benchmark returns versus full and 'smart' replication of index funds. Source: Author. Note: For illustrative purpose only

As a rule, index fund managers and their trading teams do not just sit with their feet up watching the benchmark on a computer screen. There is some heavy lifting around trading (pre-trade and post-trade analysis), cash flow management and corporate actions considered to add value to the investors and to keep the fund within a tolerance of pre-set targets. The next section describes the different processes an index fund manager undertakes to track the underlying benchmark.

3.7.1 Trading Strategies

Index-tracking managers often reflect their index's risk and return characteristics without having to choose stocks actively. However, the way they buy and sell shares can add or subtract from the performance. An index trading team is constantly investing throughout the day, looking for the best price and execution points, to minimise transaction costs and boost performance.

The life cycle of trading for index fund managers involves:

- **Cash management:** managing cash flow, subscriptions and redemptions of the funds, dividends and coupons;
- **Index rebalance or changes:** notification from index provider and corporate action database;

- **Pre-trade analysis:** analysis performed by fund manager/index analyst;
- **Implementation strategy:** decide what to trade based on market conditions (e.g. liquidity) and security attribution analysis of the change and execution of the trading plan;
- **Risk management:** managing the tracking error and index risk and return profile within set appetite and risk tolerances.

3.7.2 Securities Lending

Securities lending is another mechanism that can help enhance the performance of an index fund. It involves the owner of an asset temporarily passing the title of the asset to a borrower (while keeping economic exposure) in return for a fee and against collateral. It can aid greater market liquidity and give lenders the opportunity to earn additional income.

For an equity index manager, securities lending can be quite appealing. An index fund is unlikely to sell a stock unless that stock is going to leave the index. This means the fund can lend those shares to someone for a fee and enhance returns. However, there are risks involved in the stock lending process.

The Three Key Consideration from Securities Lending

- **Counterparty risk**—the risk that the borrower defaults while in possession of the securities. This is the critical risk with respect to future financial loss if the borrowers default;
- **Conduct risk**—can arise as a result of conflicts of interest between the lender and its agent. Sharing revenue between the lender and its agent could encourage the agent to compromise on the quality of both the collateral and the counterparty;
- **Corporate Governance Risk**—a potential loss of voting rights during the period of the loan.

Typically, some fund managers split the securities lending revenues with investors and some pass it all to their investor. In either case, it is crucial that there is an alignment of economic interest with investors.

For a global index fund (e.g. mutual fund and ETFs), the value from stock lending can be on average three basis points—see Rowley et al. in 2016. Often the fund managers split the revenue with their clients—the revenue split varies between different asset managers. Some pass all the revenue to their clients to manage any conflict of interest. The custodian bank also takes a portion that can be up to 20 per cent of the profit share for administration and other charges.

3.7.3 Cash Management

In a bull market, hoarding cash has a price, especially when dividends and new subscriptions emerge. Actively investing new money is an integral part of managing an index fund. Waiting to put cash in the market could cause a significant drag on the fund performance, especially for index funds, such as S&P 500 or FTSE All Share funds, which often attract lumpy inflows of cash on a daily basis. Being out of the market could be a painful exercise. One way to minimise cash drag in funds is known as equitisation. By equitising, the fund manager invests in derivatives (equity index or bond futures) to reflect accruals that are pending dividends or coupons. These are effectively dividends that are paid in the future (pay date) rather than invested on the ex-date (i.e. dividend entitlement cut-off date) that most mainstream indices assume.

3.8 Crowding Risk of Index Funds

Overcrowding risk in index strategies is a concern for many. A crowded investment strategy involves a large pool of capital following the same or a similar strategy. It is not necessarily a bad thing, and far more important to identify the asset price implications of this trading activity.

The argument is that as more and more people buy the index trackers, there are less and fewer people discovering the real price for those stocks. Before the world of the index, the stock prices were all just a "meeting point" for somebody claiming it was too high and somebody else claiming it was too low. That is called price discovery in financial market jargon. Price discovery is pretty fundamental to getting close to the market's view of the right price for the right value. Drivers of a security market price and "true value" are not necessarily the same things. The price can be higher or lower than the value. However, over the long term, the market price should reflect the fundamental value of the company.

There is less capital actually seeking the "true value" of the company as more and more people invest in an index. Although an investor may have limited exposure to the underlying constituents, the size of the exposure can be meaningful depending on the index choice. For example, this is more an issue for highly concentrated indices in a handful of companies such as market value-weighted or market capitalisation weighted indices. Theoretically, if all people only invest in indices, all the stock prices only reflect the fact that everyone's buying the index. This implies that there is no relationship between price and underlying value anymore. In such a scenario, poor managements and good ones are viewed equally by the market, and lead to poor corporate governance. Any big change in an economy or a geopolitical risk that rattles investors' sentiment and fuels their fear could make people pull out capital from the underlying index funds and in turn a trigger for a sell-off.

Currently, there is little empirical evidence on the overcrowding effect. However, precautions against crowding risks can be taken by proper implementation of factor indices. In particular, diversification can be an example of precaution against crowding risk. If investors spread their holdings across several factors, there should not be excessive crowding in a single strategy. Another precaution could be an alpha-chasing active manager.

MSCI developed a scorecard combining the trading information with the asset prices and valuations to identify crowded trades. The scorecard is based on the following four criteria to help determine when a position or a strategy is overcrowded:

- Mutual fund trading activity
- Hedge fund trading activity
- Correlations
- Valuation dispersion

The first two can be predictors or leading indicators of crowded trades historically. In the early 2009 period when the momentum strategy experienced a historical drawdown, mutual and hedge funds were actually sellers of momentum before the momentum strategies crashed.

However, those first two criteria are not always enough to identify crowded trades. If we aggregate all of the trading activity in the marketplace, then all the buyers and sellers cancel out—there's always a seller for a buyer and vice versa. Hence, the impact on asset prices and valuations of this trading activity matters. The third measure is pair-wise correlations—the average correlation among the securities in a strategy. As a large amount of capital flows into a specific set of securities, the correlations of all those securities in a strategy increase. Investors' could end up focusing on the capital flow rather than the content of investment.

Valuation is the final measure and focuses on the movement of securities' valuations further from fundamentals. This is measured by the valuation spreads of securities in the top versus the bottom deciles of an investment strategy. The valuation spread is the difference of the average book-to-price ratio of top and bottom decile of the stocks.

3.9 The Capacity of Index Funds

Capacity can mean various things to different practitioners. The definition can vary from the maximum amount that can be invested into a strategy to distorted pricing or unbearable transaction costs. Capacity could be a result of crowding into a strategy.

Typically, a fund manager concerned with capacity would close their book to new capital as the assets under management (AUM) reaches a certain level. They do this in order to prevent a potential impact on investment returns by the capital flows (with too much capital bidding-up the prices of securities to unsustainable levels, for example). This can also be related to liquidity conditions prevalent in the underlying market. In addition, the capacity problem is apparent when an index has to rebalance. If all index investors have to buy and sell the same stocks on the same day, notable price distortions and transaction costs could erode expected returns. While capacity concern in the index funds might be a nice problem to have from a commercial perspective, it can be harmful when everyone is running for the exit—a common phenomenon in momentum strategies that will be discussed in the later chapters.

As a practical example, we can consider small capitalisation stocks as a segment of the size factor. As pension funds move toward the 14% small capitalisation target allocation, they face a potential roadblock: there are not enough small capitalisation index funds investing outside the U.S. to meet potential institutional demand. Pension funds may need to look at both passive and active managers to fill what we calculate could be nearly a USD 750 billion gap in non-U.S. small-cap equity fund capacity.

Overall, factor-based index strategies still represent a small portion of the equity and bond market, and there is enough capacity to handle growing assets in these strategies. At the end of 2017, factor investing was still between 1.0–1.5% of the global equity AUM. However, this does not mean that it has unlimited capacity. For every factor-based investor who is overweight a security relative to market capitalisation, there must be another investor who is underweight it. If factors outperform over time, this is likely to create more buyers than sellers, distorting the pricing and lower the future expected return (e.g. factor premium over the market capitalisation).

Capacity risk can be managed either through the index construction, the ways in which an index is managed or through asset allocation (diversifying across various investment styles). On the index construction side, various measures can be taken into account: starting from setting concentration limits and extending it to managing liquidity.

One of the ways to manage liquidity from the index management side is to increase the rebalance window. By spreading the implementation of index rebalancing over multiple trading days, index fund managers can increase the threshold capacity. An experienced index implementer would manage the costs by implementing rebalancing in portions and slightly deviating away from the benchmark. Investors, from their end, could give the index manager a tracking-error bandwidth, take more risk around the review period and manage the transitional period as they see fit.

3.10 Concluding Remarks

We discussed the importance of index construction and how it can impact the investor's outcome. The evolution of new indices and fragmentation between various providers has added layers of complexity. Many index strategies aim to do the same thing but end up with different outcomes which are often a result of different index methodology and approach.

Not only is the index choice relevant to index-tracking investors, but so too is the practical matter of index replication. We discussed key features that an efficient index manager undertakes to replicate the index efficiently and add value to the investors. This involves smart and efficient trading as full replication of the index is likely to be a drag on performance for investors. We also discussed common topics around crowding and capacity risks for index fund management. The takeaway from this debate is that crowding is inevitable and not an issue if the fund manager is doing their job in replicating an index. While capacity risk comes down to how the fund manager is trading and implementing the strategy. Next time you meet an index fund manager—ask them how they replicate an index.

Part II

Equity Factor Investing

There are many factors and investment styles in the world today. This part focuses on five well-established factors in the academic literature that have been persistent for decades. These include value, momentum, quality, low risk and size factors. Harvey et al. in 2015 identified in a comprehensive analysis a much larger list of 295 factors across various assets classes and strategies, but their research shows that between 80–158 are false discoveries and have worked for a limited period of time or just in backtests. Research by McLean and Pontiff in 2014 found that a factor's return declined by c.56% following the publication of academic research of the identified factor. Even after adjusting for the possibility of data mining, the researchers estimated the "publication effect" to be a 31% reduction in return.

4

Equity Factor Investing: Value Stocks

Value investing is one of the most traditional and familiar factor strategies among academics and practitioners. Arguably, one could potentially categorise most active investors as value investors, because in general, value investing is about buying the stocks that are trading below an intrinsic value (also known as the real value or fair value). A value investor aims to buy bargains in the financial markets—paying 50 cents, say, for a stock that is worth a dollar. So, value investing focuses on understanding the underlying business behind the stock and deciding whether it is cheap, fairly valued or expensive.

Value investing belongs to the genre of fundamental investing, and generally employs a buy-and-hold strategy until the value of the investment plays out. In this case, you are likely to make your investment judgments based on the value of assets today and consider asset growth as a realisation of the value in the future. Hence, an investor wants to buy a business only if it trades at less than the value of the assets in place and view growth as a reward for taking the risk. The fact that a stock is trading at discount leads to the debate as to whether markets are efficient.

For many years, efficient market investing has been the dominant theory of investing. The idea is that the investor is not going to be able to collect information better than the consensus (i.e. the information everybody else had collected). Therefore all investors should worry about is minimising transaction costs and allocating assets in a way that creates an appropriate risk profile. Value investing is often mentioned as an argument against the efficient market hypothesis. In its most strict version, the efficient market hypothesis entails that all public and non-public information is in the security price. This implies that there is no way for an investor to outperform the market consistently.

If markets are efficient, we should not be able to profit from bargains. But as we know, financial markets are not always efficient because people are complex creatures with emotions—"greed and fear". As Warren Buffet phrased it, "I'd be a bum on the street with a tin cup if the markets were always efficient".

The inefficiency and the sentimental nature of financial markets are among the key drivers of the value factor premium. Benjamin Graham described the market like a partner who is manic-depressive. Every day "Mr Market" comes to you and offers a price for your shares of a business. If "Mr Market" feels good that day, then the price is extremely high. If the market is depressed, then the price can be remarkably low. Hence, "Mr Market" is a very weird partner and there is overwhelming evidence for that. If the market is fluctuating a lot and you think that the fundamental value of a stock is stable, then prices are going to diverge regularly from fundamental values.

A range of academic and empirical research shows that a portfolio with "cheap" stocks (based on various characteristics such as price-to-book or price-to-earnings) has historically outperformed the market capitalisation indices over the long term. These studies were born in the 1930s and revisited from the early 1950s to today. Among the most referenced research is by Fama and French in 1992. It showed the importance of value along with other factors in explaining market returns. Their approach to defining the value factor in an index strategy is widely adopted in the industry today. Common definitions used by index value strategies, for example, are to buy stocks with low price-to-earnings or low price-to-book ratios.

Today value investing is among the most popular factor investing index funds. This is evident with the increasing availability of diversified value strategies and asset under management growth. Figure 4.1 shows the growth in the U.S. listed ETFs since 2007. The total assets managed at the end of 2017 exceeded USD 180 billion.

This chapter offers an overview of value investing and how it is translated into systematic factor strategies. As value investing is a broad topic, the main focus is on the main characteristics that are part of value index strategies. We will also highlight some key debates and considerations of the strategies and discuss the key drivers of the risk and returns.

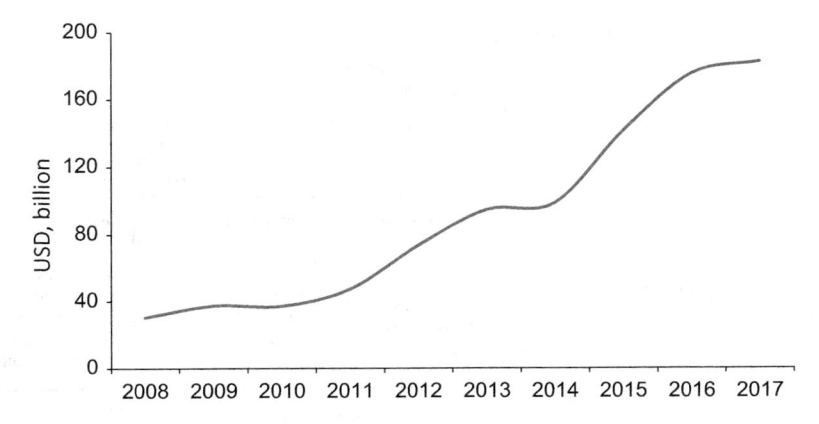

Fig. 4.1 Value U.S. listed ETFs. Source: Bloomberg, Dec. 2008–Dec. 2017

4.1 Schools of Value Investing

Benjamin Graham's investment career span from the 1920s to 1950s. During this time he also lectured a popular course on finance at Columbia Business School. Many of his students went on to practise his method of security analysis and achieved outstanding results over a number of decades. In 1934 he published his book "Security Analysis" and later in 1949 published "The Intelligent Investor", which set out an intellectual framework for value investing.

A few schools of thought have evolved post-Graham's era (Table 4.1). The first school deals with a modification of Graham's philosophy to value investing. The elite group of this branch and discipline includes Warren Buffett, Walter Schloss, Irving Kahn, and Charles Munger. They stand as a testament to the brilliance of Graham. Some of their modifications to Graham's approach look at the franchise value, management quality and capital allocation in the assessment of intrinsic value (used interchangeably with fair value).

The second school of thought is highly empirical and is based on professional and academic studies that show that value stocks outperform bonds, growth stocks and traditional stock market indices (e.g. market capitalisation) over the long run. This includes studies by Sanjoy Basu, Eugene Fama, Kenneth French and many other academics.

Another empirical and academic branch of value investing is influenced by behavioural finance, a favourite topic of conferences around the world. Behavioural finance addresses human biases and anomalies when making investment decisions. These ideas are often associated with Daniel Kahneman

Table 4.1 Schools of value investing

	Benjamin Graham *Traditional value investing* Assessing intrinsic value and set the foundation and philosophy for value investing				
	Investors *Concentrated strategies*		Empirical and academic branch *Diversified strategies*	
	Refining valuation	Special situation	International	Academic
Neo-classic value investing	Modified Graham's approach for example, franchise value, management quality and capital allocation to assess intrinsic value	Bankruptcy securities, spinoffs, and complex structures	Global stocks including emerging markets	Academics research on various value characteristics (accounting ratios)
Example of prominent figures	Warren Buffett and Charlie Munger	Joel Greenblatt and Seth Klarman	John Templeton	Sanjoy Basu, Eugene Fama and Kenneth French

Source: Author
Note: This list is not exhaustive as value investing is practised in various ways. There are psychological branches of value investing that may not necessarily be related to systematic index strategies

and Amos Tversky. The focus of this section is more on the empirical screens and studies. We will discuss later some of the behavioural aspects of value investing and how it influences the risk and reward.

Most of the schools in value investing would be considered contrarian in nature—some are more extreme than others. They often invest in companies or securities that others have given up on, either because of poor performance or feeble future prospects of the business or sector. A typical strategy involves contrarian belief that losers will do better than loved stocks in the market over the longer term. There is empirical evidence that prices recover in the long term for entire markets. De Bondt and Thaler in 1985, for example, constructed an extreme "loser" (stocks that lost value over the previous year) and "winner" (stocks that had gone up over the previous year) portfolio of 35 stocks between 1933–1978. This study examined the portfolio returns over the 5-year holding period and showed that the "loser" portfolio clearly outperformed the "winner" portfolio during the holding period. The loser portfolio is a representation of value stock where the price reverted to a long-term value (also known as mean-reversion). Similarly, the winner portfolio is a representation of expensive stocks. This concept is different from momentum, which is short-term and will be discussed in the equity momentum chapter.

In the real world, it important not to overstate the potential returns of "loser" portfolios, especially for small-sized companies with low price denomination. In general, "loser" portfolios are more likely to contain low priced stocks (for example, less than USD 5 or less), which generate higher transactions costs and are also more likely to offer asymmetric return profiles. This means that the excess returns over the market come from a few stocks that are making phenomenal returns rather than from those with consistent performance. In general, being a contrarian, an investor needs a long time horizon for the loser portfolio to win. Over the short term value stocks may still underperform. Occasionally, entire markets can simply disappear—in 1917, the St Petersburg index went to zero, and even the most committed value investors would have been wiped out.

Being a contrarian value investor often begins with the proposition that markets overreact to good and bad news. That is often inherent in the design of most value factor strategies. Consequently, stocks with negative headline news (earnings declines in one quarter or bad investments by the management) are likely to be undervalued. Empirical studies established that good years are more likely to be followed by bad years for specific stocks or sectors over the long term, and vice versa.

Sir John Templeton said that there are two ways that you can beat the market. You must hold a non-consensus view, and you must be right. Because if you do what other people do, you will get what other people get, and then if you are wrong, then you are wrong. Exceptional investors know that they have to hold non-consensus views, but they know that being a contrarian can also be very damaging to your portfolio and reputation. A successful example of holding the contrarian view is personified by John Paulson, a relatively unheralded hedge fund manager. Mr. Paulson became convinced that the housing market was wildly overvalued around 2005. He made a principled and significant bet against it by using credit derivative instruments on the U.S. subprime mortgage lending market. Today it is referred to as the greatest trade of all time. However, being a contrarian investor is not for the faint-hearted. It requires discipline, self-confidence, patience or being able to stomach market volatility.

4.2 The Value and Growth Debate

Having described value, the natural questions most people ask: what is non-value investing? The opposite to value is often seen as growth investing. To put it bluntly, growth investing may be more a philosophy of buying what is popular and thought most likely to grow while value investing is more about buying what is out of favour. Hence, a pure growth investor targets companies that may have little intrinsic worth currently, but are experiencing or might experience a high degree of future business growth. These companies typically have higher market price relative to its earnings (price-to-earnings) than those selected by value investors. These two investment disciplines are often regarded as two different ways of investing in the asset management industry and often central to many debates.

However, the debate is often blurred in the press and media. Value and growth may not be mutually exclusive—any value strategy needs growth to realise its potential in the future, and a growth company could become a value after experiencing strong earnings growth. Growth can be a component in determining value, which can influence a decision in either a negative or positive way. That is why both strategies tend to perform differently in various market conditions and years. This is illustrated in Fig. 4.2 between 1963–2017.

It can be a bit extreme to classify value and growth as two opposite sides of a coin. A corporate's fundamentals are a mix of value and growth. The question is, how much of each? It is not uncommon to think that growth investors also want to buy stocks at a good value. This desire is also expressed by many accomplished fundamental growth investors such as Philip Fisher, who is considered to be the father of growth investing. Yet, the classification between growth and value in many funds and index registers is a reflection of how asset

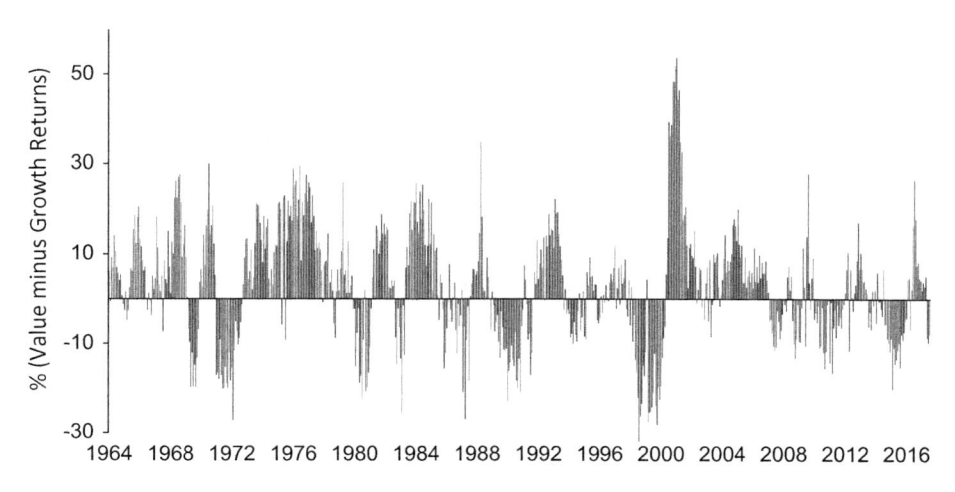

Fig. 4.2 Value versus growth performance. Source: Author's calculations, Kenneth French database, Jul. 1963–Dec. 2017 for the U.S. Note: The figure represents the difference in total returns of low value ("value") and high value ("growth") using combined screens of top 30th and bottom 30th percentile of price-to-book, price-to-earnings and price-to-cash flow. The performance difference between value and growth is calculated as the rolling 12-month total returns. Historical returns are not a leading indicator of future performance

managers bucket themselves or index providers classify securities. The bottom line is that growth can mean different things to different people.

While there is no consensus regarding which strategy is superior, most of the academic literature seems to favour value over growth. A prominent article supporting this view is by Fama and French in 1998 showing that value stocks outperformed growth stocks between 1975–1995. Since 1963 to 2017, value outperformed growth 60% of the times over 12-month periods (see Fig. 4.2). However, there were periods when value did not beat growth stocks (e.g. post-financial crisis in 2008), where value outperformed growth only 40% of the times.

In general, a concentrated value strategy tends to avoid growth stocks for two reasons. First, a rapid increase in a security price does not keep up forever. Two, the price may already discount too much future growth: the stock may be expensive. Fundamental economic laws and experience teach us that no trend continues indefinitely; regulation changes in various industries; investor preferences change and so does the political spectrum. Many investors and analysts tend to extrapolate recent trends, but as we know, economic forces tell us that conditions for a business can change.

Industries are subject to rapid change even where demand remains stable, but a steady supply could grow faster. The growth industries of the 1920s included radio, aviation, electric refrigeration, and silk hosiery—today it is more about technology companies, the likes of Apple and Microsoft. In different periods of history all these industries saw a period of high demand followed by a period of increasing supply leading to depressed returns. In 1922, department stores were favourites due to their resilience in the 1920s depression. But they did not maintain this advantage in subsequent years. The public utilities were not popular in the 1919 boom because of high costs. They became the speculative and favourite investment at end of the 1920s, but later fear of high inflation, regulation and direct governmental competition again undermined the public's confidence in them.

However, it is dangerous to assume that a downward trend will continue forever. There are many examples in history—in 1933, for example, where the long depressed cotton goods industry forged ahead faster than most industries. Often in a downward trend, analysts typically put great emphasis on the unfavourable factor—negative news tends to capture market imagination. Of course, this is not to say that one will be able to precisely predict when a downward trend will revert. Nor is it certain that the latest earnings, whether it is higher or lower than the historical average, will be the norm in the future.

Besides the structural changes in the industry, there are other episodes in history that show us how human behaviour can create unattainable trends. Arguably, a value investor would question these price-chasing trends and link them to fundamentals. The dot-com bubble is a period named after its speculative investments in internet companies. The period started around 1997, peaked in 2000 and burst in 2002. About half of the initial public offering in 1999 were internet stocks that gained on average 150% within their first day as public companies. In general, prices went up about five times only to go down five times, and returned to their pre-boom levels from 2000 to 2002, a drop which was also exacerbated by the terrorist attacks of September 11 in 2001. Only one out of two internet companies survived with businesses such as Pets.com going from a market capitalization of over USD 300 million to zero in just 268 days. However, there are also success stories such as Amazon, which went from around USD 100 during the bubble peak down to USD 7 but then climbed back up to over USD 600 per share, and reaching USD 2000 in the middle of 2018.

The dot-com bubble demonstrated a vital difference between growth and value investing. At the time, growth stocks tended to carry overstretched earnings' expectations. Value investors at that moment believed that the current state of a company mattered more than just aiming to make earning growth projections with high accuracy. Value investors target the relationship between the "true" (intrinsic value) and the market value of a stock, and avoid crowding into short-term developments. This allows the value investor to exploit market behaviour for long-term gains. The next section continues the introduction to value investing by describing the concept of intrinsic value.

4.3 Intrinsic Value

The idea of measuring intrinsic value is to provide a rough estimate rather than a precise conclusion. This means that we are only interested in how the "true value" compares to the prevailing market price. The essential point is that stock analysis does not seek to determine exactly the intrinsic value of a given security. Instead, the idea is to establish either what the value is: adequate, considerably higher or lower than the market price. It is possible, for example, to assess if someone is taller or heavier than the average person without knowing the person's exact height or weight as described by Graham and Dodd in 1934. Their work highlighted lessons on intrinsic value, a margin of safety and earnings power. Figure 4.3 presents the top 50 equally-weighted value stocks based on price-to-book in the U.S. with a market capitalisation in excess of USD 10 billion.

In general, intrinsic value can be an abstract concept. Yet, it is core to the understanding and developing value investing strategies. Graham described it in his own words as the following: *"In general terms it is understood to be that value*

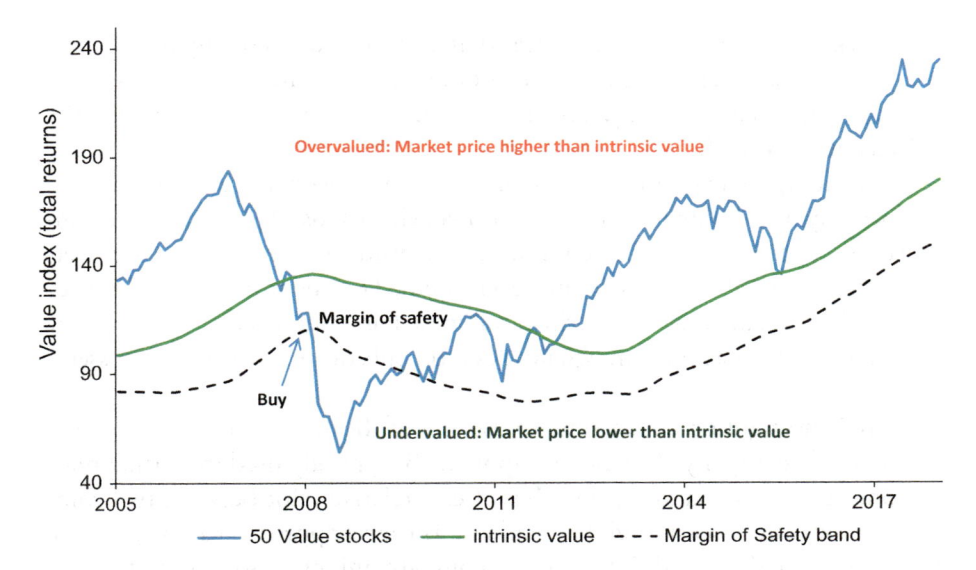

Fig. 4.3 Intrinsic value and margin of safety. Source: Author, Bloomberg data between Aug. 2005–Dec. 2017. Note: For illustrative purpose only

which is justified by the facts, e.g., the assets, earnings, dividends, definite prospects, as distinct from the market quotations established by artificial manipulation or distortion of by psychological excesses. But it is a great mistake to imagine that intrinsic value is as definite and as determinable as is the market price." (Ben Graham, "Security Analysis", 1951).

Warren Buffett, at Berkshire Hathaway, shared the following definition to shareholders in a 1996 publication: *"It is the discounted value of the cash that can be taken out of a business during its remaining life."* This means that the intrinsic value is the present value of all future earnings. There are different valuation approaches to determine what constitute an economic value (or a proxy for intrinsic value) in the finance literature often utilised by academics and professionals. To put it differently, you own a cow and want to value it. It is naive to think that we can value a cow by looking in its mouth or value a business by its front door and the people coming in and out of the door. To determine the economic value of the cow, as described to by Westbay CPAs, accounting and consultancy firm, you can consider three routes:

- The first approach estimates the amount of milk the cow can produce in the future (income or dividend approach) and the price of the milk in the market. The present value of the income stream from the milk production is referred to as the **Income Approach**.

- The second approach is to evaluate what a similar cow is selling in the market. In the same spirit, it is about finding what a company is worth when compared to similar businesses in the market. This analysis is known as the **Market Approach**.
- The third approach estimates how much a cow is worth if each part is sold separately. It is known as the **Asset Approach or Cost Approach.** The concept is to value an entity based on the market value of its underlying net assets (assets minus liabilities). This approach is based on the principle of substitution. This means that the intrinsic value or fair value is also viewed as the expected cost to acquire an equally desirable substitute of the specific asset.

There is no right or wrong time to use any of the approaches to estimating the value of a company. The income approach is typically used in normal market conditions. The market approach is often a relative value between two comparable stocks in a sector or global markets. The asset approach can be practical in distressed market conditions where a company might be sold in parts.

Successful value strategies, either active or systematic indices, target intrinsic value that is much higher than the market price for the underlying securities to ensure a margin of safety. In reality, estimates of intrinsic value could be flawed and wild guesswork: as we have seen there is no single best way to precisely value stocks. In general, value investors are not expected to come up with intrinsic value estimates for all stocks in the market. Much of the value of a security is based on unknown future results. Hence, a margin of safety between the estimated intrinsic value and the market price is essential to reduce the risk of miscalculations or worse than average luck. In practice, this means that opportunities may not arise that frequently since securities may appear only mildly undervalued or overvalued most of the time. A value investor is like a hunter—patiently waiting for these opportunities to present themselves. The next section looks at various value screens that aim to proxy an intrinsic value of portfolios stocks in a typical systematic value factor strategy.

4.4 Systematic Screening Approaches

This section covers common types of value characteristics that have been documented in the literature and often used among professionals in rules-based strategies. Common value stock screens that are considered in designing value strategies include:

Benjamin Graham screen: A classic screen based on a range of accounting characteristics and stock price behaviour.

Price-to-Book Value ratio: One of the most well-established measures for value. It measures the market value of a company relative to its accounting value (net asset value or assets minus liabilities). A low ratio indicates undervalued stock or distressed as the market price is below the accounting value.

Price-to-Earnings ratio: This measure is often used loosely for a price multiple among professionals. It measures the price paid for the company per unit of earnings. A low ratio typically may indicate that the company is undervalued. Companies with a high ratio are often interpreted as companies with high earnings growth in the future.

Price-to-Sales ratio and Enterprise Value-to-Sales ratio: Measures how much it costs to purchase a company's sales. A low ratio could imply that a company is attractive or undervalued. A high ratio does not always mean that the sales are likely to increase. The **Enterprise Value-to-Sales ratio** is similar to price-to-sales ratio but uses the enterprise value, which takes into account the market capitalization, debt, preferred shares with deduction for cash.

Enterprise Value-to-EBITDA ratio: Measures of a company value (including its debt) per unit of the cash earnings less non-cash expenses relative to Earning Before Interest, Tax, Depreciation and Amortization (EBITDA). It is often used to compare companies in the same industry. A lower ratio indicates value stock.[1]

Price-to-Cash Flow ratio: Measures the share price to its cash flow, but taking into account the operating cash flow. It can be useful valuation metrics for companies that with positive cash flow that are not profitable due to non-cash charges (e.g. depreciation, depletion of assets, among others). A low ratio could indicate an attractive valuation.

As discussed in the previous section, calculating intrinsic value is sometimes a mix of art and science. Different professionals and academics estimate intrinsic value using their preferred way and approaches. When you construct a value screen and factor-based strategy, the starting point is to acknowledge the importance of the information in the financial statements (balance sheet, income and cash flow statements). Most of the value screens look at market pricing and the components of the financial statements to infer a good or bad value stock. The idea of the screens is to search for valuable companies systematically for an index strategy that can be bought at attractive prices when investors turn away from them.

The screening approach of value stocks can be traced back to Graham. His screens aimed at finding undervalued stocks with quality features and

---

[1] EBITDA denotes Earnings before Interest, Taxes, Depreciation, and amortization. It is an indicator of a company's financial performance which is essentially net income with interest, taxes, depreciation, and amortization added back to it and can be used to analyse and compare profitability between companies and industries because it eliminates the effects of financing and accounting decisions. Enterprise value is calculated as the sum of market capitalisation, preferred shares and total debt less the total cash.

favourable long-term prospects. Generally, a successful value investing strategy requires differentiating between investment and speculation as well as adhering to a set of rules. It should be mentioned that even under a relatively rigorous set of rules for value screen there is some degree of subjectivity.

4.4.1 Benjamin Graham Screen

Some of Graham's successful students who took his classes at Columbia University include Charlie Munger and Warren Buffett. Although none of them adhered to his screens strictly, they adopted his wisdom. Figure 4.4 shows Berkshire Hathaway price relative to the S&P 500 price index over the past decades.

Graham's 10 criteria checklist for stocks includes:

- Price-to-Earnings (P/E) is less than the inverse of the yield on AAA corporate bonds;
- P/E is less than 40% of the 5-year average P/E;
- The dividend yield is higher than 2/3 of the AAA corporate bond yield;
- Price is less than 2/3 of book value;
- Price is less than the 2/3 of the net current assets;
- Debt-to-Equity Ratio based on book value is less than one;

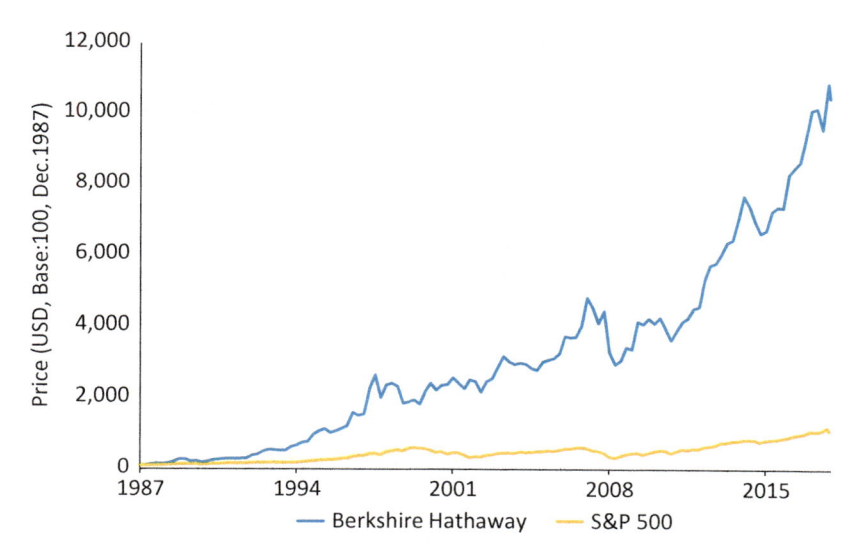

Fig. 4.4 Berkshire Hathaway share price versus S&P 500. Source: Bloomberg, Dec. 1987–Dec. 2017

- Current Assets is two times larger than current liabilities;
- Debt is two times less than the net current assets;
- Historical growth of earning per share (over last 10 years) is higher than 7%;
- No more than two years of negative earnings in the past 10 years.

The views and evaluation of the screen have been evaluated and tested after Graham. The results are mixed. A study by Henry Oppenheimer in 1984 concluded that stocks that passed Graham's screen outperformed the broad market.[2] The screen is still being evaluated and modified among professionals. James Rea ran the screen on actual mutual funds and showed that it failed to deliver the promised returns. Societe Generale has modified and used the screen as a part of their Quantitative Strategy unit and found a mixed result.[3] In the end, it depends on the time period to which the screen is applied.

Furthermore, Graham proposed a simple valuation formulation based on the AAA corporate bond yield prevailing in 1962, which is used in the formula below:

$$\text{Value} = \text{EPS} \times (8.5 + 2 \times g) \times (4.4 / Y),$$

where g is the expected annual earnings growth rate for the next seven to 10 years, EPS is the Earnings per Share for the most recent 12 months, Y is the current interest rate on AAA-rated corporate bonds, and $(8.5 + 2 \times g)$ is the earnings multiplier that assumes price-to-earnings ratio of 8.5 for a 0% growth company, 4.4 was the prevailing AAA yield in 1962 on the 20-year U.S. Treasury. The value of a stock is sensitive to current bond yields. If bond yields rise, the value of the stock goes down and vice versa.

In this valuation approach, the expected annual growth rate over the next seven to 10 years is critical. Historical rates provide a starting point, although they may not be indicative of future rates. However, using the proper historical rate requires considerable investment judgment. This approach is different from the concept of intrinsic value. It provides another check on valuations.

The Graham formula indicated that around end of December 2016 the S&P 500 appeared undervalued. This is based on 31 December 2016, where

- The EPS is about USD 97.1;
- The 10-year historical growth is around 7.4%;
- The 20-year U.S. Treasury at 2.4%.

---

[2] "A Test of Ben Graham's Stock Selection Criteria", Financial Analysts Journal, 1984.
[3] "Popular Investment Screens for Developed Markets – Performance update", April 2009.

The formula indicates an S&P 500 level at 4148 then while the actual S&P 500 was at 2239 and as a result, the formula indicates that the S&P 500 is undervalued. This formula is sensitive to the interest rates. If the interest rate component is excluded, as in the original formula by Graham, the implied S&P 500 is 2262, indicating that S&P 500 is fairly valued.

4.4.2 Price-to-Book (P/B) Screen

A low P/B value ratio has been considered a reliable indicator of systematic value strategies among many professionals and academics. The P/B (the inverse of the book-to-market) ratio gauges the degree of value for a stock relative to its accounting value. The ratio is defined as:

$$\text{Market Capitalisation} / (\text{Total Assets} - \text{Total Liabilities}),$$

where the denominator is the shareholders' equity, measured at book valued. Intangible assets include goodwill, trademark among others.[4] What this ratio ascertains is the price an investor is paying for a company relative to what it owns today.

The lower the P/B (or high book-to-market) ratio, the more likely that a stock is undervalued, and the higher, the more likely it is overvalued or just a reflection of a healthy company in anticipation of future growth. Of course, to analyse stocks, this ratio should be taken in context with other stocks in the same sector because P/B will vary by industry and sector.

In general, the empirical evidence suggests that low P/B values stocks have outperformed high P/B stocks and the overall market (traditional market capitalisation index) over long time periods. Figure 4.5 illustrates the dynamics between stocks with low, medium and high P/B against a market capitalisation index. Fama and French point out that low P/B ratio may operate as a measure of risk—stocks that are trading at a significant price below book value are more likely to be in trouble and go out of business if the market is correct in its valuation. Investors need to evaluate whether the additional returns made by such firms justify the additional risk taken on by investing in them.

---

[4] The price to book ratio for a stable growth firm can be written as a function of its Return On Equity, growth rate and cost of equity: P/B = (Return on equity − Expected growth rate)/(Return on equity − Cost of equity). Companies that are expected to earn low returns on equity will trade at low price to book ratios. In fact, if you expect the ROE < Cost of equity, the stock should trade at below book value of equity.

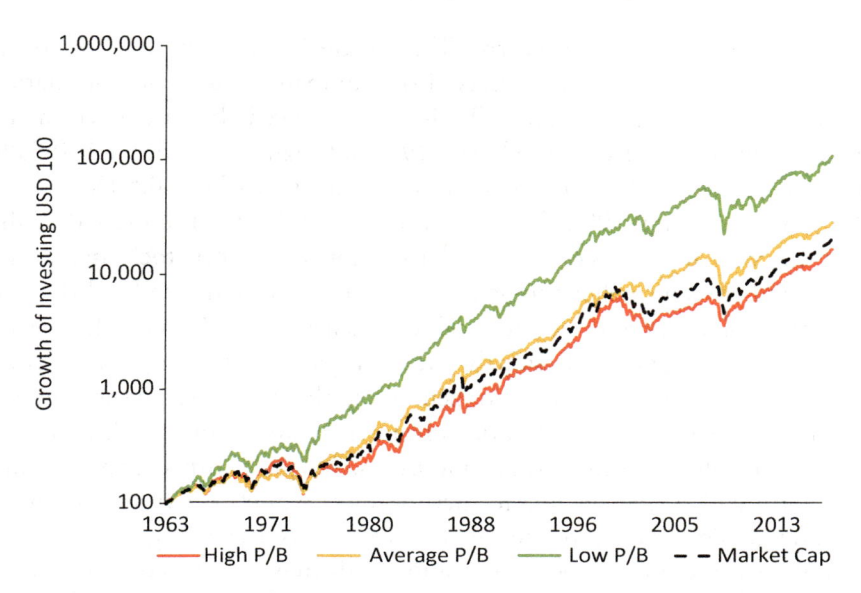

Fig. 4.5 P/B portfolios for the U.S. versus the market capitalisation. Source: Author's calculations, Kenneth French database, Jul. 1963–Dec. 2017 for the U.S. Note: The time series are logged and rebased to Jul. 1963. The high P/B is top 30th percentile, the average P/B is 40–70th percentile, and low P/B is the bottom 30th percentile. The stocks are market value weighted within each percentile bucket

Why do P/B advocates use the ratio? A P/B ratio could mean many things. For example, you are getting a lot of assets relative to the amount you are paying, a dream for a lot of value investors. But it can also suggest that the assets are depreciating; that there is something wrong or it is driven by short-term market mechanics. It can turn out as either a great value deal or a horror story. The P/B can be combined with other information to see the real story behind a low ratio.

Value investors believe that book value is cyclically less volatile than earnings or dividends, and so is a better guide to the underlying value. In practice, book value is far from fixed. It can grow with retained earnings—and can also be hit hard by asset write-downs, which in fact were the source of the biggest fall in earnings historically in 2008/2009.

A study by Rosenberg, Reid, and Lanstein in 1985 showed an outperformance of a portfolio based P/B ratio of 1400 securities in the U.S.[5] The portfolio had an average monthly return of 0.36% during the 12 year time period and was positive 38 of the 54 months. Fama and French document in 1992 the relative success of using value characteristics to explain average portfolio

---

[5] The portfolio has equal long and short positions and attempts to control for a number of factors such as size, earning per share, share turnover, and industry classification.

returns compared to market returns. They create 100 equally weighted portfolios, using the intersection of ranks of the company's size (based on market capitalization) and the P/B ratio. Their study showed the difference in the average monthly returns for the lowest P/B and highest P/B decile is 0.99% compared to the size decile of smallest minus largest stocks of 0.58%.

Fama and French in 1992 also showed that the P/B effect is impacted by the size of the company—it is even more positive for the smaller stocks due to the strong link between smaller and value stocks. The question whether P/B ratio represents a risk factor or is indicative of mispriced securities is still up for debate among academics and professionals who complement the ratio with other screens—we will continue to discuss them in the chapter. The Fama and French research excluded financial institutions from their stock universe due to their fundamental difference from other industries. Financial firms such as banks have typically high leverage due to their business models based on borrowing and lending. High leverage to the size of a firm's assets over a long time for non-financial institutions could be an indication of distress, which is not necessarily the case for financial institutions. Hence, a screen with financials could distort the overall P/B screen. Mitigation for this could apply to a sector relativity measure or complement the P/B ratio with leverage and fundamental adjustments, which will be discussed in the chapter dedicated to the quality factor.

As a drawback of the ratio, the book value excludes intangibles asset. This is particularly relevant in economic environment where many technology companies have a lot of their value in intangible assets and P/B may erroneously classify them as expensive. Another drawback of P/B ratio is that it could pick up "cheap stocks" of companies in distress conditions (sometimes referred to as junk).

4.4.3 Price-to-Earnings (P/E) Screen

A stock priced at USD 150 is not necessarily cheaper than a stock priced at USD 15. The P/E ratio is one of the simplest but most popular screening criteria for value strategies, often used loosely as "multiple of equity earnings" and the king of all ratios. The P/E ratio measures the price of a stock to its recent earnings per share. A stock will often move in the direction of its earnings over time—when a company makes money, its price eventually goes up, and the other way around: when a company loses money, its stock price goes down. If a company's stock price is 20 USD and reports earnings per share of two USD, then it has a P/E ratio of 10. This means that if investors buy the stock at the current price, then they are prepared to pay for 10 times the recent trading earnings. If a company has a high P/E ratio right now but a lower forward P/E (market analysts' estimates), then this implies that analysts are expecting the earnings to go up soon.

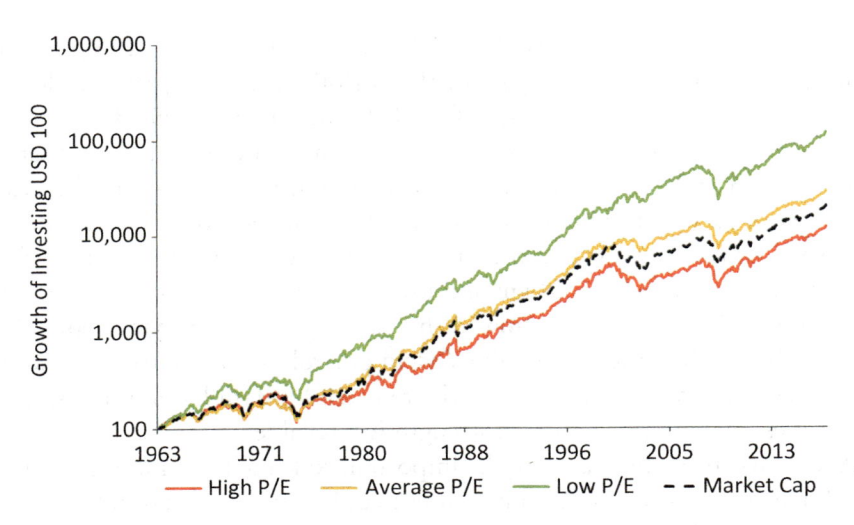

Fig. 4.6 P/E portfolios for the U.S. versus the market capitalization index. Source: Author's calculations, Kenneth French database, Jul. 1963–Dec. 2017 for the U.S. Note: The time series are logged and rebased to Jul. 1963. The high P/E is top 30th percentile, the average P/E is 40–70th percentile, and low P/E is the bottom 30th percentile. The stocks are market value weighted within each percentile bucket

This ratio has historically been successful in delivering value screens. Figure 4.6 illustrates the dynamics between stocks with low, medium and high P/E against a market capitalisation index. In recent history, stocks have averaged a P/E ratio between 15–20, but often it makes more sense to compare the P/E among peers in a sector. For example, the average P/E ratio in the technology sector could be higher than the health care.

A company like Tesla might have been able to grow its earnings by double digits since its initial public offering in 2009, but there comes a time when that growth must slow down, and the stock price will have to adjust. No company can keep its growth going versus value exponentially. So for certain growth investors, a P/E ratio of 29 might be perfectly reasonable, and the importance of the P/E ratio like all ratios will depend on the industry. Indeed a high P/E ratio can indicate a company is growing fast whereas a low P/E ratio can indicate that a company is doing poorly. There will always be differences in P/E ratios, which may stem from market expectations and random fluctuations in earnings or seasonal factors. Hence it is for a reason why combination all of the various financial ratios can be used as a compliment for P/E ratio.

Academics and professionals have long argued that stocks with low P/E ratios are more likely to be undervalued and earn excess returns in global financial markets. P/E was one of Ben Graham's primary screens. Empirical researchers have continued to study value investing as well as others in the past decades. For example, Basu in 1977 showed that low P/E ratio portfolio earns 6% more per year than a high P/E portfolio in the 14-year sample. He also looked at the inverse measure of the P/E ratio (earnings yield). He demonstrated that the P/E for various market capitalisations of the companies (often known as the size effect) can affect stock returns in long-term. In 1983, Basu examined whether high earnings' yield (the inverse of P/E ratio) of the U.S. small stocks is related to the high returns also known as the size effect. Basu compares the return of high and low earnings' yield portfolios of stocks with similar size.[6] The result showed that the high earnings' yield portfolios perform better than the low earnings' yield portfolios. Of course, the success of the P/E ratio is time-dependent. The research by Basu has a much smaller time-series, making the empirical strength less reliable.

A few caveats for P/E ratio can be important to keep in mind. First, the tax cost for investors—a low P/E ratio stocks could have a substantial dividend yield. This could create a significant tax burden for investors since dividends are taxed at higher rates. Second, P/E ratio could be low because the market expects low or negative future earnings growth. Many low to modest P/E ratio companies are in mature businesses where the potential for growth is minimal.[7] Finally, P/E is also sensitive to cyclical earning variations. For example, during the Global Financial Crisis, earnings for financials dried out and P/E alone would not pick up the financial sector rebound in 2009.

4.4.4 Price-to-Sales (P/S) Ratio

The P/S ratio can be a useful measure to decide whether a share is cheap or expensive, which has historically worked as a good predictor of future share price performance. It is a simple ratio calculated as **Market Capitalisation/ Total Sales,** where the sales figures are typically given over 12 months or more extended time period. For example, if a firm's market capitalisation is USD 1 billion and the sales figure is USD 800 million, then the price to sales ratio is 1.25. The advantage of sales ratio compared to earnings reduces the risk of manipulation of accounting figures. The disadvantage is that a business without sales may indicate that a business is not worth much over some time,

---

[6] In this study, stocks are ranked annually using the E/P and size data.

[7] Generally, markets tend to place too much importance on current year earnings and the earnings trend of the market and become overly optimistic or pessimistic. This criticism goes back to Graham's era and could apply equally today. Analysts should be focused more on the historical record of the company. Therefore, a thorough analysis of the past can provide some degree of confidence in the future. This thought process inspired the concept of earnings power. It combines a statement of actual earnings shown over a period of years with a reasonable expectation that these will be approximated in the future, unless extraordinary conditions change.

which may not be the case. To smooth out the noise and the seasonality in sales data, a screen could be based on 12 months or years of historical averages.

The ratio is useful for firms with rapid business growth and may have little or no earnings. Alternatively, it can be useful for stocks or sectors where earnings are volatile, which can make it hard to interpret the results. During the dot-com bubble, there were many companies with no earnings. At that time, many investors' substituted sales with earning to create a relative price to the market. It resulted in a confusion that P/S ratio of 20 is a better value than a company with P/S ratio of 50. While generally this is true, this time it was not a bargain or a value stock.

Senchack and Martin in 1987 compared low P/S ratio and low P/E ratio portfolios with the broad market benchmark. They showed that low price-sales ratio portfolio outperformed the market but not the low P/E ratio portfolio. Later on, Jacobs and Levy in 1988 concluded that low P/S ratio portfolio yielded an excess return over the market of 0.17% a month between 1978–1986. Even when combined with other factors in the analysis, the P/S ratios remained a significant factor in explaining excess returns together with the P/E ratio and the size of the company.

However, it is not all sanguine for the P/S ratio, it has some drawbacks. First, sales are not necessarily profits. Going back to the cow valuation case—a cow farmer can sell a cow for USD 4000 (revenue), but when it comes to calculating profit, the farmer has to factor in costs such as food and shelter for the cow to calculate the profit. Hence, P/S may need to be complemented with other measures such as earnings.

Moreover, when a firm is substantially leveraged, it is entirely possible that its market value will trade at a low multiple of revenues. Hence, if you pick stocks with low P/S, you may very well end up with a portfolio of the most highly indebted firms. That is why some investor may use the enterprise value instead of market capitalisation to capture the value of the debt and preferred shares relative to sales, which help to adjust for the leverage issue. Furthermore, a low-margin business that operates with little pricing power and poor profit margins will trade at low multiples of revenues (i.e. price-to-revenue). The reason is intuitive. The value ultimately comes not from the capacity to generate revenues but from the earnings.

4.4.5 Comparison and Combination of Screens

Table 4.2 compares rules-based value screens based on various ratios for illustrative purposes, using data between 1963–2017 in the U.S. The

Table 4.2 Comparison of value characteristics

		Market value weighted			Equal weighted					
		Low 30	Mid	High 30	Low 30	Mid	High 30			Market cap
P/CF	Total return (%)	13.6	10.8	9.6	18.1	15.1	10.5			10.3
	Volatility (%)	15.1	14.7	16.4	18.7	17.0	20.3			15.2
	Risk/return ratio	0.9	0.7	0.6	1.0	0.9	0.5			0.7
	Max drawdown (%)	−49.1	−52.7	−48.8	−59.4	−54.7	−68.4			−50.4
	U.S. recession return (%)	2.9	1.8	1.1	11.0	8.6	0.8			0.8
P/E	Total return (%)	13.9	11.0	9.2	17.6	14.5	11.0			10.3
	Volatility (%)	15.8	14.3	16.4	18.1	16.9	20.6			15.2
	Risk/return ratio	0.9	0.8	0.6	1.0	0.9	0.5			0.7
	Max drawdown (%)	−55.9	−47.0	−50.7	−54.3	−51.5	−67.1			−50.4
	U.S. recession return (%)	3.1	3.3	−0.3	11.2	8.5	1.4			0.8
P/B	Total return (%)	13.7	10.9	9.9	18.6	14.5	8.0			10.3
	Volatility (%)	16.6	14.7	16.0	19.5	18.6	22.6			15.2
	Risk/return ratio	0.8	0.7	0.6	1.0	0.8	0.4			0.7
	Max drawdown (%)	−61.7	−55.9	−51.5	−64.8	−56.4	−67.7			−50.4
	U.S. recession return (%)	3.9	0.5	1.7	9.6	7.5	−0.5			0.8
		Top value	Mid value	Low value	Top value	Mid value	Low value			Market cap
Combined value screen	Total return (%)	13.9	11.0	9.5	18.1	14.7	9.9			10.3
	Volatility (%)	15.9	14.4	16.2	18.7	17.4	21.1			15.2
	Risk/return	0.9	0.8	0.6	1.0	0.8	0.5			0.7
	Max drawdown (%)	−57.8	−49.8	−47.9	−61.5	−54.5	−67.2			−50.4
	U.S. recession return (%)	3.3	2.4	0.4	10.6	8.2	0.6			0.8

Source: Author's calculations, Kenneth French database, Federal Reserve Bank of St. Louis, Jul. 1963–Dec. 2017

Note: The low 30 is the bottom 30th percentile, the Mid is the 40–70th percentile, and high 30 is the top 30th percentile of each ratio. The U.S. recessions are based on NBER. The recession analysis is based on the average return during each recession since 1960th. In the combined screen, Low Value, Median and Top Value represent an average combination of P/B, P/E and P/CF screens with the bottom 30th percentile, 40–70th percentile and top 30th percentile, respectively comparisons are made with market capitalisation and equally weighted portfolios. The value characteristics such as low P/B or P/E in the table have historically improved the risk-adjusted returns. The securities that do not exhibit value characteristics have in fact underperformed both the value and the market capitalisation index over the long term. Most value characteristics have performed well through the economic recessions since 1960s in the U.S. as stock sell-offs in aggregate tend to recover faster than the economy. Combining the screens can intuitively provide some diversification—the combined screen is an average of three characteristics: P/B, P/E, and P/CF at the bottom of Table 4.2. The combined screen tends to do well during the recessionary period with similar risk-adjusted performance to P/CF screen.

The results are consistent even when applying an alternatively-weighted scheme, such as equal weighting with the screens. The volatility tends to increase in the portfolios due to increased exposure to smaller companies with the equal weighting but the equal weighted scheme has improved the risk-adjusted returns compared to market value-weighted factor strategies. The investor may decide to combine a mix of weighting schemes that we discussed in Chap. 3 to enhance further diversification around the factor. Different market indices utilise different weighting schemes in the factor index design.

Some of the popular index strategies tracked by many value funds are quite common among different index providers. Typical household names are RAFI, MSCI, Russell, FTSE, Scientific Beta and Solactive. There is no unique approach among the various providers as some have biases towards some screens. Some use P/B only through academic evidence while others combine various characteristics to create the index strategy—see Table 4.3.

Table 4.3 shows that commercial indices are not all the same. They have different inputs and methodologies, which often lead to different outcomes as discussed in Chap. 3. The definitions are not always consistent with the academic literature as professionals often choose to adjust the value characteristics and sometimes enforce unnecessary complexity to the subject, which could lead to data mining. Hence, it is critical to ensure that the index of choice is diversified enough to mitigate the risk of data mining and investment rationale.

Table 4.3 Comparison of commercial value indices

Index provider	Factor characteristics	Methodology
FTSE value factor	Cash flow yield, earnings yield and P/S	Tilt the market capitalisation index by using a composite score
FTSE –RAFI	Sales, cash flow, book value and dividends	Weights stocks based on a composite score
MSCI Enhanced value	Forward P/E, P/B, and Enterprise value-to-operating cash flow	Tilt the market capitalisation index using the composite score and target a fixed number of stocks based targeting 30% market capitalisation coverage
MSCI value weighted	Book value, sales value, earnings value and cash earnings value	A ratio of a composite score and market capitalisation
S&P Enhanced value	P/B, P/E and P/S	Tilt the market capitalisation index by targeting a fixed percentage of constituents in the market capitalisation index
S&P Intrinsic value weighted	Book value and discounted adjusted earnings	Weight the universe based on a score
Scientific Beta value multi-strategy	P/B	Excludes stocks with poor multi-factor characteristics and focus on value with a range of weighting schemes

Source: Author, methodology and factsheets from various index providers

4.4.6 What Constitutes Good Screen Criteria?

Now that we discussed some common value characteristics that are often included in value index strategies, it is apparent that there is no perfect financial or market ratio on its own. The most important feature of a value characteristic is whether it makes sense and has a rationale rather than just being selected due to backtests. The mix of value screens, the diversification of portfolios and a robust weighting approach can assist in devising a good value strategy. This section provides an overview of the criteria for a value screen.

In general, all value characteristics are cyclical and may perform differently in various market conditions. On the one hand, using one value characteristic such as P/B could exhibit high cyclicality in performance. On the other hand, combining too many characteristics can wash out the effectiveness of individual value metrics like P/B and reduce diversification. Hence, it is essential to understand the limitations and strengths when presented with the various screens.

A long-term investment horizon is necessary for the rules-based value index screens in this chapter, long-term is typically considered as five years and beyond. It is essential to be cognisant that low price-to-book or earnings based ratio could underperform high price-to-book based index over a shorter time period. Rather than focusing on the current year's ratio, taking an average of past earnings for three or four years as a guide to the future could reduce the noise, cyclicality and index turnover. Hence, rather than trusting the current earnings, a value strategy could focus on two versions as an example:

- Normalised earnings—using average earnings over a period of time to reduce cyclicality;
- Adjusted earnings—where investors use their own measures of earnings that correct what they see as shortcomings of the accounting earnings or consensus estimates.

A popular measure to forecast long-term equity returns (typically over 10 years) is the cyclically adjusted price-earnings (CAPE) ratio introduced by the Nobel-award-winning financial economist Robert Shiller. The CAPE ratio is a valuation measure and represents the market capitalisation index price level over its 10-year average inflation-adjusted earnings. The rationale for CAPE has its root in the concept of mean-reversion in earnings. Elevated stock prices relative to earnings are likely to gravitate to a long-term historical average.

Finally, the degree of diversification could play an integral part in the risk management of value strategies. The excess returns from these strategies often come from a few holdings in a broad portfolio. Holding a concentrated index with few holdings may expose investors to unintended stock-specific risks and may impede performance relative to the broad market, particularly during market downturns. Hence, a diversified value strategy could help avoiding long-term or permanent losses.

4.5 Behavioural Drivers of Value Factor

We have discussed value characteristics and how they can be used in a rules-based index strategy. This section discusses the behavioural explanation of the value factor premium. As we mentioned before, the value factor aims to exploit shortcomings of market behaviours by targeting cheap stocks that are out-of-favour. Some behavioural biases in the market tend to influence the value factor premium.

We describe a limited number of behavioural anomalies and concepts that can link to the value factor premium. These include:

- **Representativeness bias:** is a mental shortcut and is defined as the tendency to irrationally make judgements based on few observations to draw a general conclusion about the market. We tend to form a representative opinion about events by how much they resemble other events as a holistic conclusion;
- **Recency bias:** a tendency to believe that what has been happening recently will keep on happening on into the future. Warren Buffet points out that "investors project out into the future what they have most recently been seeing. That is their unshakable habit".

Representativeness is a term that Tversky and Kahneman in 1982 defined as a relation between a hypothetical process and some event associated with it. From an investment perspective it can mean that when a company announces poor yearly earnings, the next earnings announcement is expected to be poor too, or assuming that one poor earnings announcement represents a "bad stock".

Recency bias tends to exacerbate a stock market downturn in volatile market environments, creating a value premium. These value stocks may look risky compared to the general market. However, the higher the risk of a stock does not necessarily mean a higher risk-adjusted return compared to the broad market. The expected returns may be higher than the broad market benchmark but not necessarily on a risk-adjusted basis. In terms of stock prices, recency bias is a short-term behavioural bias that applies both on the way down and way up (when recency bias fades away) for the value factor.

During the global financial crisis in 2008 investors' emotions were dominated by fear and heightened risk aversion, which prompted them to dump securities as fast as possible, and that phenomenon added impetus to the drop spiral as the media and mediocre investor thought the drop would continue forever. The panic phase was followed by the phase of stagnation, during which fear prevented investors from returning to the stock market even though the valuations of numerous companies had fallen a long way.

Like any investment strategy, successful value investing is all about controlling emotions. At a time when markets are nervous with low investor confidence, value investing can be used as a guide to form investment decisions. Of course, irrational behaviours could prevail in the market for an extended period of time and performance may take time to come through. Just because "Mr. Market" is irrational, you do not need to follow him. The next section provides an overview of the market structures and rewards for risk as an additional explanation of the value factor premium. We will give an overview of the market structures and rewards for risk as an additional explanation of the value factor premium.

4.6 Market Structure and Reward for Risk

An important aspect driving the value factor premium is the shorter time horizons of the investors compared to what is required for value strategies, this shorter time horizon leads to investors missing out on the potential long-term payoff. Therefore, short-term performance targets could encourage many fund managers to look for securities that will earn high abnormal returns within a few months, rather than 3% per year over the next five years. Additionally, some investors may be pressured to window-dress their portfolio by altering their fund ahead of the year-end to make them look more attractive for the reporting.

Even institutional asset managers can have short-term investment horizons, given that they often cannot afford to underperform the index or their peers. Underperformance could discourage asset owners or the investment sponsors, and lead to the withdrawal of funds. Many investors and sponsors may see such a strategy as risky, and from the investment manager's point of view, sticking to the strategy might lead to reputational damage. An investment manager may avoid value investing altogether and follow more glamourous stocks to keep up with peers and to have happier sponsors. When both individuals and institutional money managers prefer glamour and avoid value strategies, value stocks will be cheap and earn a higher average return.

Depending on how the value is structured or implemented, in some cases a value premium (i.e. excess return over a traditional benchmark) is a reflection of reward for risk. Arguably, if markets are efficient there is a possibility that this will be reflected in the valuations, and the value premium would disappear over time. If value stocks are riskier than growth stocks, it is the same as saying they have a higher cost of capital (i.e. higher rate of return that could have been earned by putting the same money into growth stocks with equal risk). Moreover, the inherent risk of a value stock could emerge from the fact that these companies may be reorganising their business.

4.7 Considerations for Value Investing

So far we have discussed the power of systematic value screens and drivers of the value factor premium. This section continues the discussion around the issues and considerations that are required for a successful value strategy design. Companies are cheap for a reason and may stay so for a long time due to business environments and a struggling sector. Banks, for example, in 2008 and oil and gas in 2015 were trading at a very low P/E. Some of these companies did recover, but some companies in these sectors still struggled for many years or even went out of business. Next time you see a cheap stock, ask why? For how long has it been cheap? Is it in a struggling sector? Is the company struggling financially? Is there any disruption to the company's business?

Often too much emphasis on low prices can mislead, particularly, retail investors. A low price does not always lead you to a bargain nor does it constitute a value characteristic in itself. It makes sense to consider attributes that can assist in understanding the financial health of companies in portfolios. Keeping Warren Buffett's wisdom in mind, "It's far better to buy a wonderful company at a fair price than to buy a fair company at a wonderful price."

In the absence of quality checks, focus on price alone could lead investors to poorly calibrated value portfolios. This is typically a problem for highly concentrated value strategies where one of the constituents in a portfolio has a large allocation (also known as idiosyncratic risk). This can damage the long-term performance of a portfolio. Most portfolio construction that we have discussed in this chapter assumes a high degree of diversification, which is central to the long-term outperformance of traditional market capitalisation strategies. Lack of foresight in the portfolio construction approach can often lead to value traps—undervalued stocks that are cheap for a reason over a long time period. Such a problem tends to emerge with stocks traded at a low valuation for a long period after the time of purchase. This type of issue comes up in discussion with investors and is often very specific to single-stock or concentrated strategies.

Often, stocks that look cheap based on metrics, such as P/E ratio or other indicators may not be really "cheap". There are risks that the earnings of the business can continue to drop. As a result, the P/E ratio of the business increases, but the stock price remains stable or continues to fall further to distressed levels. As a good reminder, a single stock can often be cheap for a reason, although it may not be straightforward to know that it is a trap. As a rule of thumb, if a company has been trading at an average price-to-earnings ratio of five in the last 10 years, it is doubtful that that stock is suddenly going to start trading at a price-to-earnings ratio of 10 or 15. This is a sign that a company might be a value trap. However, the effect of a value trap to specific securities can be again reduced with high diversification, where one or few securities in the index do not pose the risk of long-term damage to the portfolio performance.

While a properly devised strategy can provide a reduction in so-called idiosyncratic risk, risks that are specific to securities or a sector, the investor is still exposed to the general economy and market cycles that can directly impact a value portfolio. Value investing tends to suffer during market panics and in some stages of an economic recession or bear market. Prices can still drop in a bear market despite appearing undervalued in the short term.

Moreover, short-term approaches to investing can aggravate the problem if the manager does not have the skill to navigate the market. In the design of a strategy, it is important not to just relay on earning forecasts for stocks. This type of exercise can be speculative, and most analysts, in aggregate, are often optimistic in their recommendations (Fig. 4.7). Historically, most market consensus based on market analysis tends to consistently provide an overoptimistic outlook. Figure 4.7 shows the median 12-month price targets for top 500 stocks in the U.S. All analyst estimates were consistently overoptimistic every year compared to the most recent stock price. Due to over

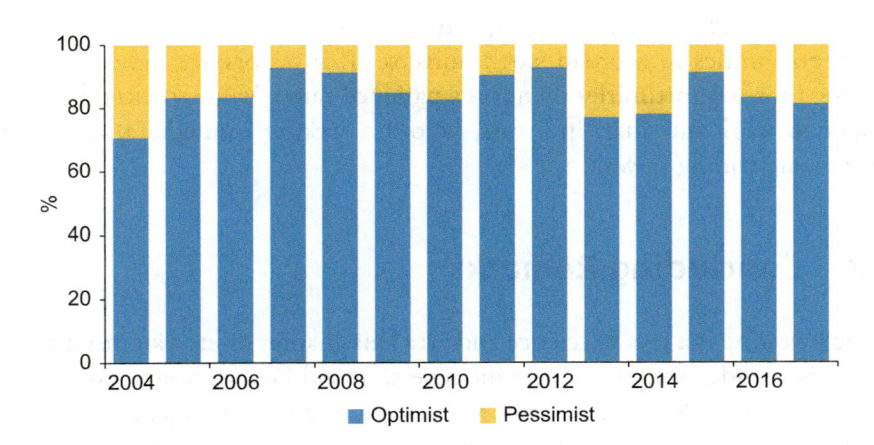

Fig. 4.7 Optimist and pessimist price targets for the largest U.S. 500 stocks. Source: Bloomberg, analyst reports, Dec. 2004–Dec. 2017. Note: The optimist and pessimist price targets are based on the median estimate of market analysts. The sample of analysts includes at least five price targets per company

optimism about 40% of the estimates never reach the 12-month targets. These mistakes do not stop the market from rising in most years—suggesting that the market is not priced on analysts' numbers only.

Another issue with value investing along the lines of the risk of value trap is linked to the estimation of intrinsic value. Intrinsic value estimates often require assumptions. There are risks that we may be wrong in our judgement, which can create an issue with the method of calculating intrinsic value. We discussed alternatives to intrinsic value by using accounting figures for rules-based screens. It is essential to recognise the limitations of value screens on firms in nascent industries with rapid growth. These firms are often subject to high levels of uncertainty. For this reason, any estimates or accounting figures should be used with caution. In cases like these, value investors should recognise the limits of their abilities and move on to evaluate other companies.

Finally, academic and market research has shown that sectors and country-specific accounting rules have an impact on financial ratios due to market structures and internal regulation. A study by Foye and Mramor in 2016 demonstrated that country-specific factors have a strong influence on measures of value (such as the price-to-book). Their conclusion is that value stocks' outperformance is country-specific and impacted by economic structures such as access to capital and the sophistication of capital markets in a country. For an excellent illustration as to how accounting measures which are used in value investing can differ and impact a strategy by country—see Brandes in 2004. Some aspects remain relevant today, although the harmonisation of accounting standards has moved on since publication.

The principle of value investing is to intelligently and systematically look for opportunities in a broad stock universe. If investors are rigorous about valuing those opportunities then it is a patience game. Value stocks often take longer to work out than investors, who are seeking immediate, abnormal returns, are willing to wait.

4.8 Concluding Remarks

Value investing is a mix of science and art. This chapter offered an insight into rules-based index strategies for value investing and how they are constructed as well as the challenges that come with them. Today investors have access to information on companies to help in constructing a strategy of value stocks. To process all the information you would need substantial resources and have a credible investment approach. That credibility can only be created in the way you design the value strategy.

The success in value investing is patience. It is not unusual to go through disappointing years as a value investor, but if you have constructed your strategy with an established and inherent value characteristic in a diversified portfolio, it is likely to be a rewarding opportunity in the future. The key to success in value investing is to adopt a long-term horizon (often five years and beyond) and stay patient even during uncomfortable times in the market. As the American economist, Paul Samuelson, once said: "Investing should be more like watching paint dry or watching grass grow".

5

Equity Factor Investing: Quality

In this chapter we continue the journey with high-quality factor investing. While value investing is a well-understood concept among professionals and academics, the definition of investing in high-quality companies is much broader and less consistent. On the one hand, quality often means investing in companies with sustainable business models and competitive advantages. On the other hand, these investments could include companies with old lines of technology or businesses that do not change much over time. Elevator, escalator or healthcare businesses could serve as examples—for many of us, it would be really hard to imagine people moving up and down the buildings in different ways years from now, or stop buying medicines in coming years.

This chapter will discuss how the quality factor is measured and what drives the (apparent) premium (the excess returns over a broad market benchmark). Since quality investing is a broad topic, the focus is on key characteristics as a part of quality factor strategies. I will also highlight some key debates and considerations, both qualitative and quantitative, for the strategies and discuss the key drivers of their risks and returns.

In general, a quality factor strategy targets stocks that tend to be profitable and generate value for the shareholders through the various market and business cycles. As we mentioned, this factor is not consistently defined and varies across quality investing strategies. Firstly, it can be derived from many financial statement attributes, such as profitability or return on investment as well as corporate governance expressed through the treatment of company shareholders. Some characteristics are quite straightforward. Consistently profitable companies have historically done relatively

© The Author(s) 2019
F. Zaher, *Index Fund Management*, https://doi.org/10.1007/978-3-030-19400-0_5

well compared to a broad market index over the longer term. Other characteristics, such as low asset growth (or low investment), are less intuitive when it comes to why this would generate an excess return over the broad market. Secondly, some academics consider the quality premium as an anomaly. This also tends to differ depending on the quality definition. It falls under the genre of anomalies as Modern Portfolio Theory is not able to explain the entire premium from all quality screens. Some of the explanations are partly evident from the general market risk while others emerge from market frictions and behavioural biases.

Regardless of the definitions, quality investing gained attraction after the dot-com bubble in 2001 as investors experienced the failures of Enron and Worldcom. These, as well as other financial failures in history, are due to lack of attention to the quality of balance sheets, earnings and corporate governance. After the global financial crisis in 2008, when cash was king, the popularity of higher-quality companies increased—some call it "flight to quality". Separating the wheat from the chaff proved to be a good risk dampener in the portfolio. Quality-focused investment managers were chasing businesses that generated a lot of cash, especially when financial stocks lost popularity, and their business models were questioned. For example, companies like Unilever, Nestle, Apple, and Berkshire Hathaway generate a lot of cash. Mining and smaller businesses generally do not.

The origin of quality investing, similar to value investing, goes back to Benjamin Graham. He recognised the importance of quality characteristics of stocks in the 1930s. In Graham's thinking, the most significant losses emerge from investing in low-quality stocks with attractive valuations and not necessarily from expensive quality stocks. In the post-Graham era, academics and professionals have documented the presence of a quality-factor premium. Today, quality factor investing is considered as the latest new joiner among the suite of index styles. It is increasingly popular in index funds and as a compliment with other factors such as value or size factor. The availability of diversified quality strategies is increasing with the double-digit growth of assets under management in these strategies between 2007–2017. As a result, the number of listed ETFs and index funds is increasing too. Also, more funds are blending the quality with other factors such as value and other multi-factor approaches that will be discussed later in the book.

5.1 Investment Horizon for Quality

Stock markets can rise and fall quickly over the short term. Historically, a diversified and broad stock investment has performed well over the long term. Quality investing is no different. In principle, a tactical investor aims to time the entry into the quality factor, either by replacing another strategy or adding more weight to quality in the portfolio. To remain invested in the market, the manager has to search for buy and sell opportunities of securities constantly. Strategic investors, on the contrary, avoid timing the market. They select quality securities or a quality index and aim to hold these investments for a long time, and as a result, cut down the cost of running the portfolio. A typical turnover (buying and selling) for a diversified quality index in the market is about 40% with semi-annual rebalancing.

As the saying goes, "you pay for quality". Quality factor strategies would be inherently more expensive than the broad market or value factor. In the short term, a quality stock may look expensive compared to the broad market but may be relatively inexpensive in the long run. Investors could pay on average a higher price for quality companies in terms of price-to-earnings or price-to-book. The price to pay for quality varies over time. Yet, an investor can still break even or outperform the market over 5–10 years investment horizon. For example, the MSCI World quality index has historically about two to three times the price-to-book of the market capitalisation index and about 20% higher in terms of price-to-earnings. Yet the index has delivered higher risk-adjusted returns in the past two decades.

Figure 5.1 shows the frequency of global quality outperforming the market capitalisation index over various holding periods. The likelihood of outperforming the market over the short time horizon such as 3-month or 1-year ranges between 38–46% based on historical data from 1990–2017. Quality has outperformed the broad market over 5-year to 10-year horizon. The result is also consistent in developed and emerging market indices.

When making strategic quality investments, compounding matters. Investing USD 1000 for 10 years, for example, with an expected return of 5%, would generate a value of USD 1629 at the end. However, investing at 10% rate of return with a potential drawdown of 40% in the portfolio would deliver an end value of USD 1415, which is slightly less than a consistent quality portfolio. A well-constructed quality strategy can benefit from a compounding rate of return with less frequent and severe drawdown in the long-term. This can help to explain the relative performance success to the broad market. The next section will cover some of the common screens that are linked to quality factor strategies.

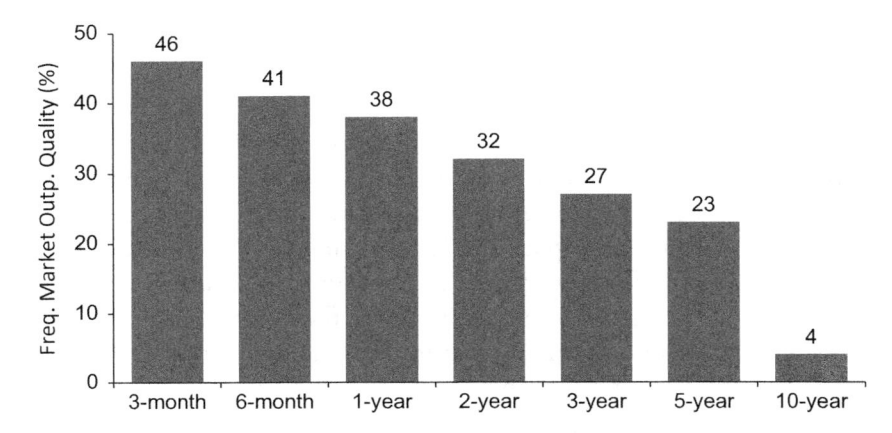

Fig. 5.1 Global quality relative to market capitalisation over holding periods. Source: Author's calculation, Kenneth French database, Jan. 1990–Dec. 2017 for global equities. Note: The construction of the quality factor is equal weighting of high profitability measures, low investment and low earnings variability portfolios. Historical returns are not a leading indicator of future performance

5.2 Quality Factor Screens

Academic literature and factor-based indices include some common quality characteristics. The classification of quality is often based on accounting figures such as profitability, qualitative aspects or a mixed approach. Examples include:

Profitability screen: focus on profitable companies;
Asset growth and investment screen: focus on companies with low asset growth;
Leverage screen: focus on companies with sustainable debt;
Accrual screen: focus on companies' earnings quality (cash versus accounting items);
Equity issuance screen: focus on companies with share buybacks;
Corporate governance: focus on attributes of well-run companies;
Combined characteristics: a combination of the screens above.

We focus on the main rules-based quality screens for factor index design. Many of the screens here are often associated with the quality premium that has been observed in global stock markets. The underlying data is available in the public domain and more accessible than ever. Before going into the specific screens, it makes sense to understand the implications of financial accounting for each particular screen and how these screens may link.

Balance Sheet

Current Asset
- Cash
- Account receivable
- Inventory
- Pre-paid expenses
- Investment securities

Long-Term Assets
- Investment
- Property, plant & Equipment
- Intangible assets
- Others

Current Liabilities
- Account payable
- Accrued liabilities
- Short term loans payable
- Others

Long-Term Liabilities
- Long-term liabilities
- Other obligations (e.g. Lease)

Shareholders' Equity
- Preferred stock
- Common stock
- Retained earnings
- Additional paid-in capital

Cash Flow Statement

- Operating Cash Flow
- Investment
- Financing
- Net Change in Cash

Accrual Adjustments

Income Statement

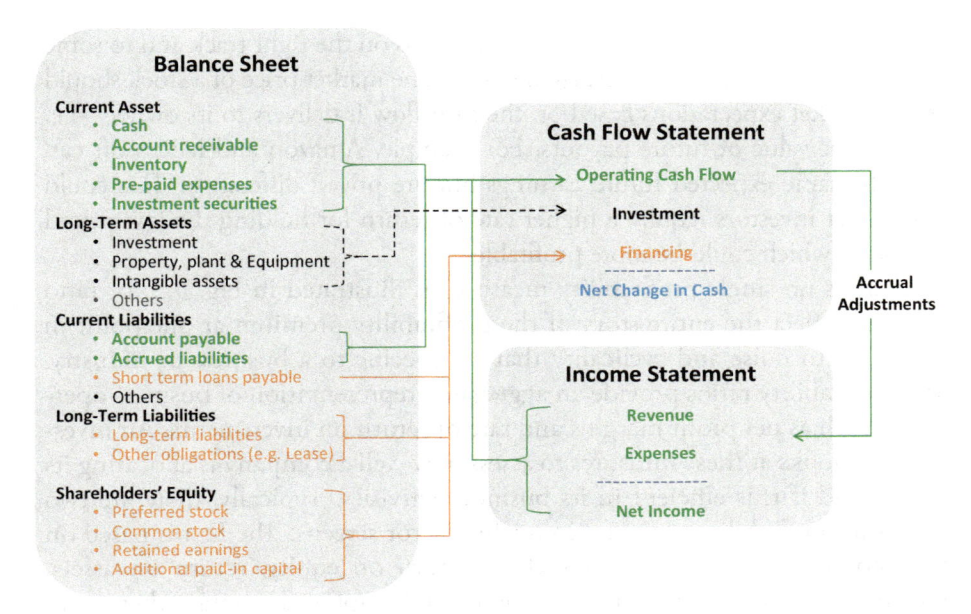

- Revenue
- Expenses
- Net Income

Fig. 5.2 The link between the balance sheet, cash flow and income statement. Source: Author. Note: For illustrative purposes only

Figure 5.2 provides an illustration of the link between the balance sheet, income statement and cash flow statement. For our context, the entire quality attribute targets these different traits of the financial statements.

Hsu et al. in 2018 finds earnings stability (e.g. earnings per share growth variability), capital structure (e.g. debt-to-equity or debt-to-cash flow), and growth in profitability (changes in profit) show little evidence of premia, whereas profitability, accounting quality, payout/dilution, and investment tend to be associated with a premium. In their research they show further that profitability levels and investment-related characteristics tend to capture most of the quality-related premia. However, the list of quality characteristics is broad and those presented in this chapter are not exhaustive.

5.2.1 Profitability Screen

This section focuses on a few profitability ratios that emerged from the academic world and got adopted among professionals. The idea is that consistently profitable companies tend to generate a so-called profitability premium (excess of factor returns over a market benchmark) over the long term. Profitability is used as financial health screen in quality factor strategies. If the profitability steadily increases over time, it is likely that the business is on the right track and to some extent explains the expected return of stocks. The market price of a stock should reflect market expectations based on the cash flow it delivers to its owner—i.e. the present value of future payouts. For example, Amazon and Microsoft can have the same expected future earnings but are priced differently. This could reflect that investors require a higher rate of return for holding the low priced company, which could be more profitable.

There is no single profitability measure, as illustrated in Fig. 5.3, or ratio that can reflect the entire story of the profitability premium at one point in time, due to noise and cyclicality that are specific to a business or industry. The profitability ratios provide an aggregated representation of business operations such as net profit margins and rate of return on investments. An investor often looks at these measures to assess how well a company is allocating its capital and if it is efficient in its business activities. Typically, there are two classes of profitability measures in quality factor screens. The first is based on profitability from investments such as return on equity, return on assets, return on invested capital or return on capital employed among other variations of these ratios. The second is focused on profit margins such as gross profit, operating profit, operating cash flow, net profit margin, among others.

A common and well-understood ratio is the **Return-on-Equity (RoE)**, the usual ingredient of investment profitability screens. It measures the profit per dollar of shareholder's equity and often used as an indicator as to how well a company is generating returns on investment by using shareholders capital. It is defined as Net Income (profit or net income after taxes) relative to

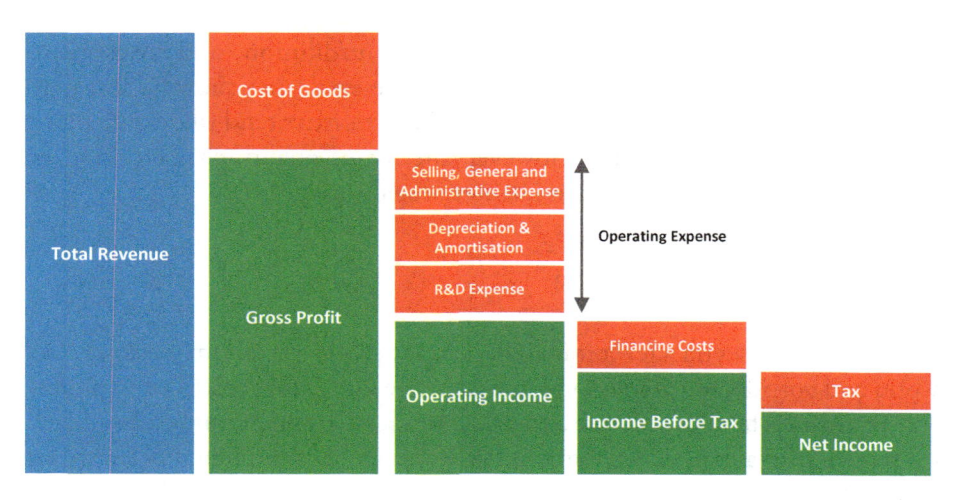

Fig. 5.3 Structure of profit measures. Source: Author. Note: For illustrative purposes only

Shareholder Equity (total assets minus total liabilities). RoE is often featured in combination with other quality characteristics. The MSCI quality indexes, for example, tend to complement RoE with leverage and earnings variability.

Another well-established metric in quality factor investing is the **Gross Profit/Total Asset** ratio. It was proposed by Robert Novy-Marx in a study in 2013 as a quality screen for stocks and used by Scientific Beta. Gross profitability is at the top of the income statement and could be a better representation of the "true economic profitability" of a company. Gross profit is measured as Revenue—Cost of Goods Sold (COGS). COGS is the cost of manufacturing or production of goods, including material and direct labour costs for a company. The total asset is the book asset value here. Since gross profit is not reduced by interest payment and book asset value, it is also not reduced by debt value. Hence, we can divide gross profit over total assets so that it is independent of leverage. Amazon is a classic example of a company that has delivered mediocre net earnings due to spending on business development—drones, robots and other assets. The company's profits look far healthier without the massive spending. However, the spending allows it to maintain a competitive advantage at the forefront of innovation. It is increasingly popular as a proxy for true economic profitability despite its limitation, where some assets in various industries such as financials, information technology or consumer discretionary are not comparable and need sector adjustments (i.e. peer-to-peer comparison).

An alternative to gross profitability was introduced by Fama and French in 2014. They suggested using operating profit instead of gross or net profit. Figure 5.4 provides an illustration of the historical performance of an index portfolio based on Operating Profit-to-Book Value (OP/BV). Historically the high OP/BV has outperformed low OP/BV and the broad market. In general, the OP/BV measures operating profitability per unit of book value (the balance sheet value of the company). It shows how efficiently the company generates profits for one dollar of book value. Operating profit is defined as the revenues after deducting operating expenses, COGS and depreciation. Despite the different profitability metrics among academics and professionals, the various measures present evidence of the existence of the profitability premium. In sum, either gross or operating profitability should help you achieve a long-term profitability screen.

5.2.2 Asset Growth and Investment Screen

Another measure of quality measures the evolution of the assets and corporate investment over time. Several academic studies identified that stocks with high total asset growth tend to underperform the general market. This has

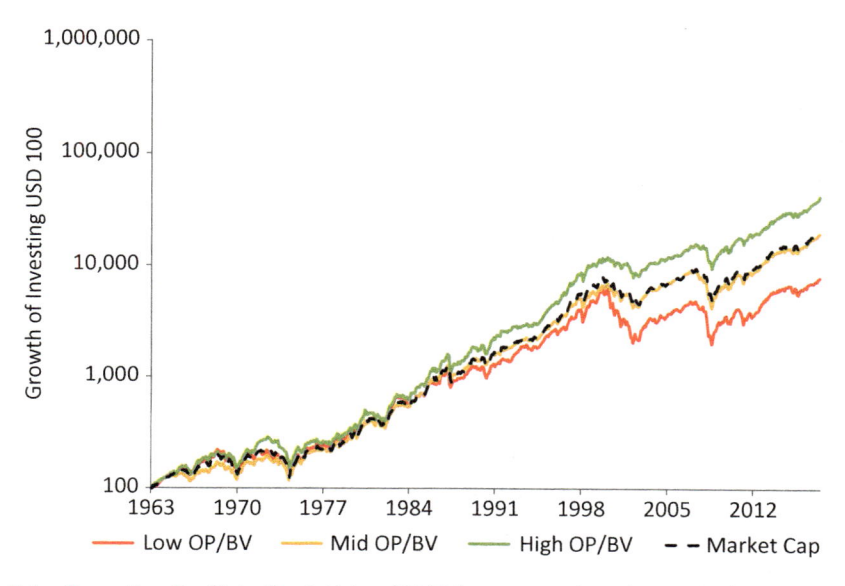

Fig. 5.4 Operating Profit-to-Book Value (OP/BV) screen and market capitalisation strategies. Source: Author's calculations, Kenneth French database, Jul. 1963–Dec. 2017 for the U.S. Note: The time series are logged and rebased to July 1963. The high OP/BV is 30th percentile of the companies with highest OP/BV, the Mid OP/BV is 40–70th percentile, and low OP/BV is the bottom 30th percentile. The portfolios are market value-weighted based on each stock's market capitalisation. Market Cap is the market capitalisation portfolio. Historical returns are not a leading indicator of future performance

been attributed to corporate events associated with asset expansion (e.g. acquisitions, public equity offerings, public debt offerings). Events associated with asset contraction—e.g. spinoffs, share repurchases, debt pre-payments and dividend initiations have historically featured "abnormally" high stock returns. Total asset growth is defined as the changes in assets between periods. The total asset can be decomposed both from the asset and liabilities side of the balance sheet.[1] While the profitability screen in the previous section is intuitive, the low investment phenomena are often classified as an anomaly among many academics and professionals, simply because companies that refrain from growing their asset base may not do well over the long term.

Asset growth effect is weaker in times of increased corporate oversight. This is consistent with the evidence that the asset growth effect can emerge from managerial overinvestment. In 2008 Cooper et al. demonstrated that between 1963–2003 periods with high asset growth tended to follow low stock returns

---

[1] Total asset growth based on the liability side of the balance sheet = Operating liabilities growth + Retained earnings growth +Stock financing growth +Debt financing growth. Operating liabilities are defined as total assets less all the asset categories mentioned above.

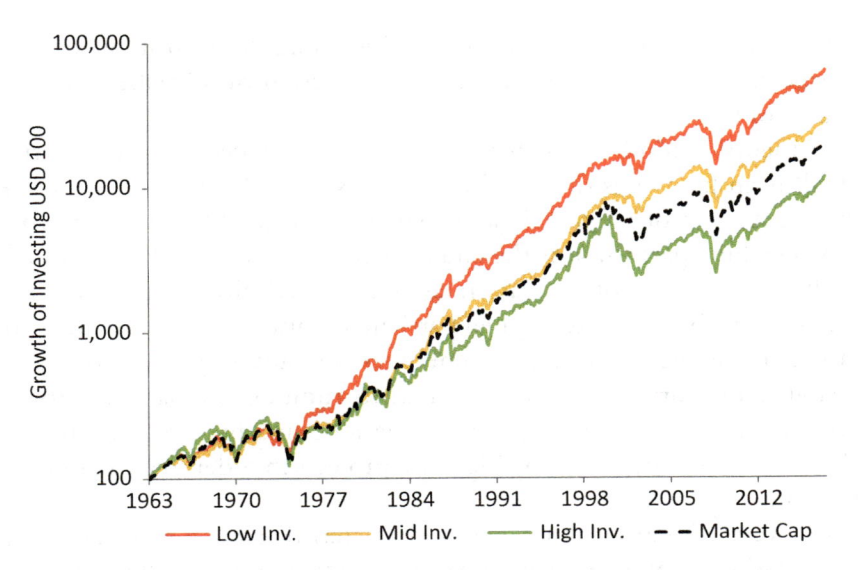

Fig. 5.5 Low, average, high investment and market capitalisation portfolio. Source: Author's calculations. Kenneth French database, Jul. 1963–Dec. 2017 for the U.S. Note: The time series are logged and rebased to July 1963. The high Inv. is 30th percentile of the companies with the highest investment, the Mid Inv. is 40–70th percentile, and low Inv. is the bottom 30th percentile. The portfolio is market value weighted based on each stock's market capitalisation. Market Cap is the market capitalisation portfolio. Historical returns are not a leading indicator of future performance

in the U.S. Similarly, companies with low asset growth tend to outperform those with high asset growth.[2] This observation has also been established for global stock markets.

Figure 5.5 shows a screen of year-on-year total asset growth rate for companies in the U.S. with low and high investment portfolios versus market capitalisation index.

5.2.3 Leverage Screen

Leverage is another dimension from the balance sheet that can also be a source of quality. A firm may increase its leverage beyond a certain affordable point. This is particularly the case for a firm with debt exceeding the market value of its assets for some period of time. Leverage can incentivise

---

[2] The approach is to rank portfolios based on past asset growth over the previous year and hold that portfolio over the next year and rebalance the portfolio annually. Various weighting were used by Cooper, Gulen and Schill (2008) such as equal weighting, value weighted, capitalisation weighted portfolios to reduce biases driven by small capitalisation stocks.

shareholders to accept high-risk projects, including those with low or negative expected future value. Such behaviour is driven by a "make it or break it" frame of mind.

The theory behind this behaviour can be illustrated by the American football term known as the "Hail Mary" pass. The "Hail Mary" pass often occurs at the end of a football game, which is executed by the quarterback throwing a long pass towards the end zone in the hope that the ball will fall into the hands of one of his team members. Statistically, the success rate of this pass is low but tends to happen particularly often for a losing team. The idea is that the high-risk play is sometimes the only way, even with a low probability of scoring quickly compared to running the ball or throwing short-passes. Hence firms that have large amounts of debt may increase their risk tolerance by accepting high-risk projects in order to outmanoeuvre bankruptcy.

Low leverage is considered a quality characteristic among many academics and professionals. Studies have shown that companies with a stable and sustainable leverage level relative to their equity capital tend to generate excess return over the market in the long term—see George and Hwang study in 2010 and Penman et al. in 2007. At the same time, excessive leverage may jeopardise a company's ability to service its debt. Academic research shows that firms with low leverage tend to generate a high excess return over the market. Albert Altman's research from 1968, with his famous quality screen (discussed in the fixed income chapter later) showed that consistently high corporate leverage tends to increase credit risk and these companies tend to underperform over time.[3] Also, a company with the high cost of capital may choose to maintain low leverage or deleverage to reduce the likelihood of distress.

Leverage comes with a range of measures for rules-based index construction. Among these that complement that total level of debt as a safety measure includes high current ratios (current assets to current liabilities), high-interest coverage ratios and high credit ratings. These ratios can be affected by the choice of accounting method and vary across industries—banks are naturally overleveraged and utilities tend to have long-term debt. Typical metrics to construct a systematic rank or alternatively-weighted index includes:

$$\text{Total Leverage} = \text{Total Debt} / \text{Total Assets}.$$

---

[3] Altman (1968), Ohlson (1980), Campbell, Hilscher, and Szilagyi (2008).

In addition to the level, the change in these ratios can also be used as safety indicators.[4]

Change in Net Leverage $= \text{Change}\left[(\text{Total Debt} - \text{Total Cash})/\text{Total Assets}\right].$

Of course, a low level of debt may not tell the entire story of a company's performance. For example, take a farmer with a small amount of debt that is faced with bad crops due to the weather for two years in a row. The farmer can always sell a piece of land to repay what is owed to the bank. But if the same farmer has a lot of debt, then liquidating enough land to repay the debt is going to eradicate the farming business. As long as the farmer has a good year of crops, he can keep farming the land and service the debt. Now suppose the farmer wants to diversify the business and decides to buy cows that produce milk with borrowed money. The milk business may take off well, and the leverage may not harm the overall farm business at all, assuming the cows are healthy. In the end, it is about the corporate strategy and finding the balanced line between reasonable and unreasonable leverage.

5.2.4 Earning Accruals Screen

We discussed the ability of profitability to assist in generating a quality factor portfolio. Though the way earnings are booked and represented in the financial accounts can be a leading indicator of quality in itself. Another quality screen includes forensic accounting particularly focused on accruals. Accounting accruals simply mean how much accounting income exceeds cash income. This is a result of revenues and expenses being recognised as soon as they are incurred, as opposed to when the cash flow takes place. A firm typically recognises the revenue when an invoice is drawn as opposed to when an invoice is paid and also recognition of expenses that might be either incurred early or delayed. If a company were to incur an expense but not have to pay until a future date, the expense would be recognised when it is incurred. Earning accruals is defined in a study by Sloan in 1996 as:

Accruals = Change in Operating Working Capital
− Depreciation, Depletion and Amortization,

---

[4] Asness et al. in 2014 used similar approach.

where,

$$\text{Operating Working Capital} = \begin{pmatrix} \text{Current Assets} - \text{Cash and Short} \\ -\text{Term Investments} \end{pmatrix}$$
$$- \begin{pmatrix} \text{Current Liabilities} + \text{Short} \\ -\text{Term Debt and Taxes Payable} \end{pmatrix}.$$

Decomposing total profit into the net cash flow and accruals components can be an insightful practice, given that the net cash flow is more informative than actual economic performance, whereas the accruals component of profit can be potentially manipulated. Systematic stock screening based on accounting accruals can help reduce or avoid companies that report a large portion of accruals as part of their net profit, and, as a result, tend to underperform. Academic studies by Sloan in 1996 and Hafzalla et al. in 2011 have demonstrated that companies with low accruals are likely to provide better risk-adjusted returns longer term. High net cash flow as a part of total profit may reflect a "true" measure of economic performance while the accrual component is subject to adjustments and does not necessarily reflect the actual performance of a firm. Figure 5.6 shows the historical benefits of screening based on earning accruals. The index portfolio with low accrual has consistently outperformed the broad market and the companies with high earning accruals in the U.S. Similar results are evident from other global stock markets and documented in a range of academic and market studies.

5.2.5 Corporate Governance Screen

Now we move to a qualitative dimension of quality, which is represented by the actual management of a company. Any shareholder or creditor wishes to invest in well-governed companies. Corporate governance proved to be important through various episodes in history, especially in times of corporate default and crisis.

A corporate governance-based screen looks at characteristics such as the independence of the board of directors, audit aspects, the risk committee, transparency and shareholders' rights. An earlier study on corporate governance by Gompers et al. in 2003 provides examples of the level of shareholder rights and how it relates to company performance. They constructed a "Governance Index" based on various company governance provisions that are perceived to increase or decrease shareholder rights. Brooke et al. provide a range of corporate governance factors attributed to portfolio construction in their research in 2015.

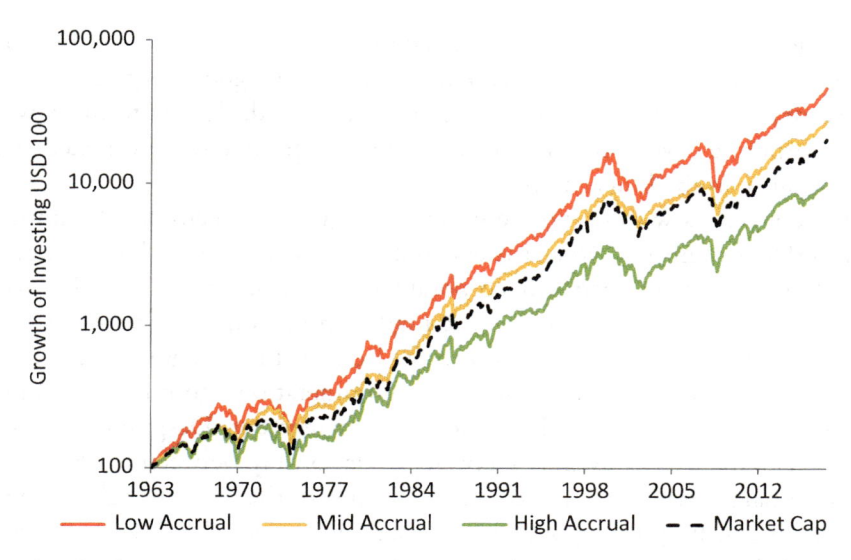

Fig. 5.6 Accrual portfolios versus market capitalisation. Source: Author's calculations. Kenneth French database, Jul. 1963–Dec. 2017 for the U.S. Note: The time series are logged and rebased to July 1963. The high accruals is 30th percentile of the companies with the highest accrual, the Mid accruals is 40–70th percentile and low accruals is the bottom 30th percentile. The portfolio is market value weighted based on each stock's market capitalisation. Market Cap is the market capitalisation portfolio. Market Cap denotes the market capitalisation portfolio. Historical returns are not a leading indicator of future performance

Active equity managers tend to factor corporate governance factors in and pay attention to it as they hold fewer stocks than an index fund manager, who may hold up to 1000 stocks. It is impossible for an index manager to meet the management and conduct a corporate governance review on each company in a broad index. Hence a systematic screen could capture some of this by using external corporate governance ratings such as "QualityScores" by Institutional Shareholder Services or an in-house developed score based on governance data and/or direct engagement with companies by a stewardship team.

Empirical evidence shows that there is a relationship between corporate governance and subsequent returns. The theory behind modern corporate governance is often referred to as the agency theory. Agency theory says that the role of the board of directors is to be the independent intermediary, the broker, the referee between the principals (the people who contribute resources and capital to the corporation) and the agents (the people who utilize those resources to get things done). Shareholders and managers have different needs, expectations and interests. The role of corporate governance and the board in agency theory is to arbitrate between them and to make decisions about resource allocation.

Agency theory suggests that potential costs can be incurred due to the separation of ownership and management, whereby with good corporate governance practices in place these costs can be mitigated. Therefore firms with weak corporate governance might expect higher agency costs and hence poor performance in the longer-term.

The challenges with corporate governance quality screens are the limited data and lack of history. Nevertheless, in 2015 Brooke et al. and others examined the relationship between corporate governance and returns between 2003–2013 for the Australian stock market based on the S&P/ASX 300 index. This study derives a composite score from six internal governance areas: the board of directors, audit committee, remuneration committee, nomination committee, external auditor and risk management. Despite the limited history of data, this study shows a positive relationship between stock returns and internal governance and vice versa. This means that that the value of governance is not fully incorporated into share prices, which allows for such a premium during the 10-year sample data history. Irrespective of the quantitative aspect of corporate governance, a well-run company with strong internal governance should provide more confidence to investors.

5.2.6 Combined Quality Screens Among Practitioners

We have discussed individual traits of the quality characteristics of a company. Each of them is attractive and serves a certain purpose at different times. Hence, many quality factors tend to combine some of these financial traits. This section provides examples of combined quality screens used by some investors and factor index providers. Graham's and Piotroski's quality screens are among the popular quality screens in the industry. These screens involve multiple accounting measures. We will discuss these two particular screens, but the list is not exhaustive. In a later section we will discuss the multi-characteristic screen by various index providers.

Joseph Piotroski, the accounting professor, created in 2000 the "Piotroski F-Score". The score is derived from nine criteria from three areas: profitability, capital structure/financial liquidity, and operating efficiency. These criteria are described below.

Profitability

- **Net Income (NI)**—Defined as profit (taking into account all income and expenses) is a sign of strength. So, positive net income from the most recent financial statement is awarded a score of one;

- **Operating Cash Flow (OCF)**—OCF is important for internal financing (pay bills and expenses) and a sign of strength or weakness. Positive cash flow from operations is awarded a score of one;
- **Return on Assets (ROA)**—Defined as net profit divided by assets for the past two years and provides a sign of the trend in asset returns. If the ROA has increased year-on-year, a score of one is assigned;
- **Earnings Quality**—Defined as a comparison between OCF and NI. The OCF is usually higher than NI as NI includes non-cash items. If OCF is greater than NI, then a score of one is awarded.

Capital Structure

- **Long-term Debt-to-Assets ratio**—If the long-term debt-to-equity ratio for the previous fiscal year is less than the ratio two-years ago, then a score of one is assigned. Decreasing leverage is interpreted as a positive sign;
- **Current ratio (Change in Liquidity)**—If the current ratio for the previous year is higher than the current ratio for the two years ago, then a score of one is assigned;
- **Change in Average Shares Outstanding**—If the average number of shares outstanding from the previous year is less or equal to the average number of shares outstanding from two years before, then a score of one is assigned. An increasing number of shares outstanding is interpreted as negative due to dilution.

Operating Efficiency

- **Change in Gross Margin**—If the gross margin has increased in the past two years, then a score of one is assigned. A rising gross margin indicates increasing prices or decreasing costs, which is a positive sign for the firm;
- **Asset Turnover**—Asset turnover ratio is the total sales divided by the total assets. If the asset turnover ratio has increased over the past two years, then a score of one is assigned.

The objective of the screen is to assess if a company has solid financials and if those financials are improving or deteriorating. For each criterion that a stock passes it gets one point. A company can have an F-score between zero and nine. As a rule of thumb, a score between 7–9 it is good—a firm is more likely to be financially stable and is expected to perform well in the future. A score of less than three for a company is considered to be very weak with deteriorating financial conditions.

An investment strategy that only bought companies with Piotroski scores of at least 8 outperformed the benchmark by an average of 13.4% annually between 1976–1996. While Piotroski initially analysed stand-alone strategies based on quality scores, Piotroski and So in 2012 showed that quality with attractive valuation performed even better than the stand-alone quality screen.

The F-score and modified versions are commonly employed by professionals and widely available on internet stock screeners. Societe Generale uses the F-score as its primary screen when constructing its Global Quality Income Index, while Morgan Stanley has offered products linked to strategies that combine the F-score with other characteristics.

Other composite quality score frameworks, often used in conjunction with value investing, include:

- The Graham screen, often associated with value-quality screens. This screen tends to focus on seven metrics with value and quality features—enterprise size, financial condition (asset and liabilities), earnings stability, consistency of dividend, P/E and P/B ratio.
- The Joel Greenblatt's screen. The logic of Greenblatt's "magic formula" is that of combining quality and value, in the spirit of Graham's belief in buying good firms at low prices. The "magic formula" ranks companies based on their Return-on-Invested-Capital (ROIC) and earnings yield. ROIC is the return that a company makes from invested capital. The idea is only to buy stocks with the highest combined ranks. The formula is explicitly intended to ensure that investors are buying quality stocks at good bargain prices—see Greenblatt 2010 for more details.

Novy-Marx in a quality review paper showed the correlation between the Piotroski, Graham and Greenblatt approach using U.S. data from 1963 to 2013. The highest correlation is between the Piotroski and Greenblatt's screen—about 56%. The average correlation between the three screens is 34%, which indicate that they do not necessarily generate similar trends of quality assessment in general.

Moreover, a composite quality score is also common among the majority index providers and asset managers. Asness and his colleagues at AQR Capital Management define quality based on profitability (e.g. gross profit, margins and other measures), profitability growth, safety (low volatility, low leverage, stable earnings) and payout ratio (profits paid out to shareholders). Table 5.1 provides a comparison of standard metrics in composite screens among index providers. For example, MSCI quality index series aims to identify quality growth stocks by calculating a quality score for each security in the eligible equity universe based on three main fundamental variables: high RoE, stable year-over-year

Table 5.1 Market indices for quality

MSCI	FTSE-Russell	EDHEC-SciBeta	FTSE-RAFI	S&P Dow Jones
RoE	Profitability (return-on-assets)	High profitability	Sales	RoE
Earnings variability		Low investment	Cash flow	Earnings quality
Leverage	Efficiency (changes in asset turnover)		Dividend & buybacks	Leverage
	Earnings quality (accruals)		Book value	
	Leverage			

Source: Author, methodology documents and factsheets of various index providers

earnings growth and low financial leverage. FTSE-RAFI quality index weight stocks based on sales, cash flow, dividend, share buybacks and book value while S&P-Dow Jones uses return on equity, earnings quality and leverage.

5.3 Drivers of the Quality Premium

Most of the quality characteristics seem to be in the league that people would rather choose to invest in instead of avoiding. Among the larger stocks, high-quality stocks may not always outperform in the short or medium term but over the longer term. This was evident in the past decades across global stock markets.

Quality, in general, should display lower volatility over a long period compared to more risky factor strategies and a broad market index. It is difficult to attribute full risk-based explanations as to why high-quality stocks outperform low-quality stocks. For example, in the period between 1963–2017 short-term interest rate, economic growth and inflation explain only about 10–17% of various quality premia (excess return over the market returns for fundamental characteristics, such as profitability, low asset growth). Even in subsamples since 1990 the quality premium can only partly be explained by macro-factors.

Among the macro-factors, inflation is consistently more significant for the quality factor. This reflects a consistent tilt to companies with the ability to maintain pricing-power and grow with inflation over time. At the same time, interest rates seem to be more significant for the profitability-screened factor, this means that companies with high profitability tend to also benefit or remain profitable in a rising interest rate environment.[5] The typical sector

---

[5] The analysis was conducted using quality premium (return difference between quality factor and market capitalisation index) in the U.S. The statistical regression analysis involved regressing the premium on annual change of industrial production, consumer prices index and short term interest rates.

where this applies to is the banking sector which historically formed an integral part of the quality factor. However, at the end of 2007, for example, the Global MSCI quality index was tilted to the technology sector.

While the macro and risk-based explanations are weak, the unexplained part of the quality premium can be attributed to behavioural drivers and to some extent to market structures. Quality stocks are often dull due to the lack of exciting stories compared to the big headline stocks. Investors tend to ignore and not incorporate the firm's quality into stock prices. Psychologically, the more information we have on an event, the more likely it seems to occur. If we hear negative news about a shark attack on a lovely golden sandy beach, even if the likelihood is small for such an event, we are unlikely to go there any time soon. When we hear about a company from our friends over dinner, it may influence our judgement. This is known as the **availability bias**. It happens when investors judge the likelihood of an event or the frequency of its occurrence with the ease and examples that are available to our mind by remembering the shark attack or the dinner conversation with friends. In the context of the quality premium, events or lack of interesting stories mean investors pay little attention to quality stocks in good market conditions.

Moreover, based on a range of studies the market structures are perhaps more significant. We have touched on some of the market structures as a part of the earning accrual screens. It is not unusual that revenues and expenses are recognised on the financial statements as soon as they are incurred instead of when the cash flow is actually taking place. Companies with high net positive accruals have historically underperformed relative to those with high net cash flow as a part of total profit.

Other market structures involve corporate management, who tend to be overconfident in their ability to grow the business. There are few studies that document this behaviour. A study by Malmendier and Tate in 2008 shows that overconfident Chief Executives Officers (CEOs) are more likely to undertake a Mergers and Acquisition (M&A). The market reaction to the M&A had a more negative impact on the share price than the acquisition undertaken by less overconfident CEOs. The theory is that management overconfidence can lead to overpaying for M&A or excessive spending on capital-intensive projects that can be dilutive to the shareholders' value. Other studies showed that overconfidence could also lower the average M&A deal quality. This is not to say that this decision-making is deliberate, management believes their actions lead to positive outcomes. This observation is often referred to as the low investment premium, which is considered a positive quality characteristic.

5.4 Quality and Valuation of Stocks

A group of academics and professionals argue that using a quality factor should be combined with another factor by taking into account the valuation of the underlying stocks. This is important in order to avoid overpaying for the quality stocks. One of the better explanations of how to think about valuation and quality is attributed to Kalesnik and Kose in 2014 at Research Affiliates. They use a baseball analogy, based on a story of Billy Beane, the general manager, of the Oakland Athletics baseball team in the 2002 season.

The challenge for Mr. Beane was to create a competitive team with a limited budget. He built a successful team of undervalued talent based on statistics to select and analyse players. Mr. Beane's objective was to win games as cheaply as possible. The story is subject in the best-selling book Moneyball by Michael Lewis and it was later made into a movie with Brad Pitt. The philosophy is similar for the former Manchester United soccer coach Sir Alex Ferguson who recognised value for money—I am not a Manchester United fan, but rather am acknowledging the consistency of their success for decades.

From a finance perspective, the quality screens emerged from well-established academic research that are used by professional investors to devise a variety of investment strategies. Some companies deserve higher prices while others are just overpriced or may be cheap and have every reason to be so. There are cases, for example, when a quality company becomes a value company, especially during volatile market periods or when a company's valuation becomes overstretched which can undermine long-term performance. In 2018, a study by Frazzini et al. showed that the performance of companies held by Berkshire Hathaway (Buffett's primary investment vehicle) looked more like high-quality stocks despite being seen as value stocks.

Historically, the quality factor exhibited low correlation to value. Figure 5.7 shows the 5-year correlation since 1960 between value and quality premia (measured as an excess return to the market capitalisation index in the U.S.). It is historically evident that the quality and value factor premia vary and tend to be negatively correlated. During periods of high market volatility and crises value stock tends to sell off, while quality stocks may sell off less than value.[6] Nevertheless, the long-term correlation is close to zero. In general, it indicates that the two factors are good diversifiers in portfolios and may complement each other over the long term.

---

[6] It is important to acknowledge that quality can experience severe drawdown. During the global financial crisis quality lost as much as 50% from peak to trough in developed markets compared to 60% of the broad market capitalisation Indices.

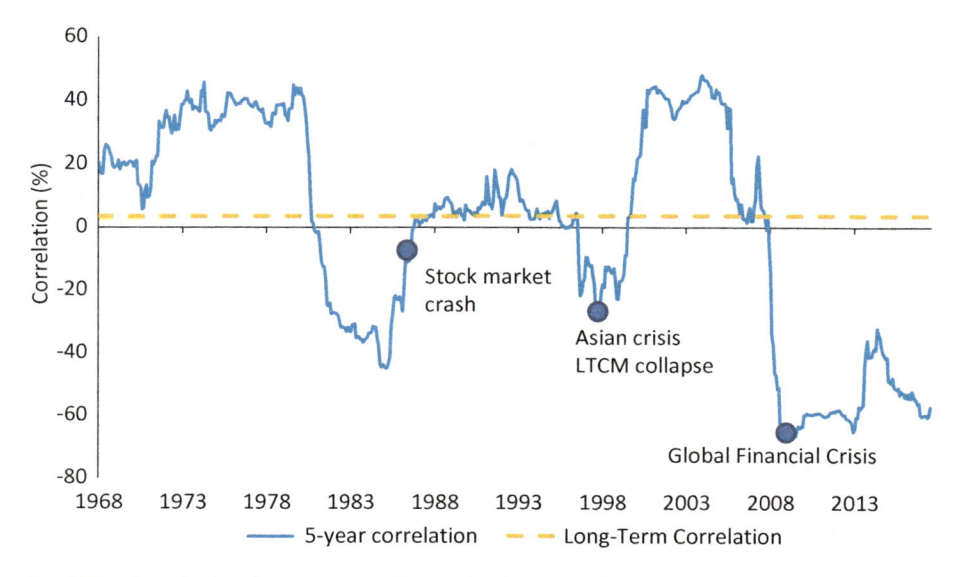

Fig. 5.7 Correlation between quality and value premia. Source: Author's calculation, Kenneth French database, Jul. 1963–Dec. 2017 for the U.S. Note: The quality premium is defined as the difference between the quality portfolio and the market capitalisation index total returns. Quality is defined as an equally weighted portfolio with high profitability, low asset growth and low accruals

Overall, high-quality firms tend to be more expensive and less cyclical than a value stock. Consequently, the two tend to do well precisely when the other underperforms, making them attractive for diversification in a long-term investment strategy. Capturing both high quality and highly undervalued companies may not be achievable in all market conditions. Therefore it can be rewarding to find the crossroad that provides the balance between value and quality.

5.5 Consideration for Quality Strategies

I am always suspicious of claims that higher quality companies consistently provide higher returns. When looking at the quality factor, there are few considerations that investors need to keep in mind, particularly around cyclicality, applicability to specific sectors and whether it should be combined with other factors. For a quality factor strategy to provide a persistent future excess return (returns over traditional market capitalisation index), one has to ask what the drivers of the quality premium is. The results are most likely to be different depending on the choice of design of the quality factor.

The quality premium could reflect an "insurance", risk premium against poor economic and market conditions. It tends to pay off relative to the broad market during volatile market conditions as more investors look for these stocks. In normal market conditions, quality is not always rewarded as economic sensitivity is not necessarily the primary driver of stock returns. We discussed earlier that company-specific variables and behaviours in the market are drivers of the premium.

It is important to acknowledge that quality is not exclusive or specific to one industry, although it is human nature to build affection and biases to specific sectors and stocks. We live in an evolving world with new companies taking the lead on the quality scoreboard. Sony, for example, dominated mobile music through the walkman before the rise of the MP3 player and the iPod. Yahoo was among the favourite web-search engine before Google came along and destroyed their business.

Being open-minded and challenging the systematic screen can save investors from unrecoverable or long-term losses in the market. Table 5.2 provides an example of companies that filed for bankruptcy in the U.S. Many of these companies had decades of history and were profitable quality, companies at some point in time. Changes to the sectors and the general economy changed the viability of these companies for the worse. Although we have discussed diversified quality index strategies here, having a concentration in one company that runs into bankruptcy can lead to permanent or long-term capital damage. This reinforces the importance of diversification as quality screens tend to be more concentrated than the broader market.

Table 5.2 Example bankruptcy filings

Stock	Sector	Total assets before bankruptcy (USD)	Year of bankruptcy
Lehman Brothers	Banking	691	2008
Washington Mutual	Banking	328	2008
Worldcom	Telecommunications	104	2002
General Motors	Car manufacturer	82	2009
CIT Group	Banking	71	2009
Enron	Energy trading	66	2001
MF Global	Financial broker	41	2011
Chrysler	Car manufacturer	39	2009
Pacific Gas and Electric Co.	Utility	36	2001
Texaco	Oil & Gas	35	1987
Global Crossing	Telecommunications	30	2002

Source: Author's compilation from news and media, including New York Times, Wall Street Journal and Financial Times

Finally, some characteristics used for the quality screen may be limited and not comparable between industries. Financial institutions such as banks have fundamentally different business models (e.g. borrowing and lending). Hence, it is essential to understand how the factor strategy design is distinguishing between financial and non-financial companies. For example, working capital, CAPEX and debt are not clearly defined under the International Financial Reporting Standards (IFRS) or the U.S. Generally Accepted Accounting Principles (GAAP) for financial institutions. Consequently, a number of quality measures discussed, such as gross profit, operating cash flow and accruals are not always applicable to financial companies, where return-on-asset might be a better reflection of profitability.

5.6 Concluding Remarks

Quality factor investing is not a new concept. It goes back to Graham advocating for buying quality stocks at low prices. Like most of the well-established factor strategies, quality has emerged from active managers who typically use it with value strategies. With technological advancement and availability of data, it is possible to generate a systematic quality factor screen for a global stock universe. Despite the rich choice of characteristics in systematic factor strategies, not a single measure of quality is superior to another, and different characteristics may do better in various market conditions. In the end, there are many ways to prepare a nice salad, and it may taste different depending on which vegetables are used.

Depending on the choice of characteristics, performance can differ tremendously between various quality definitions. The common objective is to capture the quality factor premium over a more extended time period as investors do not fully incorporate quality characteristics into market prices or recognise the importance of them before the rainy days. The price for the quality stocks tends to be higher during risk-off periods and lower during normal market conditions. In general, investors should keep an open mind as to whether a quality factor makes a good investment on its own and whether it should be combined with other factors in the overall portfolio.

The bottom line is that companies that have poor profitability are often cheap for a good reason. Companies that are playing games with their accounting statements, again, are cheap for a good reason. A company with sustainable leveraged, profitable, "clean" financial statements as well as being cheaply priced is the nirvana of investing. Such opportunities are often hard to find or may not be in the public domain for purchase.

6

Equity Factor Investing: Low Risk

The low risk factor, interchangeably known as the "low volatility" factor, is the story of the risk-return paradox in finance literature and the finance industry. This paradox has shaken up the fundamentals' theory of higher risk and higher reward. This factor targets securities or portfolios with low volatility characteristics. Historically, these characteristics have rewarded investors with higher risk-adjusted returns compared to a broad market capitalisation strategy over the longer term.

This chapter offers insights into low volatility factor investing, how these strategies are constructed and why the premia exists. We will discuss the drivers of the factor premium and the factor's pros and cons in portfolios. The benefits of using low volatility factor investing emerged among institutional investors in the wake of the financial crisis in 2008 and the euro debt crisis, and recently among retail investors. These crises were a reminder of the importance of capital preservation and diversification. In the past years, the availability of systematic low volatility funds has increased through mutual funds and ETFs. The number of low risk or volatility index funds is over 60 listed ETFs with assets under management of over USD 200bn in 2018.

Although this asset growth is new to index-tracking funds, low volatility portfolios came into the spotlight in the 1970s when academics started to challenge the assumptions of the traditional asset pricing models—the Capital Asset Pricing Model (CAPM). As discussed earlier, the CAPM assumes a world with efficient markets and rational investors. It also predicts a positive linear relationship between risk and returns—i.e. high risk should provide higher expected returns. This is not always necessarily the case in the financial market, and standard financial theory is not able to explain the low volatility paradox.

In 1972 Haugen and Heins showed that there was a positive alpha for low beta stocks (a proxy of low volatility relative to the market) between 1929–1971. Subsequent studies by Frazzini et al. in 2014 and others reiterated the existence of the low volatility anomalies in the U.S., Europe and emerging markets. Today low-volatility investing has gained broader acceptance within the academic circles and investor base. Similar to the other factors in the book, the low volatility premium has persisted for decades despite going in cycles. Figure 6.1 shows the long-term performance of low, medium and high volatility portfolios versus the market capitalisation index. From 1963 to 2017 the low and medium volatility portfolios have outperformed the high risk and market capitalisation index.

Today, the low risk factor strategies come under few names and variations such as "low volatility", "low beta", "minimum variance", and "minimum volatility". The common goal to all of them is to win by losing less. Investors should suffer less drawdown in a declining market and gain less in rising markets. This is one of the reasons why investors are looking at low volatility factor in their portfolios, irrespective of valuation during volatile market conditions.

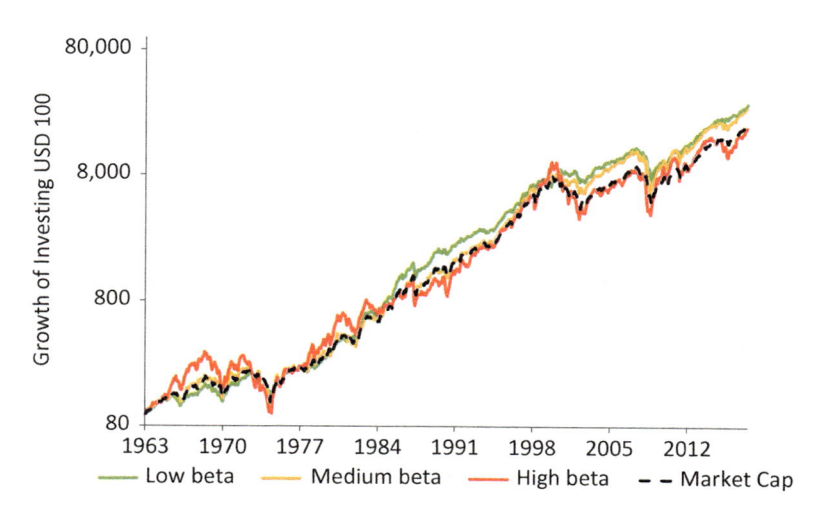

Fig. 6.1 The low volatility premium for the U.S. and portfolios with different risks. Source: Author's calculations, Kenneth French database, Jul. 1963–Dec. 2017 for the U.S. Note: The time series are logged and rebased to July 1963. The low beta portfolio is the bottom 30th percentile, the medium beta is 40–70th percentile and the high beta is the top 30th percentile. The portfolios are market value weighted based on each stock's market capitalisation. Market Cap is the market capitalisation portfolio. Historical returns are not a leading indicator of the future performance

6.1 Why Considering Low Volatility Factor Investing?

Given the increasing acceptance of the low volatility premium, why do not all investors pile into it? In reality, a decade ago low volatility mutual funds and ETFs were not readily available to investors, which has changed in the new era of index investing. At the same time, many investors ignore or simply do not like low volatility. Some investors may oversee the low volatility stocks as they are limited to investing in market capitalisation benchmarks due to tracking error constraints (deviations from benchmark) or investment management guidelines. Periods of long and severe underperformance relative to the benchmark, which are more likely to occur for the low risk strategies, can lead to career risk for the fund manager. Other reasons for a premium can be attributed to behavioural reasons such as overconfidence or risk seeking to cause a bias towards more popular risky stocks. For these reasons, investors are likely to remain attracted to and willing to overpay for high-risk stocks. There are market micro-structures and market behaviours that drive the low volatility factor premium that makes it persist over time, which will be discussed later in the chapter.

Typically an asset allocator would consider low volatility strategies to help free up risk budget that could be allocated to higher returning strategies in an asset allocation framework of different risk categories. Figure 6.2 shows how low volatility is expected to shift in a risk-return spectrum from a traditional market capitalisation index. Most institutional and retail investors deploy low volatility factor to de-risk their portfolio or to manage their risk budget. In general, the decision to integrate low volatility is a function of a retirement fund's investment horizon, risk tolerance and age. Investing in

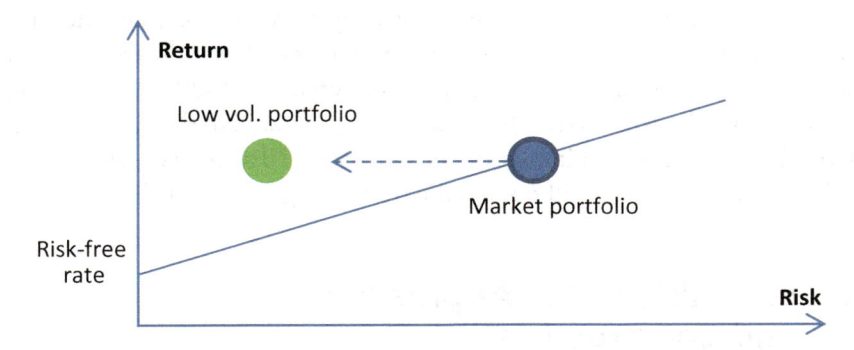

Fig. 6.2 The risk-return relationship and the market. Source: Author. Note: The market capitalisation index is typically the representation of the broad market portfolio. The risk-free rate is often short-dated Treasury bill

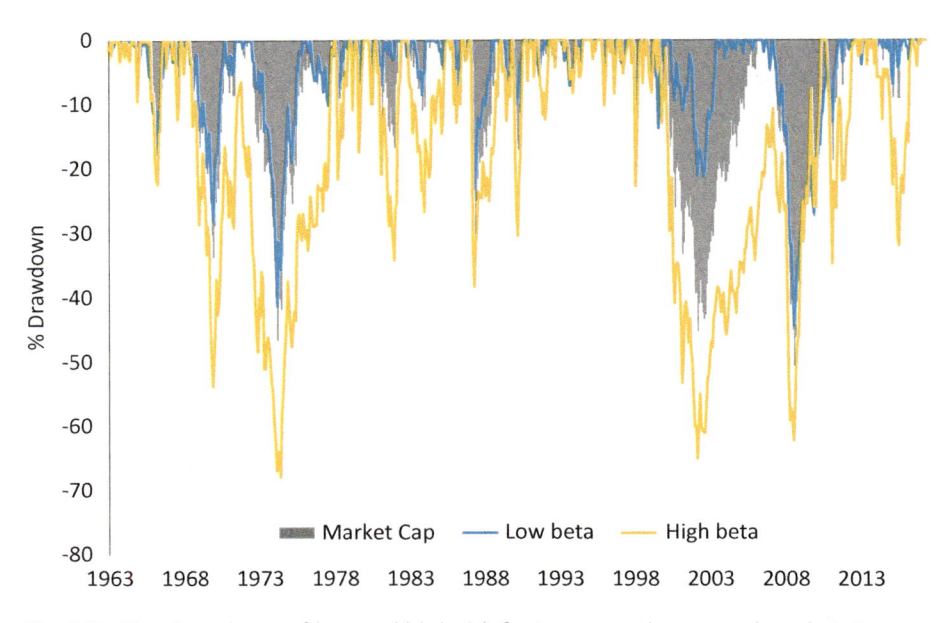

Fig. 6.3 The drawdown of low and high risk factor versus the general market. Source: Author's calculation, Kenneth French database, Jul. 1963–Dec. 2017 for the U.S. Note: The low beta portfolio is the bottom 30th percentile and the high beta is the top 30th percentile. The figure is based on rolling 12-month cumulative drawdown

purchasing a car in the next six months is different from investing in a retirement fund which requires a long-term horizon. A mature retirement fund where members are close to retirement may consider de-risking their portfolio and looking into a diversified low risk equity strategy.

Figure 6.3 shows the drawdown of the low and high risk factors compared to the broad market index, which is critical for long-term capital preservation. The maximum drawdown for the low volatility factor is less than the broad market. For example, the monthly and annual drawdown difference to the broad market is 7% and 4%, respectively between 1963–2017. Historically, the high beta stocks exhibited higher drawdown compared to the low beta stocks and the broad market capitalisation index—over 70% drawdowns on four occasions since 1963. We will discuss the underlying drivers of this anomaly.

6.2 Low Risk Factor Approaches and Construction

This section provides insight into types of rules-based low risk factor strategies and design. The construction of these strategies is quantitative in nature as it relies on statistical measures and techniques. Some approaches require more

Table 6.1 Common low risk factor approaches

Portfolio construction approaches	Risk measures	Weighting
Low volatility	Standard deviation of returns (σ)	• Market-value weighted • The inverse of risk ($1/\sigma$) or ($1/\beta$)
Low beta	Beta (β) of stock returns to a general market benchmark	• Tilting or ranking of securities by low risk (e.g. 30th percentile) • Equal weighting of lowest risk stocks
Minimum variance	Standard deviation and correlation between stocks	Minimisation of volatility subject investment objectives and targets
Semi-variance (downside volatility)	Standard deviation of stock returns with negative returns	• Similar stock weightings to low volatility and beta • Minimisation of volatility subject investment objectives and targets

Source: Author

inputs than others, but the central measure to all approaches are standard deviation and beta of returns. We will focus on four common approaches for construction of low volatility portfolios. Table 6.1 provides a summary for those.

The first approach is straightforward as it ranks securities based on their standard deviation of historical returns. This approach does not take into account the correlations between stocks in the selection process. The second approach is a comparable version to the first one but measures the sensitivity of each security directly to the general market (market capitalisation index) also referred to as beta. The third approach is more sophisticated and involves optimisation techniques that aim to minimise total portfolio volatility by taking into account the correlations between securities in the universe. The fourth approach is known as downside volatility. Unlike the standard volatility approach, which uses both positive and negative returns, downside volatility considers only negative returns. This approach aims to reduce the downside risk without limiting the long term upside potential.

The first two conventional ("rank-based") approaches for low volatility are the standard deviation and market beta weighting of securities. These are among the most common approaches due to their simplicity and transparency. The first, volatility-weighting approach creates the factor to target stocks with the lowest volatility directly without additional assumptions or models. For example, if a stock has 20% volatility compared to another with 10% volatility, the latter stock will have a proportionally higher weighting in an index that is rebalanced every quarter or six months. With the simplicity comes some limitation. First, the strategy does not take into account the correlation between securities or a direct risk measure to the broader market (beta). This matters as high correlation between securities can create portfolios that are systematically sensitive to the broader market, which is an undesired outcome for the tilting or ranking approach. The second approach is an alternative to simple standard deviation and involves weighting by using the security market beta, which implicitly takes into account the correlation of individual securities to the broad market.

The optimisation techniques approach allows for more precise control of constraints on a sector, securities, regions or target volatility. This approach is often seen as more efficient in generating optimal portfolio weightings to achieve a targeted volatility factor portfolio. The drawback is the complexity of implementation and low transparency of the calculation. While the high-level portfolio volatility of the factor portfolio might be small, the security selection may not always include stocks with the lowest volatility compared to the rank-based approach, described earlier. A study by Chow, et al. in 2016 analysed the impact of constraints in a minimum variance approach. They showed that the effect of constraints improves investability for global stock market strategies. However, the improving investability could come at the cost of higher volatility.

In general, these approaches depend on the historical total return volatility as input over a typical time window of 1–5 years of daily or weekly data. The idea is that if past volatility is a good predictor of future volatility, then low volatility techniques will work very well. However, there is a distinction between different portfolio constructions approaches, especially how historical or expected volatility is used in weighting the securities.

In terms of outcomes, the different approach can provide vastly different results. The following example illustrates a simple construction of a factor strategy:

1. Define the starting universe—For example, U.S., developed or global market stocks universe;
2. Calculate the desired risk measure. For example, standard deviation or beta of each security;
3. Selection and weighting of securities in a portfolio—either narrow or broad stock universe based on weighting schemes and exclusions;
4. The final low risk factor portfolio.

The narrow universe option in step three involves a reduction of the starting security universe by exclusion criteria, which can apply to all factor constructions discussed in this book. A typical method is through a rank approach, deciles or percentiles of highest risk stocks. The broader universe option is simply an alternative weighting of an existing index such as market capitalisation index but with limited or no exclusion. The weightings can either be based on the inverse of risk measure or minimise the risk measure subject to various objectives such as return, concentration, turnover to manage the index transaction costs.

For example, suppose you have a market capitalisation portfolio of largest 1000 stocks for an opportunity set. You can select the 30th percentile of lowest return volatility of the 1000 stocks. The volatility can be the last 12-month daily volatility, 2–5 year weekly returns volatility as examples. This is a type of ranking approach and provides 300 stocks after removing 700 stocks from the starting universe. To complete the design of a low volatility factor strategy, the constituents are either weighted equally or by market capitalisation (market value weighted) or by the inverse of security volatility. The same exercise can be repeated for the semi-variance approach (downside volatility), which only calculates the standard deviation of the negative returns. The factor construction on a broad or narrow universe is a common distinction among index providers. The next section provides an overview of factor indices in the market that are tracked by mutual funds and ETFs.

6.3 Common Low Volatility Factor Indices

Despite the strength and short-coming of various approaches, there is no unique approach among investment managers and index providers. This section describes the different types of indices in the market and how they differ. Table 6.2 offer examples of common indices among index providers that are tracked by mutual and ETFs in the market.

These indices created by various providers use different approaches, as described in the previous section. The descriptions of these major indices are as following:

- The S&P 500 Low Volatility index narrows the S&P 500 index to 100 least volatile stocks. The low volatility index weights the constituents relative to the inverse of their corresponding risk using 1-year daily return volatility. The least volatile stocks receive the highest weights as described in previous sections.
- The MSCI Risk Weighted index is similar to the approach of the inverse of the security risk presented in the previous section. The index reweights the constituents of the market capitalisation index using 3-year historical returns to calculate a risk ratio such as the inverse of the security variance to the sum of the inverse of the security variances of all securities in the market capitalisation index.

Table 6.2 Example of low volatility and variance indices

Category	Index series	Objective	A typical number of stocks
Low volatility	S&P 500 low volatility	Selects the 100 least volatile stocks in the S&P 500 index	100
	MSCI risk weighted	Reweight market capitalisation index and weight low-risk stocks higher	2400–2500 for developed markets
	FTSE RAFI volatility	Apply fundamental stock methodology with low volatility	300–400 for global markets
	FTSE volatility factor	Apply fundamental stock methodology with low volatility	800–900 for global markets
Minimum variance/volatility	MSCI minimum volatility	Optimised portfolio	300–400 for global markets
	FTSE minimum variance	Optimised portfolio	2000 for global markets
	Solactive regional minimum downside volatility indices	Optimised portfolio using semi-variance	50–100* for regional markets

Source: Author, methodology documents and factsheets of various index providers
Note: The indices tend to have rebalancing frequency ranges from 3–12 months. The one-way turnover tends to hover around 10–20% among the various providers and historically have a tracking error in excess of 4%

- The FTSE RAFI All-World Low Volatility applies a fundamental screen (such as sales, book value, cash flow and dividend features, similar to what we discussed in Chap. 4, with low volatility. The fundamental screen is applied before the low volatility ranking criteria. The RAFI approach uses up to 5-year return history in regression analysis and a stock's relative volatility to the global stock universe. The aim of the fundamental screen is to reduce exposure to stocks trading with a high valuation that can undermine the benefit of low-volatility strategies.
- Another version of MSCI's low volatility factor index is the MSCI Minimum Volatility index series. These are designed to provide the lowest return volatility with a covariance matrix of stock returns by using a market capitalisation index as the starting universe. An optimisation technique is deployed to achieve the lowest absolute volatility with a pre-defined set of constraints.
- The Solactive approach is slightly different from other providers and focuses on the downside volatility. Their approach estimate security risk based on its negative returns, also known as semi-variance. The risk measure is used in an optimisation framework to create the weights of the low volatility risk factor index.

The bottom line is that the indices in the market are suitable for a risk-averse investor who aims to harvest the low volatility premium in their own way. In the next section, we will discuss the drivers of the low volatility anomaly and the premium.

6.4 Behavioural Drivers of the Factor Premium

If the low volatility premium exists, why has it not been arbitraged away? Most anomalies which have been identified in the market tend to be swiftly arbitraged away. It is the behaviour of market participants and the limits of arbitrage that explains and make us believe the low risk anomaly is likely to persist over time. Common questions among investors are: why does a premium exist for low volatility? What is the investor psychology that leads to a preference for volatile stocks? What forces prevent "smart" institutions from taking advantage of the low volatility premium and restoring the risk-return trade-off? This section aims to answer some of these questions.

As we know, "smart money" does not always offset the price impact of any irrational demand for securities. A study by Karceski in 2002 showed that mutual fund investors tend to project the future based on short-term moves in the market (extrapolation bias) with their sticky fund flows. These often force fund managers to care more about outperforming during bull markets than underperforming during bear markets, increasing their demand for high beta stocks and reducing their required returns. In general, low volatility can come across as boring and less exciting in the mind of the market. Investors' behaviour and biases often lead to seeking high volatility stocks relative to low volatility stocks. Behavioural biases that can help to explain the low volatility factor anomaly include:

Lottery demand theory (Preference for lotteries): Investors do show a clear preference for stocks with lottery-like payoffs;
Representativeness bias: Investors tend to look at high flying stocks and conclude that these stocks are the representative way of making money or outperforming the market while ignoring the possibility that it may not be the case in the future;
Overconfidence bias: people are overconfident in the accuracy of their information or judgment.

When it comes to the lottery demand theory, individuals seek "a shot at riches", and they believe that higher volatility provides the possibility of higher returns. This can lead to an asymmetric payoff to investors and mimics a lottery ticket. There is some small chance of gaining quadruple the price paid for the lottery ticket in the near future with a high probability of winning little or nothing. For example, most people would decline to buy a lottery with 50% chance of losing USD 1000 and 50% chance of winning USD 1100 despite the positive expected payoff (USD 50). The possibility of losing USD 1000 is enough to deter participation.

Kahneman and Tversky referred to this phenomena as "loss aversion" in 1979. Loss aversion suggests investors would shy away from volatility due to fear of losing. Loss aversion makes low risk stocks more popular during times of nervous markets, which makes the investor shift from riskier stocks. Investors typically place a premium on stocks with lower chances of losing money relative to stocks with a higher chance of losing money.

Now, what if the probabilities shift? Suppose you are given a lottery with a 99.95% chance of losing USD 1 and a 0.05% chance of winning USD 1000. In this example, the expected payoff is USD –0.50. Most people would buy this lottery. That is why many people get excited about the casinos and national lotteries. The amounts spent on lotteries and roulette wheels, which have negative expected payoffs, are a clear manifestation of this tendency.

Moreover, Tversky and Kahneman in 1974 highlighted representativeness as a bias in decision-making experiment. People will often exhibit insensitivity to sample sizes when establishing judgment probabilities. In other words, investors look at successful stocks like Microsoft, Amazon and Apple and assume these companies are more often the rule rather than the exception to the rule. In the example of Microsoft, Amazon and Apple, despite looking at a sample size of just three, investors will tend to conclude that most technology companies are successful stocks. Ericsson, the Swedish technology firm, share price traded over SEK 800 in 2000 and valued 80–90% lower since the collapse of the dot-com bubble and never recovered. In 2000 there was an Ericsson fever—everyone was talking about it as the prime company in the Swedish stock market. The competitive landscape to the telecommunication landscape and business environment has kept a lid on the share price for almost two decades.

Other academic studies in the 1970th and early 1980th provide overconfidence as another bias that explains investors' desire for high-risk stocks—see Fischhoff et al. from 1977, and Alpert and Raiffa in 1982 for experimental research on overconfidence bias. This bias could lead to underestimation of the time required to perform a task and overestimate our own abilities to perform or deliver on a task. My plumber, Billy is always late and often takes longer than anticipated to fix the problem, although he does not charge me more. A survey in the U.S. showed that 93% of drivers rated their skills above average. This means that 43% of them must have been wrong. Similarly, an overconfident investor can have an overoptimistic assessment of his own knowledge and control of a situation, which can be detrimental to stock-picking if they believe they can choose the best stocks at the right time. Overconfident investors are likely to disagree with this.

Forecasting a company's share price over five years is tough. Some are confident they can. An overconfident forecaster will agree to disagree by sticking with the false precision of their own estimate. The extent of disagreement is greater for more uncertain outcomes far out in the future. At the same time, a cautious or pessimistic forecaster often acts less aggressively in markets than the optimist. Many investors have a general reluctance or inability to short stocks relative to buying them. Empirically, the relative scarcity of short sales among individual investors and even institutional investors is evident. It means that prices are generally set by optimists, as pointed out in a study by Miller in 1977 and what we described for the value factor in Chap. 4. Typically, stocks with a wide range of opinions will have more optimists among their shareholders and sell for higher prices, leading to lower future expected returns.

Furthermore, studies have shown that overconfident investors conduct more trades, although more trading does not necessarily mean better results. Generally, investors that over trade often tend to receive lower returns on average. This leads us to discuss the market structures that complement the behavioural drivers of the low volatility premium.

6.5 Market Structures Driving the Factor Premium

As established in the previous section, the average investor has a psychological demand for high volatility stocks. In addition to the behavioural debate, market structure plays a part in explaining the low volatility premium. As mentioned earlier, the anomaly has historically gained force with the growth of the asset management industry.

Yet, many institutional investors do not short the very poor performing top volatility stocks. This is sometimes a limitation rather than a preference. In the full CRSP data, for example, the top volatility quintile tends to be small stocks, and they are costly to trade in large quantity both as long and short positions. The volume of shares available to borrow is limited, or the borrowing costs are often high for these stocks. The same frictions are present in large capitalisation stocks but on a smaller scale. If this is the case why do institutional investors not at least go overweight the low volatility quintile of the stock universe? One of the main reason could be due to benchmarking.

In addition, a typical investment management mandate contains an implicit or explicit objective to maximise the excess return versus the portfolio relative risk to a benchmark (the information ratio) and relay on stock selection without using leverage. This objective leads managers to neglect considerable profit opportunities among low beta stocks and prefer high beta stocks that tend to exhibit a lower tracking error.

The limit to borrowing, the importance placed on benchmarking and substantial tracking error budget (deviation from benchmark) in the asset management industry should support the persistence of the low volatility premium over the longer time periods. Given the lower absolute return, but a higher risk-adjusted return of low volatility stocks, leverage is required in order to arbitrage the anomaly. Borrowing restrictions will limit this arbitrage. Ultimately, investors who seek higher returns will continue to chase high-risk securities. Furthermore, Roll analysed in 1992 the distortions that arise from a fixed benchmark mandate and similarly by Brennan in 1993 in stocks. Their research showed that a benchmark makes institutional investment managers less likely to exploit the low volatility anomaly. Many institutional investors are in a position to offset the irrational demand for risk which discourages investments in low volatility stocks in order to hug their benchmark. Other studies show that the anomaly exists in sectors and various segments of the market. The low volatility anomaly within a sector might even be more noticeable by limits imposed on how far a fund manager can deviate from the sector benchmark.

6.6 Considerations When Implementing Low Volatility Strategies

Like for any factor strategy, there are considerations required for effective implementation to the choice of strategy. This section outlines a set of issues and features of the low volatility factor on index construction and market conditions. This should assist investors in judging and assessing whether a specific low volatility factor strategy fits their need and purpose.

By now the reader is familiar with the fact that a low volatility factor aims to select stocks or portfolios based on the risk of past returns. These have been successful in delivering a factor premium over the past decades. However, historical returns may not always reflect future risk or immunise investors from loss of equity capital. The low volatility factor can undergo a pre-longed underperformance, particularly in bull market condition historically.

Therefore, enhancing the low volatility factor by complementing it with other factors such as value and or quality could help overcome the shortcomings of just relying on historical risk data. It is unwise to select stocks purely on risk and ignoring the price you pay for them. Utilities and consumer staples can be relatively expensive to other sectors, especially post the 2008 financial crisis. These sectors frequently feature in low volatility factor strategies. Hence, investors are essentially taking a bet by seeking exposure to low volatility sectors and sometimes overpaying for these stocks. This is a classic way of translating volatility risk into valuation risk.

Meanwhile, consideration around sector bets in low volatility strategies compared to a broad index can support an informed decision on overall sector allocation in portfolios and also avoid unintended exposures. Naturally, one would expect some sectors and securities to exhibit low volatility based on their business model or sector. This is the nature of targeted security selection based on stock characteristics. Utility companies, for example, are often seen as low volatility, which makes these securities a perfect candidate for such a strategy. For example, in December 2012 most unconstrained indices had around 60% invested in only two sectors, utilities and consumer staples. This means that any sector rotation or sector-specific developments can have a significant negative impact on the performance of the strategy. If you do not have visibility of the overall sector allocation in your portfolio, then it makes sense to look at constrained factor strategy to limit any sector-specific risk.

However, the constrained sector approach can be costly, but then again it comes down to your total sector exposure and investment guidelines. In 2002 and 2003 the technology sector made up roughly 20–30% of the S&P 500. This means that you would have had a high exposure to the sector in a constrained low volatility strategy when technology lost three-quarters of its value when the dot-com bubble burst. Similarly, in 2008 the financial sector had substantial weight in the low volatility index. For illustrative purposes, Fig. 6.4 shows the sector deviation between a low volatility factor index against its global market capitalisation parent index. It is evident that some sector overweight and underweight allocation varies in some cases and consistent in some others over time due to the nature of the factor strategy. The global low volatility index in this example has included and excluded industrials and consumer discretionary in some periods. At the same time, it is consistent in overweighting the utility sector and underweighting financials. On regional and country-specific indices, the low volatility factor indices could exhibit high cyclicality irrespective of index provider.

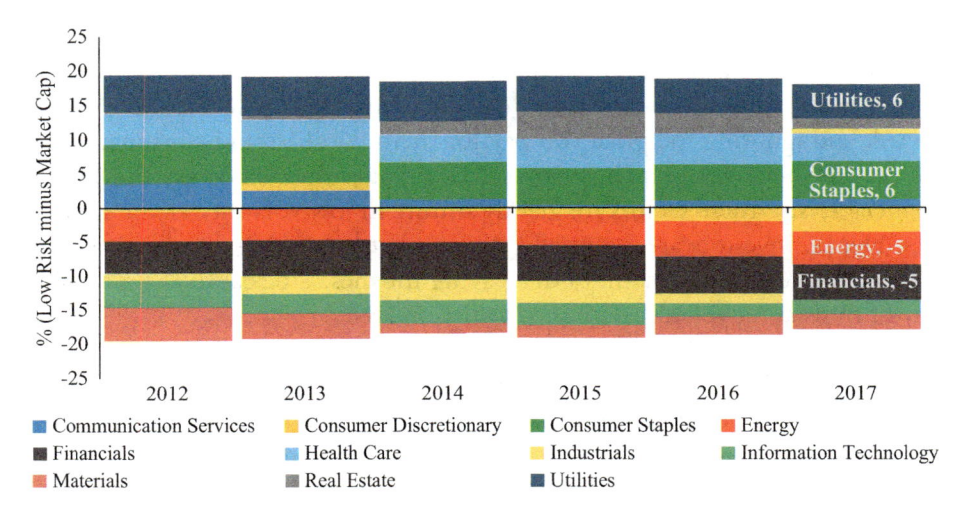

Fig. 6.4 Relative sector allocation: low volatility factor and market capitalisation index. Source: Author's construction of global low volatility index and market capitalisation index and Solactive, Jan. 2012–Jan. 2017. Note: The 100 stocks are narrowed from the largest 1000 stocks in the U.S. with free-float of 80%

While sector exposure matters for the low risk strategies, the trading turnover is equally important. The best way to reduce turnover is always to hold on to a security longer since transaction costs can erode long-term portfolio performance. It is well-known that index low-volatility strategies have high trading costs compared to a market capitalisation index—typically two-way turnover (buying and selling) of 50–90% per annum. This can vary by region and sector—emerging market stocks typically have inherent higher trading costs compared to developed market equities. Typically, the fund manager would look to hold depositary receipts instead of the underlying local shares in emerging markets to reduce the market impact, currency conversion costs and taxes.

As we established earlier, sector allocation matters and low volatility could mean different things at different times. Low volatility factors tend to gravitate around sectors that have exhibited low volatility. Given that the long portfolio of the low volatility factor highlighted sensitivity towards interest rates it is interesting to analyse the sector composition. We also showed that utilities and financials have historically featured in unconstrained low volatility factor strategies.

The low volatility factor, like other factors, is cyclical and depends on the market conditions and the allocation to the specific sectors. Often we hear that the low volatility strategies tend to do well during rising interest rate cycles.

This is not necessarily the case and depends on the composition or biases to sectors of the low volatility screen against the market capitalisation index. In periods where utility stocks with long-term debt, for example, have a large allocation in the index, the factor strategy is likely to underperform the broad market. If financials have a larger allocation in a low volatility factor index compared to the market capitalisation index, a rising interest rate is likely to benefit the factor as banks' profit margin tend to increase.

However, a diversified and balanced low and high volatility index shows clear differences historically. Figure 6.5 illustrates 5-year rolling correlations between volatility factor indices (low and high volatility) and the U.S. short-term interest rates between 1963–2017. The low volatility index tends to exhibit positive correlation on average with interest rates—i.e. positive stock performance when interest rates are high. High volatility stock returns have historically been negatively correlated to interest rates. However, the relationship between volatility factor returns and interest rates has not been consistent after the financial crisis in 2008. This period is characterised by falling interest rates all the way down to zero. During this short period, the sensitivity to interest rate is almost invisible.

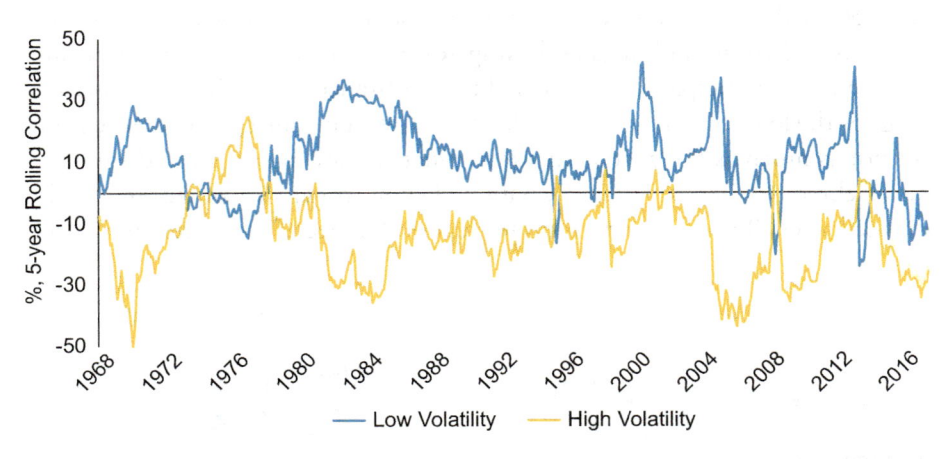

Fig. 6.5 Correlation of volatility strategies and short-term interest rates. Source: Author's calculations, Federal Reserve of St. Louis, Kenneth French database, Jul. 1963–Dec. 2017 for the U.S. Note: The short-term interest rate is the 3-month Treasury bill rate, the factor premium is the difference between volatility and market capitalisation returns on a monthly basis. The definition of 'high' and 'low' interest is based on Z-score of short term interest rates

6.7 Low Volatility in Asset Allocation

We all want higher returns with lower risk, but of course, the two are seen as a trade-off in traditional asset allocation as the idea is to strike a balance between risky and less risky assets, typically between stocks and bonds. An allocation of 60% to stocks and 40% to bonds is a pretty standard in the investment world for a "balanced risk" portfolio. The idea behind this typical weighting is that these two allocations (stocks and bonds)—balance each other in terms of risks. For simplicity, we present a standard asset allocation for a balanced risk portfolio of about 60% in equities and 40% in bonds and alternatives to demonstrate the impact of the low volatility factor. The low volatility factor is not a substitute for bonds but used as a substitute for some of the equity allocations in this example. Figure 6.6 shows the base asset allocation (without low volatility) and a modified asset allocation (with low volatility factor).

By modifying the asset allocation and embedding the low volatility factor (with 15% allocation) into the equity segment, the volatility tends to decrease for the overall portfolio. Figure 6.7 shows the modified asset allocation and how the risk-return profile changed.

A reasonable way to look at this problem is to allocate capital and manage this presumed trade-off between returns and risk. Low volatility does participate in the overall equity holdings and mitigates broader losses in asset allocation. Many market participants argue it is like an insurance hedge. It is not a perfect hedge as the low volatility stocks are likely to lose value during a market sell-off, but not as much as the general market—what we saw in 2008 and during the euro debt crisis in 2011. Low volatility factor strategies can improve risk-adjusted asset allocation over a long-term period, especially at different parts of

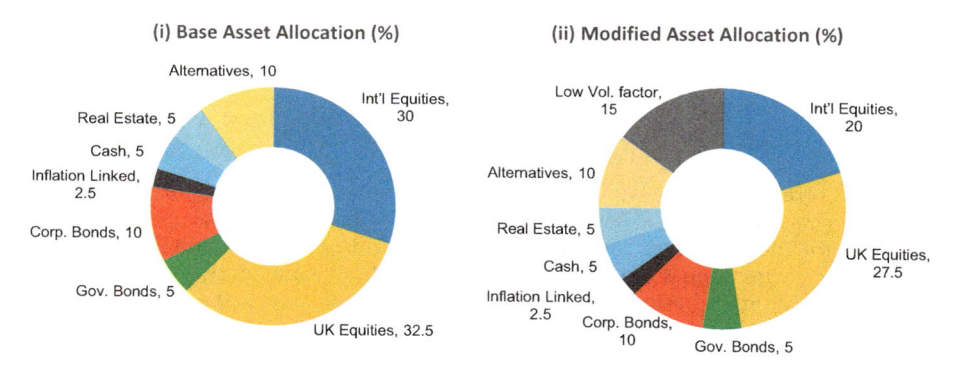

Fig. 6.6 Balanced asset allocation with factors. Source: Author's construction. Note: The asset allocation is a compilation of typical "balanced" portfolio allocation (base asset allocation) of Wealth Managers in the United Kingdom in 2017

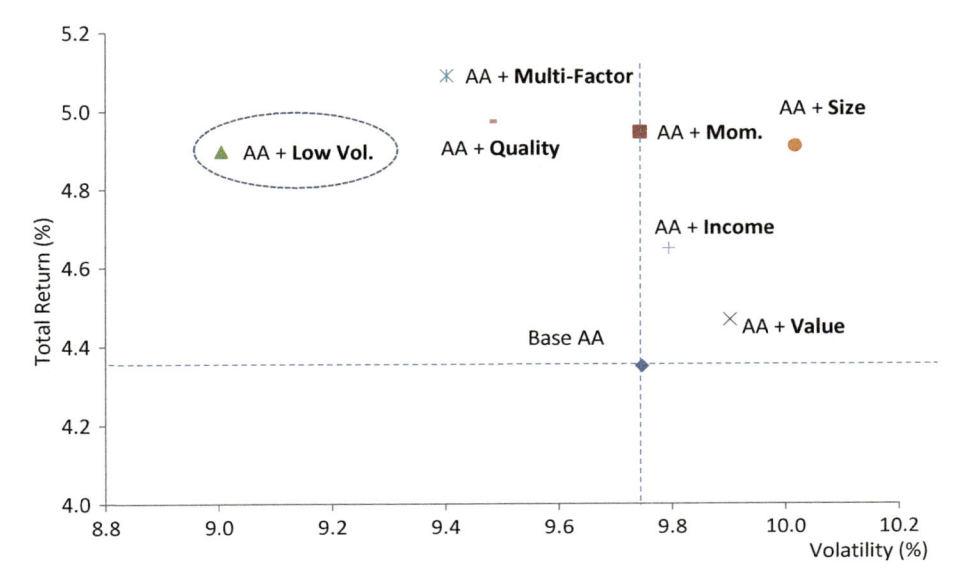

Fig. 6.7 Integration of factors into the asset allocation. Source: Wealth Management Association Asset Allocation, Solactive and Bloomberg-Barclays bond indices. Note: AA denotes Asset Allocation. GBP hedged returns, Jul. 2005–Dec. 2017. Regional allocation is kept similar in the overall asset allocation. This example is for illustrative purposes only

the market cycle. However, it is important to keep in mind that low volatility equities are not a substitute for high-quality bonds and not as effective as a plain tail hedge (buying protection through options that can be costly).

6.8 Concluding Remarks

The low volatility effect is still the largest anomaly in theoretical finance and remains the one factor with the most possibilities to explore in the coming years. It is important to recognise that low volatility investors typically do not expect market-beating returns. Instead, the aim is to create a smooth investment journey with the potential to outperform the broad market on a risk-adjusted basis over a long-term period.

Following the success of active managers, passive managers have now also jumped on the low volatility bandwagon by introducing ETFs and index funds. The market is expected to continue to grow as new providers come up with new solutions. The demand from institutional, retail and asset allocators for low volatility factor is unlikely to abate any time soon. It is instead an integral part of portfolio decision and complementary strategies with other factors such as multi-factor, which will be discussed in a later chapter.

7

Equity Factor Investing: Momentum

Momentum investing is one of the most popular investment styles among professional and private investors. It is not an enigmatic investment concept. The term momentum was borrowed from Newton's first law of motion where an object in motion tends to stay in motion unless an external force is applied to it. The concept can be applied to financial markets—an asset or security in motion also tends to stay in motion. In other words, a momentum stock is likely to continue in the same direction as its most recent past. Stocks that go up in value are likely to continue to go up and stocks that are falling in value to continue to go down over the short term. The concept is as simple as it sounds.

Due to the simplistic nature of momentum, it has been deployed by many in the finance industry including hedge funds and mutual funds for decades. According to the efficient market hypothesis momentum premium should not exist. But momentum effects are pervasive in financial markets. In fact, it is so pervasive that even the Nobel laureate Eugene Fama, the creator of the efficient market hypothesis, says that momentum is "the premier market anomaly". As described in previous chapters, an anomaly is a phenomenon that cannot be explained with theories and that defies rational markets. There are psychological explanations as to why momentum occurs. The simplest explanation is that rising prices attract buyers and falling prices attract sellers. Most of the time when stocks are going up in price people tend to crowd into the market at any price. Conversely, when the market is going down people tend to want to exit the market and sell at any price.

The persistent momentum effects preside in regions and sectors of the financial markets as well as various asset classes. Examples of this are presented in Asness et al. in 1997 and Rouwenhorst in 1998 and 1999. Stocks with low returns over the past year tend to have low returns for the next few months, and stocks with high past returns tend to have high future returns.

This chapter offers insight into the equity momentum factor. We will also discuss the construction approach, drivers of the momentum factor and other considerations such as the strengths and weaknesses of momentum strategies.

7.1 Evolution of Momentum Investing

Momentum investing is perhaps among the most intuitive investment styles. The field of momentum investing goes back decades, but the discussions and arguments sound eerily similar to the same arguments and discussions that go on in the current market. Isaac Newton's first law was that a body in motion tends to stay in motion. This does not just apply to physics but also to financial markets. This section discusses the historical milestone of momentum.

Many of those who had money in 1720 invested in the South Sea Company in England, whose share price is presented in Fig. 7.1. The South Sea Company was an English merchant company with an official monopoly to trade with Spanish colonies in South America and the West Indies. The company was founded in 1711 to buy the outstanding debt financed by shares with 6% interest. As many investors believed in the benefit from the richness of the new world, the demand for the stock pushed the price to artificially high levels. Isaac Newton was among the investors and doubled his money within a year.

However, as he was sitting on his assets watching his friends getting rich, he decided to re-invest all his money. Everything went well for a while until the South Sea stock started to fall due to fraud (arguably the fraud predated much of the rise). Newton thought it was going to bounce, but it never did, and he sold all his holdings short after at a loss. It is not a surprise that Newton's third law of motion implies that "for every action, there is an equal and opposite reaction".

However, later in history, momentum investing was formalised. In 1931 Richard Wyckoff, founder of the Magazine of Wall Street and known as one of the prominent technical analysts and momentum investors contributed to its formalisation. He would buy a stock only when the market was

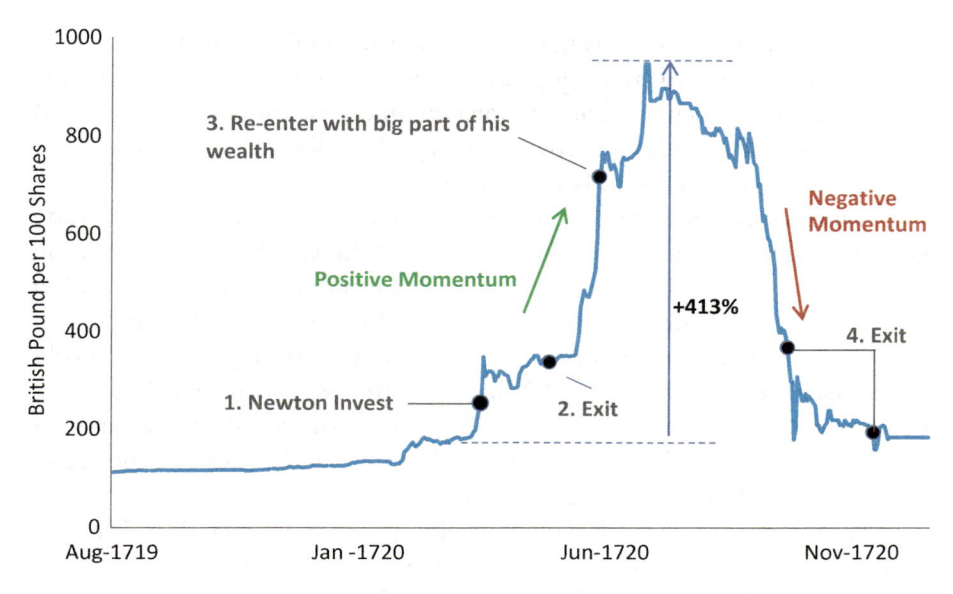

Fig. 7.1 Newton's momentum trade of South Sea Company. Source: Author's creation, stock price data from Frehen et al. in 2013

trending up and sell when the market was trending down. Wyckoff's research claimed many common characteristics among the greatest winning stocks and market campaigners of the time. Furthermore, he also pinpointed the necessity of stop-losses to manage the risk.

Another iconic work in the field of momentum is attributed to H.M. Gartley who published his expensive book "Profit in the stock market" in 1935. The book was priced at USD 1500; equivalent to USD 30,000 at the end of 2017. Gartley came up with velocity ratings for stocks, now called relative strength within the family of momentum strategies and technical analysis. Relative strength strategies measure the price trend between two or more stocks.

Wyckoff and Gartley provided a practical insight to momentum, but at that time a more scientific or academic rules-based approach was missing at that time. Two prominent economists Alfred Cowles and Herbert Jones published one of the main iconic academic research papers in 1937. Their work analysed the performance of stocks listed on the New York Stock Exchange from 1920 through to 1935. This research established that stocks that exceeded the median performance in one year also exceeded it in the following year. This was a significant finding, which is the basis for modern-day momentum in academic literature.

Momentum became increasingly accepted in academic circles a few decades later. In the 1970s two psychologists, Kahneman and Tversky showed that people consistently behave in an irrational manner.[1] People follow a trend and fail to realise that trees do not grow to the sky. We will discuss the behavioural biases around momentum in later sections.

This opened the door for further momentum research. The seminal study on momentum by Jegadeesh and Titman in 1993 showed that best-performing stocks in the past 3–12 months continued to perform over the following 3–12 months. This study is based on U.S. data from 1965 to 1993. Jegadeesh and Titman noted poor performance of momentum strategies in pre-World War II data for the U.S. Figure 7.2 illustrates the performance of U.S. stock top, average, low momentum portfolios versus market cap index between 1963–2017. In general, momentum has also done well relative to the broad market over the longer term (see Fig. 7.2).

Today, momentum is a common factor strategy in index investing. The asset growth in momentum strategies has grown by 53% per annum between 2011–2017 with listed ETFs in the U.S. and Europe obtaining assets under

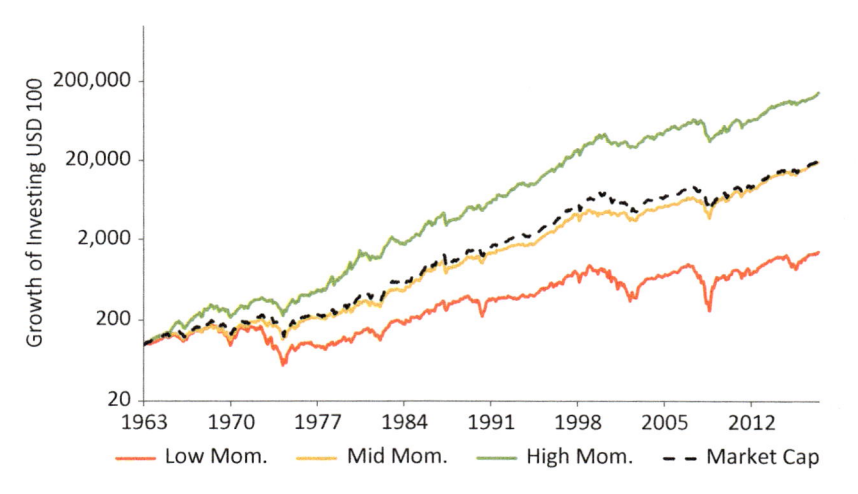

Fig. 7.2 Momentum portfolio and market capitalisation historically. Source: Author's calculations. Kenneth French database between Jul. 1962–Dec. 2017 for the U.S. Note: The portfolios as market value-weighted (market capitalisation weighted) portfolios. Low Mom is the bottom 30th percentile, and High Mom is top 30th percentile, Mid Mom is the 30–70% percentile. The price returns are monthly prior (2–12) return. For illustrative purposes only. Historical returns are not a leading indicator of future performance

---

[1] Book in 1979 called "the prospect theory" 1979.

management in excess of USD 12 billion and at least 30 listed funds. It is also increasingly being included in combination with other factors as well as used by many asset allocators.

Before going into details, it is important to distinguish momentum investing from other types of investments that might be confused or have some similarities. First, momentum investing is not necessarily growth investing. Growth is characterised by high historical or projected earnings growth and high historical or projected revenue growth, while momentum is essentially the strength in price relative to itself or relative to other securities. Second, momentum refers to, in this chapter, as the short-term momentum of stock price and return behaviour within a 1-year time window. This is different from intermediate to long-term momentum (3–5 plus years). The long-term time windows are often attributed with value investing under the banner of mean-reversion trading (security prices tend to rise over the long-term to their long-term average). The next section will focus on short-term momentum that tends to form the main momentum factor strategies.

7.2 Rules-Based Momentum Index Strategies

This section aims to provide insight into two momentum factor approaches. In general, there are two prolific momentum approaches in factor investing.

- **Cross-sectional momentum (also known as relative momentum)**: Compares the best and worst performing stocks in an index based. The stock performance is ranked from top to bottom performers to create a relative screen in the portfolio construction.
- **Time series momentum (also known as trend-following or absolute momentum)**: Creates a portfolio based on historical winners (or losers for a short strategy). Unlike the cross-sectional momentum, this approach includes stocks with positive stock returns for winners and stocks with the most negative returns for the losers.

7.2.1 Cross-sectional Momentum Strategies

Cross-sectional or relative momentum is the most common approach in index factor investing and well-established among academics (Jegadeesh and Titman in 1993) and index providers. This strategy aims to slice the stock universe

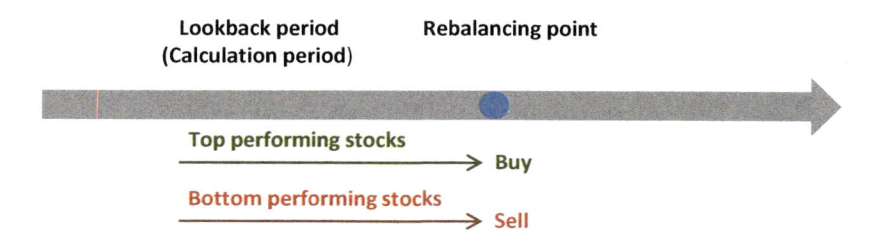

Fig. 7.3 Cross-sectional momentum. Note: For illustrative purposes only

into the best and worst relative performers over a lookback period (also known as a formation period) and hold for a future period (see Fig. 7.3). It also applies to sectors, regions or global stock universe. If the entire index or stock universe has negative returns during the lookback period, then cross-sectional momentum would select the stock that is losing the least.

For illustrative purposes, suppose, we have two companies: Technology Corp and AI Corp. The 12-month total returns for Elevator Corp and AI Corp is 5% and 50%, respectively. For simplicity, the 12-month momentum is the 12-month return. In this case, we would buy AI Corp due to its higher return relative to Technology Corp. You may either sell or short Technology Corp.

The lookback period is central to many factor strategies among professionals and academics. It measures the stocks' past stock performance while the holding period is the investment horizon and the strategy is re-evaluated at the end of it (the rebalance period). Common lookback periods range 1–12 month with the exclusion of the latest month. For example, assume it is 31st December 2018 today (beginning of rebalancing period). The lookback period for momentum calculation would be calculated as:

$$Return\ (12-1\ month) = \frac{\text{Stock price on 30 Nov. 2018}}{\text{Stock price on 31 Dec. 2017}}, \text{adjusted for dividend and corporate actions}$$

Often the lookback period tends to exclude the latest months in order to screen out companies with an abnormal or significant increase in stock price over the past month. Many studies in the literature usually found a reversal short after a strong momentum a month or two before a rebalancing period. There is no theoretical explanation for this but simply based on empirical evidence among academics and professionals.

Without going into the complexity of the construction of a rules-based momentum strategy, it involves the following steps:

1. Define a stock universe;
2. Define the lookback period, typically past 12-, 6-, 3-month, excluding the latest month or two. Table 7.1 shows simulated indices with various lookback periods;
3. Define the rebalancing period, typically 1–12 months. Most commercial momentum indices rebalance between 3–6 months;
4. Calculate the stock returns;
5. Rank all the stocks by their performance and select the top (bottom) decile, quartile or 30th percentile for long (short) strategy;
6. Apply a weighting scheme (as described in Chap. 3).

This approach is common among index-tracking funds. It allows an investor to remain exposed to the broad stock when the market is down as the stocks are ranked (from top to bottom performers during a period). Table 7.1 shows the performance over various lookback periods and rebalancing frequencies.

The selection of the lookback period differs among investor and index providers depending on what they think works best. This can, of course, provides different results. Longer rebalance periods (e.g. 6–12-month) allow for the momentum to play out with smaller turnover, while the short rebalance periods tend to erode the returns due to higher turnover. The most common way of adopting a combined rebalance and lookback tends to be 6–12 months. These are the time windows with the smallest turnover as described in Table 7.1.

7.2.2 Time Series Momentum Strategies

The classical economist and trader David Ricardo said "Cut short your losses; let your profits run on". In this context, time series momentum target winners and sell the losers over a short period of time, often less than a year. Time series momentum focus on a security's own historical returns as a leading indicator of the future. If positive, then you invest or keep the stock, and if negative, then you sell or avoid the stock depending on the time period that you are looking at. Unlike the cross-sectional momentum, for a long-only strategy, it focuses only positive returning stocks.

While the investor does not always have perfect timing on the market, time series momentum can signal an entry somewhere in the middle between the very bottom and exit just after the top (unless the prices fall sharply due to sud-

Table 7.1 Cross-sectional momentum with various rebalancing and lookback periods

			Lookback period (month)				
			[-1/-12]	[-1/-9]	[-1/-6]	[-1/-3]	Market cap
Rebalance period	1-month	Return (%, p.a.)*	7.7	6.4	7.3	7.2	7.6
		Risk (%, p.a.)	14.1	13.8	13.7	13.6	13.3
		Return/risk	0.5	0.5	0.5	0.5	0.6
		Turnover (%)	696.1	707.0	1234.3	1294.5	72.0
	3-month	Return (%, p.a.)*	8.0	8.4	6.8	6.1	7.5
		Risk (%, p.a.)	14.4	14.5	14.4	14.2	13.3
		Return/risk	0.6	0.6	0.5	0.4	0.6
		Turnover (%)	341.2	389.1	502.4	605.2	43.7
	6-month	Return (%, p.a.)*	8.8	9.4	9.1	9.0	7.6
		Risk (%, p.a.)	14.2	14.2	13.9	14.0	13.2
		Return/risk	0.6	0.7	0.7	0.6	0.6
		Turnover (%)	228.5	265.0	302.0	292.8	31.4
	12-month	Return (%, p.a.)*	8.7	8.7	8.5	9.1	7.5
		Risk (%, p.a.)	14.0	14.2	13.6	13.7	13.1
		Return/risk	0.6	0.6	0.6	0.7	0.6
		Turnover (%)	154.6	155.8	150.3	152.3	23.6

Source: Author's calculations. Stock prices from Bloomberg between Dec. 2003–Sep. 2018
Note: The table is based on author's construction of indices for the U.S. listed stocks on NYSE and other U.S. exchanges using the following assumption: minimum 80% free-float, USD 3 billion market capitalisation for inclusion. Select the 30th percentile with the highest momentum stocks. The lookback period convention is defined as:[exclusion of most recent month, 12-month performance history from the rebalance date]. For example [-1,-12] denotes exclusion of the last month and using total returns from past 12 months. This table is based on real data but should be used for illustrative purposes only. Historical returns are not a leading indicator of future performance.
*The total returns are adjusted for the turnover assuming a 5 basis points transaction cost for buying and selling a stock in the index. It is important to acknowledge that the turnover is inflated for the market and the momentum strategies due to a hard market capitalisation threshold of USD 3 billion in this example. Typically, index providers have a buffer zone for the minimum market capitalisation, which reduces the turnover

den market correction). With this type of momentum, investors would either sit out or invest into something much more conservative than stocks in the interim until momentum is positive. However, time series momentum is less common in diversified equity index strategies and more common among the Commodity Trading Advisors community (CTA). In general, trend followers focus on absolute price changes (i.e. share prices changes against itself). In other words, a trend follower takes a view on the market and could focus on a subset of stocks, while a momentum investor does not necessarily take a view on the market. This could lead to the fact that a trend follower increases the investment exposure during the market rise and decreases it during the market fall.

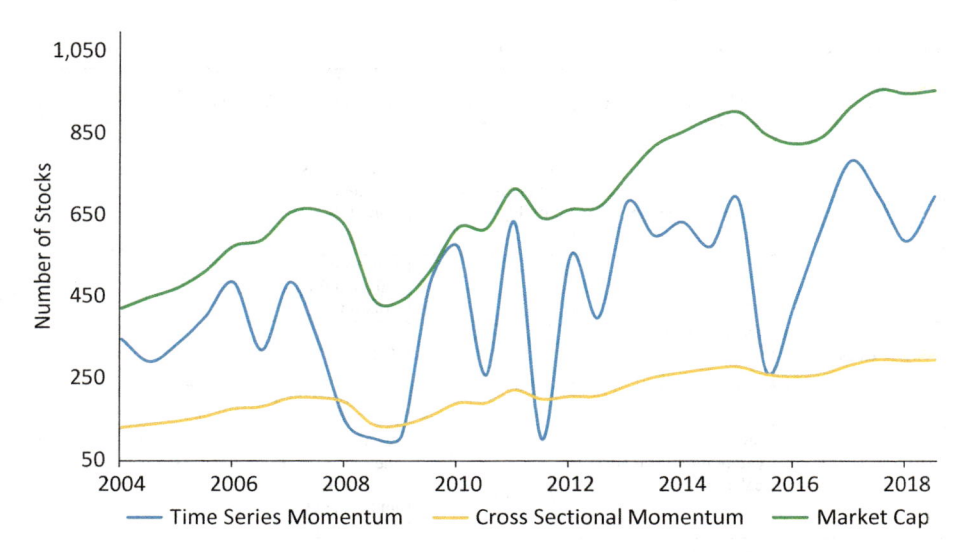

Fig. 7.4 Comparison of the number of securities between strategies. Source: Author's calculations. Stock prices from Bloomberg between Dec. 2003–Sep. 2018. Note: The lookback period and rebalancing period is six months, similar to the example in Table 7.1

Time series momentum could end up in few stocks when the market is sharply down or take short positions (e.g. global financial crisis in 2008) if the rebalancing of the strategy was taking place around the Lehman Brothers default. Figure 7.4 shows the number of stocks using the same example as above. Time series momentum is less stable and less diversified when markets are falling.

A variation of cross-sectional and time series momentum is known as dual-momentum. This type of momentum is efficient in a multi-asset context where the strategy can switch between bonds and equities, especially when the rank-based momentum includes the top performing (e.g. top decile or quartile) that may include negative momentum stocks. This concept is thoroughly discussed in Gary Antonacci's book in 2014.

7.3 Market-Based Index Strategies

The majority of the indices constructed by index providers adopt cross-section momentum. There is an abundance of methodologies for momentum strategies, all backed by professionals and academics. The MSCI Momentum indexes utilise two Sharpe Ratio measures of momentum. In other words, momentum strategies based on the total return per unit of risk.

Table 7.2 Commercial momentum factor strategies

Index provider	Lookback period	Rebalancing period	Measure	Index weighting method
MSCI	Combine 6- and -12-month, excluding the past three months	Semi-annually with conditional monthly	Price returns adjusted for volatility	Tilts from market cap weight
S&P	12-month excluding the most recent month	Semi-annually	Price returns adjusted for volatility	
FTSE-Russell			Total return	
RAFI	365 calendar days excluding recent 30 calendar days	Quarterly	Average of three scores (excess return momentum, the sensitivity of a stock to the market, and changes in the momentum)	Include top 50% of stocks with high momentum
AQR	12-month excluding the most recent month		Total return	Market cap

Source: Author's compilation from index, fund and methodology documentations

Table 7.2 provides an overview of common momentum indices among index providers and professionals. The MSCI, S&P and FTSE-Russell use a tilted index approach. S&P uses a more traditional approach by defining momentum as the 11-month total return to the month prior to the rebalance month.

Others use a combination of historical performance and risk with an optimisation approach such as Russell-Axioma. The Russell-Axioma Momentum Indexes follow a two-stage process. First, the momentum factor index is constructed using the cumulative 250 trading day performance excluding the last 20 trading days. Second, it applies an optimisation approach to derive narrower indexes whilst controlling for turnover and exposure to other risk factors.

Many of the common strategies in the market have historically been successful. The fact that something works well is good, but you really want to know why it works to make sure that it is not a coincidence. In the next section, we discuss some explanations as to why momentum works and should continue to do so as well as the key drivers of the momentum factor premium.

7.4 Behavioural Drivers of Momentum Premium

The debate about drivers of momentum is a debate between rationalists (rational investors reacting to unpredictable news) and behaviourists (i.e. the science of investor behaviour and decision making). A theory that explains momentum is that investors typically exploit behavioural shortcomings in other investors. Since the 1960s finance was dominated by the economic paradigm of traditional asset pricing models to describe the world. Often, the starting point in most finance research often derives economic theories, but later on, evidence suggested that the theories were not really supported by the data or individual behaviour in the market. Financial economists and professionals started to think of alternative paradigms that could help explain the data better. That is where behavioural finance comes in. It tells us something about the mistakes that investors are likely to make. And how those mistakes are likely to translate into stock prices, or they can just be a reflection of collective behaviour. A number of behavioural theories of price formation have been attributed to momentum. Examples include:

Herding: Investors follow the crowd by mimicking each other's behaviour;
Representativeness: Events that happen today are seen as a representation of the future;
Confirmation bias: Investor tends to seek to confirm their investment beliefs as a reassurance.

This section aims to discuss some of the behavioural biases that can help explain the momentum premium.

7.4.1 Herding Behaviour

Cafés and restaurants with a greater number of guests or schools with more students tend to appear more appealing to the observer. We copy each other and are influenced by the choices of other people in a group. This is generally referred to as herd behaviour. It is a behaviour in which individuals collaborate as part of a group rather than making decisions individually. This type of behaviour is built into our DNA. Evolutionary psychology highlights a Stone Age mentality hardwired into our brains and reflected in our behaviour and habits. It is far less dangerous to be wrong in a group than being right on our own. This explains the drive and instinct of an individual investor to follow the crowd.

There are two widely accepted explanations of herd behaviour. The first is the social pressure to conform (the desire to feel accepted and to mimic others behaviour). Often this means behaving in the same way as others even if that behaviour goes against your natural instincts. Secondly, individuals find it hard to believe that a large group of people can be wrong—three heads are better than one. Therefore, people tend to follow the group's behaviour, believing that the group knows something that the individual does not or they feel safer making decisions in a herd. This is known as the bandwagon effect or groupthink.

The herd behaviour is common in financial markets. It is a behaviour about investment decisions based on not necessarily on your own investment beliefs, but on the behaviour of others. This can be rewarding in some time periods, but damaging in others, especially when the market rallies or crashes. Evidence of herd behaviour is evident among institutional investors during financial crises and market volatility. Evidence of this is presented in a study by Papaioannou et al. from the International Monetary Fund in 2013. They described the evidence as the following for the category of institutional investors.

- **Developed market pension funds:** Net sellers of equities in 2008
- **Life insurers:** Contributed to the sell-off of the equity markets in 2001–2003 and 2008
- **Endowment funds:** Harvard Management Company reduced its uncalled capital commitments and fine-tuned its portfolio to enhance liquidity
- **Mutual funds:** Based on flow data, mutual funds shows a typical procyclical behaviour by cutting their exposure to regional exposures in bear markets and increasing in bull markets
- **Sovereign wealth funds:** Reduced exposure to banks in the first half of 2009
- **Central banks:** Collectively reduced more than USD 500 billion of deposits and other investments from the banking sector between December 2007–March 2009.

The degree at which investors are influenced by others' decisions will have a different impact on the investment outcome. This can be described with two scenarios that could lead to a different impact on the security price. The first scenario has limited herding behaviour where investors make their investment decision simultaneously while in the second scenario, investors make their investment decision sequentially with potential herd behaviour.

Scenario 1: In this scenario the likelihood of herding is limited, and investment decisions are made simultaneously. Assume that 1000 investors have individual assessments of the prospects of Eldorado Inc. at the same time. Now suppose that 300 of these investors believe that Eldorado Inc's earnings are to surprise on the upside in the coming quarter, and the remaining 700 investors believe the opposite. Every investor knows only their own estimate of the earnings and does not have visibility on how other investors think—i.e. no exchange of information. If these investors pooled their knowledge and assessments, they are likely to collectively decide that Eldorado Inc. is not a good investment and may change their expectations.

Scenario 2: Suppose these 1000 investors do not make their investment decisions at the same time and there is some visibility of the price dynamics in the market. Now the first optimistic investors from the pool of 300 make their decision to buy Eldorado Inc. As some of the 700 pessimists see the share price moving higher with upbeat headline news, these investors may revise their beliefs and also decide to invest. This, in turn, could have a snowballing effect, and lead to many of the 1000 investors to invest in Eldorado Inc. This could boost the share price in the short term. If the earnings are below expectation in the future, then the decision becomes clear, and many investors would sell their position and push the price down.

Typically, the existence of investor herding is a frequently used explanation for the volatility of stock returns. When investment returns cluster around the market consensus, the return dispersions are predicted to be relatively low. When markets are nervous, the herd split which often leads to higher volatility in expected returns and scattered consensus. The collective behaviour can lead to many rising and falling trends as many investors celebrate and panic in a herd.

7.4.2 Representativeness and Confirmation Bias

Confirmation bias is among the most widely committed cognitive biases. This is when we tend to listen to information that confirms what we already know, or even interpret the information that we receive in a way that confirms the current information that we already have. Suppose that your friend believes that sweets are unhealthy. This is generally a widespread belief, and he will only focus on the information that confirms what we already know. Your friend is more likely to click on videos that confirm that belief or read news and blogs that support the argument. In doing this, we may miss looking for any possible type of positive health effects of increasing blood glucose levels, or the positive effects of eating ice cream (at least during hot days). Instead, your friend will instinctively go to Google and search for how bad sugar is for you.

Confirmation bias is defined by Nickerson in 1998 as "the seeking or interpreting of evidence in ways that are partial to existing beliefs". Investors that are prone to the confirmation bias modify information that is consistent with the individual's prior views. Pouget et al. show in a study in 2017 that the presence of investors prone to the confirmation bias induces short-term momentum and excessive price volatility and increased trading activity. Induced momentum occurs when biased traders hold optimistic beliefs, which can increase the likelihood of exaggerated positive signals. Moreover, momentum and reversals are a consequence of the fact that when biased traders' beliefs shift from, for example, optimistic to pessimistic, these traders switch from amplifying positive news to negative news.

Another bias linked to short-term momentum behaviour is representativeness bias. This is when we see something happening in the short run, we project in our minds to keep happening. Hence, if we see stocks going up, we think they are going to continue. This gives us confidence, but it can also give us overconfidence when we get over-enthusiastic, which can cause price momentum to extend beyond what it should.

7.5 The Reward for Risk and Market Structures

In a rational market, investors demand higher returns to compensate for higher risk. Therefore, one should logically expect lower returns from safer securities and higher returns from riskier securities. Since momentum factor portfolios are sorted by past returns, the premium is likely to vary over time due to changes in the general market and economic conditions (also referred to exposure to systematic factors). Because long (short) momentum strategies are bets on past winners (losers), they will have inherently higher risk-exposure to systematic factor, which can lead to a time-varying risk premium during the momentum periods. In general, equity momentum factor can exhibit similar or higher volatility than the broad market capitalisation index. Typically, if the market went up over the last 12 months, a cross-sectional momentum factor is likely to be overweight high beta stocks (more volatile stocks than the broad market) and underweight low beta stocks (less volatile stocks than the broad market). Figure 7.5 shows the relative risk of high and low momentum portfolios to the broad market capitalisation index since the 1960s. We can see that the high momentum factor exhibits a relatively higher

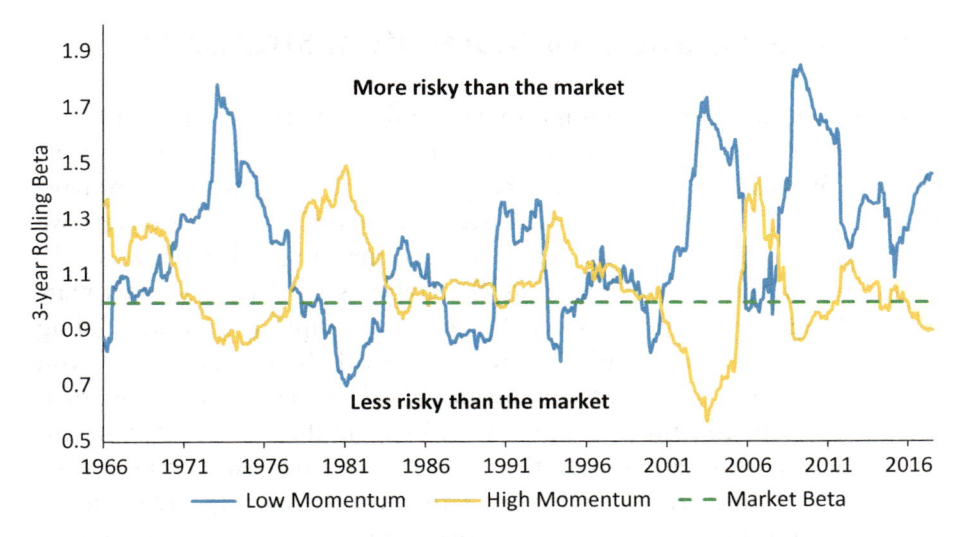

Fig. 7.5 High and low momentum relative risk to the U.S. market capitalisation. Source: Author's calculations. Kenneth French database, between Jul. 1963–Dec. 2017 for the U.S. Note: For illustrative purposes only

risk than the general market in most periods—between 66–75% of the times for both low and high momentum compared to the market.

Other aspects that can explain the momentum premium include market structure and the functioning of the financial markets. I will focus on three market structures, although the list is not exhaustive.

- **Price behaviour relative to market:** Typically, when the market falls significantly over a momentum lookback period (particularly from 12-month excluding the last months) it is likely that stocks that fell hand-in-hand with the market are the high beta stocks. At the same time, it is likely that the low beta stocks are the winners. After the market fall, the momentum factor is likely to buy the past winners that are low beta stocks, and sell or exclude past losers that are high beta stocks.
- **Benchmarking and peer comparison:** Another aspect of the market structure is that a fund manager is facing scrutiny and benchmarked against peers. No fund manager wants to be a bottom performer. Hence, it allows for short-term incentive which may create a buying pressure on trending stocks.
- **The seasonal effect** could also help to explain the effect of momentum. If a stock has been performing poorly for months leading up to tax year-end, investors may sell their holdings for tax purposes, which could add downward pressure on the stock. Once the tax-selling fades, the stocks typically start to recover. Hence, investors could be exposed to tax year rebalancing.

7.6 Consideration for Momentum Strategies

This section focus on the common issues and the risks related to momentum, namely scalability, frictions, and high volatility. The first issue is scalability. Typically, global index strategies in momentum tend to have significant scalability, mainly cross-sectional momentum. However, we established earlier that time series momentum might have few stocks depending on the market conditions. Scalability is an issue for smaller markets and segments of the market. For example, suppose you are trading momentum in a market with few stocks or small sized companies. If you decide to invest a significant amount of capital in that particular market, you are likely to encounter the problem of scaling the investment strategy. Consequently, this can impact the performance and risk profile of the momentum strategy. As we established earlier, the rebalancing and lookback period matters for momentum. These two aspects can also have an impact on the scale of a momentum strategy.

Second, momentum strategies tend to exhibit higher volatility compared to the broader market. The maximum drawdown can play an important role depending on the level of diversification. A highly diversified momentum portfolio for the U.S. based on Kenneth French database (plotted in Fig. 7.2) has similar drawdown to the broad market of about 50%. The low momentum has about 70% drawdown, which is not a surprise since these stocks tend to be losing stocks and their losses are even more magnified during a market downturn. As we established in the behavioural section, people get caught up in their emotions and behave irrationally. When stocks go down, investors become fearful and sell, or stocks go up a lot and they buy to be part of the herd. The effects are loosely consistent with several behavioural findings. In extreme situations, where individuals are fearful, they appear to focus on losses while probabilities are largely ignored. Greg Fischer said we do not have people with investment problems we have investments with people problems—the enemy is indeed us.

Third, we discussed in Table 7.1 that momentum tends to exhibit high turnover. In fact, it has the highest turnover among the equity factor family in this book. A typical momentum index by major index providers could exceed 100% one-way turnover with semi-annual rebalancing. Hence relative to other strategies it is likely to incur higher transaction costs. However, depending on the implementation capabilities and whether it is an institutional or retail investor, the costs of implementing momentum can differ vastly.

7.7 Concluding Remarks

Momentum is everywhere. Positive momentum factor for equities has delivered an excess return over the broad market historically. Also, positive momentum portfolio has also outperformed low momentum portfolios. Due to the simplistic nature of momentum, it has been deployed by many in the finance industry—hedge and mutual funds—for decades. This factor investing style has developed tremendously and the abundance of research since 1990 has led to it being broadly adopted in many index strategies today.

Although the focus of this chapter is mainly on equities, the momentum can be traced in other areas of financial markets such as bonds, commodities and currencies, which will be discussed in later chapters. The investor behaviour, reward for risk and market structures are central in explaining the momentum premium and the reasons for it to exist. In particular, behavioural finance can explain why we observe inefficient market prices and why the momentum premium are cyclical and likely to remain with us.

8

Equity Factor Investing: Size

David often beats Goliath in the stock market, as well as in the biblical field of combat, as smaller and mid-sized companies have historically outperformed the broad market over the long term. The small and mid-sized companies are classified as an investment style factor, known as the size factor. In this chapter, we will refer to the size factor as small capitalisation (small-cap) and mid capitalisation (mid-cap) stocks. These are the little siblings of large capitalisation (large-cap) stocks with more pro-cyclical performance (does well during economic expansion and poorly during contraction) and less liquid than large-cap. Professionals may blend small and mid-cap as a factor strategy or may use either of the two.

Smaller companies tend to have higher growth potential than large ones—it is easier for a small company to double its size relative to a larger company. The potential for higher risk-adjusted returns encourages long-term investors to hold some allocation of small-cap and mid-cap stocks. At the same time, small and mid-cap stocks tend to be more volatile as fewer shares are available in the market with higher drawdowns compared to large-cap.

Many academics, including Banz 1981, and professional studies would argue that the size factor performance is a reflection of the reward for risk. The "size premium", often defined as excess return over the market or large-cap, is based on the observation made by a study by Rolf Banz in 1981 for U.S. stocks. This study showed that smaller stocks had higher risk-adjusted returns than larger stocks over the longer term. Fama and French in 1992 showed the importance of the size of a company in explaining the expected return of the U.S. stocks. The size premium is also documented in other global markets—e.g. emerging markets study by Rouwenhorst in 1999. Traditional asset pricing theory explains this outperformance based on higher reward for risk compared to the broad market and large-cap stocks. This explanation is consistent with the efficient market hypothesis and financial economic theory.

Companies with smaller market capitalisations have less access to capital markets (borrowing and refinancing at favourable interest rates compared to a large-cap). These companies are often more domestically focused with one or few business lines. Hence, their revenues are typically less diversified, making them more sensitive to the economic activity. While smaller size stocks are relatively riskier than their large-cap counterparts they also come with higher expected returns as the finance theory would suggest. Figure 8.1 compares few characteristics between various company sizes.

Most great investors have bought small-cap stocks at some point, but few have exclusively focused on it as a stand alone strategy. Many famous stock pickers, Warren Buffett, Joel Greenblatt and Seth Klarman—are pronounced small-cap stock investors with value and quality styles, amongst others. For large institutional investors, typical smaller companies are satellite strategies—for an investor with USD 50 billion, it would be a fraction of the total asset allocation. Some investors focus only on mid-sized companies as a size style factor. It is often a matter of appetite and risk profile of the investor's portfolio. Yet, the reward for risk has prevailed for decades, and the size premium is unlikely to go away despite going in cycles.

Segment	Example*	Market cap
Nano-Cap	Ikonics Corp	<50M
Micro-Cap	Red Lion Hotels Corp	50-200M
Small-cap	Nippon REIT	200M-2B
Mid-cap	Footlocker	2B-10B
Large-cap	BMW	10B-50B
Mega-cap	Apple	>50B

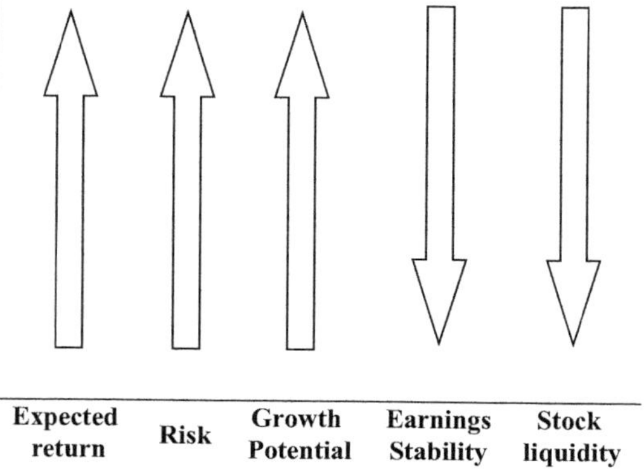

Expected return | Risk | Growth Potential | Earnings Stability | Stock liquidity

Fig. 8.1 Company profile by size factor index. Source: Author, Bloomberg. Note: *M* denotes million and *B* denotes billion in USD, EUR or GBP. The shaded area is the target segment of the size factor. *Market capitalisation in USD is as at 19 December 2018

In this chapter, we will discuss the nature of the size factor investing. We will also cover the underlying drivers of the size premium. Factor premium is defined either as excess return of small-caps over large-cap, typically the academic definition or the excess return over the market cap which is preferred among practitioners.

8.1 Defining the Size Factor

The size factor targets small and mid-size companies, typically defined by market capitalisation. In general, publicly traded companies are grouped into large-cap, mid-cap, and small-cap, but the cut-off for each market capitalisation bucket varies among researchers and professionals. Within the buckets there are sub-segments. The largest stocks are mega-cap (in excess of 50 billion) stocks such as Apple or Walmart. The smallest stocks of the small-caps world are micro-cap (USD 50–200 million market value) and nano-cap stocks (typically less than USD 50 million in market value). Nano and micro stocks are apparent hot spots for managers with the ability to pick up relevant information sooner can others to gain a significant edge.

There are currently more than three times as many publically listed small-caps than large-caps and more than 10 times the mega-caps. The selection stock universe can present a dilemma for fundamental managers and analysts simply due to lack of ability to cover the full breadth of the small-cap universe.

Every index provider or active manager has their own classification. A small-cap company definition may overlap with mid-cap from one index provider to another. It is increasingly common to separate the small-cap from the main regional or global benchmarks and put in a standalone index. For example, FTSE small-cap indices target the smallest 10% of all securities; MSCI, S&P, and Dow Jones each cover the smallest 15%. In addition, the S&P 600 U.S. small-caps ranges between USD 450 million to 2.1 billion market cap with at least 50% of shares outstanding must be available for trading (i.e. the free-float discussed in Chap. 3). Globally FTSE small-cap and MSCI small-cap cover small-cap from global markets. Popular indices to use as U.S. benchmark for small-cap performance are the Russell 2000 and S&P 600 from a wide variety of industries. The average market cap for these indices ranges from USD 800 million to USD 1.4 billion.

Moreover, the mid-cap tends to be the "sweet spot" for many factor strategies and is also considered as a part of the size factor. Typically, mid-cap stocks' market value ranges from USD 2 billion to USD 10 billion. Some index providers like the MSCI and FTSE may include large stocks rather than using a simple market capitalisation band. Instead, the index definitions allow for rank and a buffer zone for the market value of a stock.

Popular regional indices include the U.S. Russell index family for small and mid-caps. The small-cap index, for example, has about 2000 companies, twice as many stocks as the large-cap Russell 1000 index. Another popular index for developed markets excluding the U.S. is the MSCI EAFE small-cap, which has over 2000 stocks, about twice the MSCI EAFE large-cap.

A size factor strategy would buy a broad stock universe, similar to the indices mentioned earlier to harvest a premium with diversification. The ideas are that smaller stocks may be riskier with either value or growth characteristics that could assist in delivering the excess returns over the market in the longer term. Unlike an index manager, an active manager would examine thoroughly individual stocks to find the "good ones".

8.2 Construction of Size-Based Index Strategy

A size-factor index can be constructed in various ways for different objectives. The first approach is to define cut-off points with tolerances around the market capitalisation movement. This generates a targeted size-focused portfolio with pure small- and mid-cap. Alternatively, a tilting-approach (as described in Chap. 3) can be applied to a broad market universe with (large to small-caps).

A general approach with a starting index universe that includes large, mid and small-cap can be designed as follows:

1. Select starting universe
2. Rank stocks by their market cap (highest to lowest)
3. Apply exclusion or scoring approach:

    (a) Select a proportion of the stock universe for exclusion by market capitalisation limit (e.g. smallest 30th percentile of the starting universe similar to Fama and French approach) or
    (b) Translate the market capitalisation to scores (see Table 8.1 as an example).

4. If an exclusion approach is adopted, then apply a weighting scheme (either market capitalisation on the new universe or alternative weighting, e.g. equal weighting). If the scoring approach is used, then apply the score as tilt to the starting universe weights in the index. Table 8.1 provides an example of the scoring approach.

Table 8.1 Titling approach example with a blend of large, mid and small-caps

Stock	(A) Score (0–1)	(B) Market cap weight (%)	(C) Unadjusted weight (%), A × B	(D) Adjusted weight (%) C stock weight/ sum of C weights
Stock 1	0.10	46.8	4.8	24.8
Stock 2	0.18	23.4	4.3	22.0
Stock 3	0.26	14.1	3.6	18.8
Stock 4	0.33	9.4	3.1	16.0
Stock 5	0.47	4.7	2.2	11.3
Stock 6	0.77	0.9	0.7	3.7
Stock 7	0.87	0.5	0.4	2.1
Stock 8	0.93	0.2	0.2	1.1
		100.0	19.4	100.0

Source: Author
Note: For illustrative purpose only. The scores in this example range from 0–1 and applied to the market capitalisation of individual stocks in the example

The advantage of the method is a focused size exposure without dilution where large-cap is likely to be excluded from the index. However, the second approach is more common as it allows for global exposure but with reduced exposure to larger stocks. Another approach that tends to generate exposure to small and mid-cap stocks implicitly is equally weighting scheme when applied to a broad market-cap universe with no exclusions.

A typical rebalance of this indexing strategy should be 3–12 months to maintain a low turnover of the index—an active manager may rebalance their portfolio more frequently as they are not bound to set rebalancing dates. Now that readers have an idea of how a size factor can be constructed, the next sections will provide some evidence and discussions on the size premium.

8.3 The Existence of the Size Premium

The story of the size factor premium is mixed. This section discusses the success and failure of the size premium. Fama and French in 1992 included small size companies in a multi-factor context to explain the stock expected returns. Banz in 1981 showed that a firm's size matters when linked to performance. Smaller size stocks have historically generated higher returns than larger stocks. Table 8.2 compares small and mid-cap (size factor) to a large and broad market cap for the U.S. from 1963 to 2017. The size factor has historically outperformed large and market-cap strategies based on the data. However, the volatility is significantly higher for small and mid-cap stocks. Also, the drawdown is higher, particularly small-cap with a 67% drawdown.

Table 8.2 Small-, mid-, large-cap and market cap for the U.S.

	Small-cap	Mid-cap	Large-cap	Market cap
Value-weighting (market capitalisation)				
Total return (%, p.a.)	12.2	12.3	10.1	10.3
Volatility (%, p.a.)	21.1	18.2	14.6	15.2
Return/risk	0.6	0.7	0.7	0.7
Maximum drawdown (%)	66.8	52.4	49.8	50.4
Total return during U.S. recessions	1.3	3.6	0.6	0.8
Equal weighting				
Total return (%, p.a.)	13.6	11.9	10.9	
Volatility (%, p.a.)	21.9	19.4	16.5	
Return/risk	0.6	0.6	0.7	
Maximum drawdown (%)	68.6	55.6	55.5	
Total return during U.S. recessions[a]	2.7	4.9	2.4	

Source: Author's calculations. Kenneth French database, Jul. 1963–Dec. 2017
Note: The small-cap is based on bottom 30 percentile, mid-cap is 40–70th percentile, and the large-cap is the largest 30th percentile. The total return for the stocks during the U.S. recession is the average return across all recessions from peak to trough
[a]The total return during U.S. recessions (peak to through) is the average performance of the strategy during all the recessions since 1960th

Many studies report that the size premium is not robust over time and tends to be on and off. The size premium is noticeable between 1964–1981 in the U.S. but was weak between 1982–2000. During the latter period, the economy enjoyed economic growth and a bull market in stocks. The market was negative only once in 1990 and only one relatively short recession (July 1990 to March 1991 based on NBER date of recessions). However, the dot-com crash marked the end of the good times. Size premium made a comeback in global markets some years after.

The size premium has been tested regularly since its discovery. The MSCI study "One size does not fit all" used data from 1998 to 2015. The study shows that the size premium (defined as excess return over the market cap) exists across 10 deciles of the market capitalisation of tradable stock universe. The size premium is documented in the study except for nano- and micro-caps. This could be due to the fact these small stocks are inherently riskier with the highest risk of running out of business. A study by Asness and his colleagues at AQR Capital Management in 2017 demonstrated the power of controlling for poor quality (known as junk) stocks within the small-cap universe. In a more recent study, Wei Ge in 2018 examined three U.S. mid-cap equity indexes (the Russell Mid-Cap Index, the CRSP mid-cap Index, and the S&P 400 mid-cap index) reconfirms the existence of the mid-cap premium for the U.S. market.

Several explanations have been attributed to the size premium. The majority of research attributes it to reward for bearing greater systematic risk (i.e. market risk, illiquidity risk or macroeconomic risk) compared to large-caps. Others attribute the premium to non-risk based aspects such as the January effect, mispricing and behavioural drivers. These aspects will be discussed in the next section.

8.4 Risk-Based Explanation of the Size Premium

The risk-based explanation focuses on the aspects that smaller stocks are naturally riskier than larger counterparts. Hence investors should be rewarded for taking on more risk. This section provides an illustration on the reward for risk by looking at the macroeconomic environment and illiquidity.

The size premium is time-varying, similar to other factors, and influenced by the broader market conditions and economic activity. Historically, smaller companies in aggregate have provided higher returns than large-cap stocks because they are riskier, according to several measures. A key measure for market risk, known as beta (measuring a stock's risk against the market) typically shows that smaller companies have higher market risk than the general market and large-caps based on beta or volatility measures. For example, technology stocks tend to be more volatile than utility stocks. Small-cap stocks also tend to be more volatile, and usually have a higher level of market risk than well-established large-cap stock. Moreover, these firms are generally younger companies with weaker financials compared to larger stocks, and often do not pay much dividends. Hence small- and mid-cap exhibit higher market risks.

Higher risk should result in higher realised returns, at least on paper. However, in the real world, it may take years or a decade for the reward to come through—an apple seed does not carry any fruits right after it is planted in soil. Hence, it often takes a long time to capture that size premium in indices, although a concentrated portfolio strategy may get rewarded faster, but also risks of just watching the stump of the apple tree.

Like many factors, the size premium goes in cycles. In a market downturn, it is intuitive to expect that these stocks will experience higher drawdowns than the larger counterparts—see Table 8.2. Although the early studies in the 1980s showed U.S. small-cap stocks outperforming large-cap, recent data shows a lacklustre outperformance. Over the past 30 years, the U.S. small-cap just matched the performance of the large-cap but underperformed on a risk-adjusted basis.[1] However, the small-cap went through an underperformance between 1998–2002. The large technology stocks like Dell, Microsoft and Amazon did very well during the dot-com bubble, while small non-tech stocks could not keep pace with the index, leading to five consecutive years of underperformance against large-cap stocks.

In general, smaller size stocks carry higher liquidity risk. A liquid stock is one that can be sold quickly and at "fair market value". Hence, liquidity risk poses some uncertainty of trading stock with a narrow investor base. In the context here, market liquidity can be measured by bid-ask price spread and daily trading volume compared to larger stocks as well as the number of market makers in the security. The bid-ask spread is typically wider on average for a smaller and mid-cap index than the large-cap. In addition, the trading cost for the U.S. and European large-cap is estimated to be 3 and 5 basis points, respectively, and 6–8 basis points for small-cap and emerging market stocks.[2] This spread is larger during a volatile market and early stages of poor economic conditions and narrows during good economic conditions.

Structural developments have happened in the smaller size stocks, and it is constantly evolving. Historically, the mainstream small-cap stocks were rewarded from their illiquidity, but today trading is more accessible with narrower bid-ask spread compared to previous decades, as more brokers and market makers are available.

8.5 Non-Risk Based Explanation

The non-risk based explanations of the size premium include delayed price response, January effect, mispricing and behavioural biases. There is a truth in many of the explanation as risk-based explanations, and the non-risk based explanation constitute a reward for risk, market structure and behavioural drivers of market participants. Furthermore, some of the non-risk based explanations do not apply in highly diversified small or mid-cap index strategies. This section will cover some of these explanations.

---

[1] Based on Russell 2000 and Russell 1000 comparison.

[2] The trading costs are based on the U.K. FCA study in 2014, "Transaction Costs Transparency", Prepared for the FCA by Novarca.

8.5.1 The January Effect

Several studies have demonstrated that 50 to 100% of the size effect in the U.S. can be attributed to abnormal returns of small size firms in January. This does not necessarily apply in other global markets as January effect is not a consistent feature in historical data.

Tax-loss selling and window dressing hypothesis are two explanations to the January effect, described by Jay Ritter study in 1988. The window dressing hypothesis argues that in order to present "quality" holdings, institutional investors have an incentive to buy large and sell small and -mid stocks at the end of a year.

However, January effect may not necessarily feature strongly in highly diverse rules-based (none subjective) index strategy and instead more relevant to active or discretionary based strategies, which often have fewer holdings compared to an index. An indexing strategy is rules-based and tends to contain thousands of stocks. In the past few years, the size premium has been negative and decreasing over time. Table 8.3 shows the percentage of time that size premium (with small and mid-cap) outperformed the large and market cap during different decades in the U.S. This is consistent with a similar analysis for a broad index such as FTSE-Russell small and large-cap. The evidence for the January effect is not sufficiently strong for an index strategy as the investors are more directed by the index rebalance rules than managing tax losses against individual stocks.

8.5.2 Inefficient Pricing

A delayed response may leave the small-cap and to some extent the mid-cap stocks mispriced for a period of time. However, if mispricing exists in the

Table 8.3 Small and mid-cap outperformance versus large and market cap during January

	Small minus market capitalisation	Mid minus market capitalisation
1960th	100	67
1970th	90	90
1980th	80	50
1990th	50	30
2000	60	90
2010	70	50
After	43	57

Source: Author's calculations, Kenneth-French database, Jul. 1963–Dec. 2017
Note: The calculations are based on excess return between small and mid-cap over the market cap

market, they are more likely to correct when market participants realise their mistakes. An information shock such as an earnings announcement should, therefore, be a learning event that can be a catalyst for a price correction.

A study by QMA finds that about 20% of the excess returns over the market from small-cap stocks are generated during announcement periods using the Russell 2000 stock universe.[3] They find similar results for large-caps, but the magnitude of the mispricing is much larger in small-caps. The results show that the difference in return computed from the earnings announcement window is 81 bps for the small-cap space, compared to 34 bps for large-caps. Many active managers aim to find price dislocation in stocks and small-cap is most attractive. This study in particular, like many others, is a quasi-active strategy where the index is modified and narrowed.

However, similar to the January effect, the main differences between active small-cap and more diversified index strategy is how they compensate for the higher margin of error in small-caps. Concentrated managers, typically an active manager, may dig deeper into specific segments of the market for better information and allocate to regions and sectors that are more dynamic than an index fund. This exercise requires devoted resources to research the companies to gain an information edge to construct the portfolios. While the mispricing aspect makes sense for an active manager, it is less relevant for a systematic index manager whose primary target is to stay within the tracking error budget relative to the underlying index.

8.5.3 Attention, Coverage and Transparency

There are many arguments that smaller stocks lack coverage and that there is a lack of insight about small-cap stocks, which create inefficiencies in valuation and are the long-term persistent of the size premium. This creates inattention and rewards managers who know and respond to current and new information about the company. Investment bankers and brokers employ an army of research analysts, typically paid a percentage of the size of the listing deals or trades. A company with a market capitalisation of billions is a lot more lucrative for a bank or broker than a small-cap firm of millions in market-cap.

An increasing number of analyst coverage on the stocks can accelerate the incorporation of information into prices and hence reducing inefficiencies. Historically, a few analysts and brokers followed smaller companies and could

---

[3] Gavin Smith (2016) "Start of something big: demystifying the source of large alpha in small-caps", White paper.

Table 8.4 Analyst coverage by size

	Market cap (USD, billion)	Number analyst coverage
Large-cap	27.7	27
Mid-cap	8.0	18
Small-cap	2.5	8

Source: Author's collection combined with Bloomberg data. The stock universe is based on ETFs tracking small, mid and large-cap in the U.S.
Note: The security universe is based on stocks included ETFs tracking U.S. stock indices. The market capitalisation is a weighted average based including the analyst coverage as at Dec. 2017

take weeks for reports and revisions to make into the public domain and get reflected in share prices. This is particularly relevant to nano- and micro-caps that may not even make it to an investable index universe.

However, the brokerage and sell-side research coverage for standard small, mid and large-caps have been increasing over the years. The average number of coverage by analysts increased from two to six between 2000–2017. Large-caps still have consistent coverage—the largest stocks have about 27 analysts on average and the mega-cap around 40 (see Table 8.4).

It is still the case for micro and nano-cap companies to have smaller coverage and if moving into the stocks outside an index, the coverage is still small or non-existent. The low coverage may lead to a weak anchor for prices with broad estimates for growth and low consensus on the companies' earnings.

8.5.4 Behavioural Drivers of the Size Factor

Part of the size premium can be explained by investors' behaviour in the market. As mentioned in earlier chapters, these behaviours are temporary but reoccurring. These can magnify or dwarf the impact on prices of small and mid-caps. Behaviours can influence prices in many ways such as perception of a firm's business prospects. The market itself can also impact investors' behaviours, especially where information about corporate (e.g. small-caps) may be limited; emotional mistakes are even more prominent due to the high swings in the stock price.

In general, small companies often have a higher growth rate than larger stocks—the first sign of success or failure can alter investor expectation quite dramatically. In general, an increasing number of overconfident investors could push the price from a "fair value", which we discussed in other chapters.

Typical behaviours that can be attributed to the size factor include familiarity and anchoring bias. Many investors often follow popular stocks or economies that they are familiar with. We become familiar with large-cap stocks over time as they attract more news and headlines than smaller companies. Smaller companies tend to lack interesting stories and may not have as much news coverage as large companies. Sometimes this can make investors to ignore smaller companies. Also, anchoring bias may cause people to be more reluctant to update their beliefs in a timely fashion when faced with new developments or information about a stock. This can be magnified for smaller companies due to the cost and effort of accumulating information. Yet, investors can be rewarded for the cost and time to gather information.

8.6 Criticism of the Size Premium

There are few major criticisms that feature for the size factor. Among these are: survivorship bias, investability and capacity. The first critics of the size premium argue that portfolios do not take into account survivorship bias as many academic studies use survivorship-free data. Survivorship bias occurs when index performance is based on only the survivors at the end of a given period and excluding those that no longer exist. This matters because it distorts the long-term performance of the investment strategy. Therefore, some argue that the size factor could be subject to data mining. There is some degree of data mining that takes place in some research, and it is crucial to remember that the past performance does not necessarily predict the future. However, the survivorship aspect also has some truth but depends on the context in which it is criticised.

During weak economic conditions, the number of delisted stocks increases. These stocks would leave the index. Similarly, in good economic conditions, more stocks will be upgraded to the mid and large-cap indices. Hence the performance of these stocks falls out of the index on the rebalance dates. Therefore, the survivorship bias may not be an issue for index-based strategies as sometimes stated.

The index is an index, and by default, a company that grows from USD 5 billion to USD 30 billion in market capitalisation would naturally leave the size factor index. Or a stock that falls in market value may either leave the index or receive a smaller weight in an index. Furthermore, stocks in an index can be deleted from the index due to corporate action such as takeover or merger, which is typically the case among traditional benchmarks. The turnover for the U.S. small-cap universe (based on FTSE-Russell research) has 495 stocks entering or leaving the index between 1996–2005 and 237 stocks between 2007–2017. This represents about 30% and 12% turnover of the portfolio which can be defined as the market value bought (added) and sold (deleted) by the index relative to its base market value when rebalancing the index. For comparison, a global large-cap market capitalisation weighted index typically has a turnover of 6–8% per annum.

The second criticism is investability. While investability is a positive feature for index implementation, critics argue that the size premium disappears when the investability is taken into account as it eliminates tiny stocks (e.g. nano or micro-caps) that are not tradable as they lack the capacity for institutional investors. Oberoi et al. in 2016 study compare the liquidity profiles of various indices based on USD 10 billion investment shows that a global small-cap index took 3.5 days to trade 95% of the index while large-cap index can be fully traded within a day.

The third criticism is investment capacity into smaller companies. The same study by MSCI explored the investment capacity in the small-cap universe. Investment capacity has various definitions, but for simplicity, it could reflect exposure limits on ownership of underlying stocks in indices when investing. In the MSCI example of using USD 10 billion allocations, investment capacity was not an issue—maximum exposure of less than 1.5% irrespective of the weighting approach or of the strength of the size effect in the index.

In general, Beck and Kalesnik in 2014 cast doubts about the existence of a size premium emerging from small-cap stocks. Yet, their research acknowledges the diversification benefits in portfolios with large stocks and the potential of mispricing. Small stocks can serve as an alpha generating source for active managers and index strategies that primarily target factors other than size. However, the size factor (based on small-cap alone) is not sufficient to earn a higher return over large stocks.

8.7 Considerations When Investing in Small Size

The source of returns is not a mystery anymore. While the size factor could offer a reward relative to the general market or large-cap, capturing it is by no means a trivial business. There are pitfalls along the investment journey in both small- and mid-cap companies. The business may not be diversified enough, with limited access to capital. For example, small and mid-sized miners carry some risks as those tend to be single-asset companies. Hence, the main risk is whether a company is able to execute both from a technical perspective—the right geology to mine, the right engineering—and also access to financing.

Moreover, to get the most out of the large, mid and small-cap universe, managers ideally want to generate insights across the broad universe to identify investment opportunities. The same issues that account for low investor attention and transparency increase the need for extensive data integrity checks to overcome the potential of "garbage-in and garbage out" case. Managers also need to connect different data sources and analysis to obtain a complete picture of each stock. This is important from the point of view of increasing the chances of capturing the size premium repeatedly.

The importance of a separation of the "wheat from the chaff" is not a surprise by now and is a cornerstone for consistent and persistent performance. By combining the small or mid-cap with the quality characteristics (discussed in the previous chapter) is a way to achieve this. Hence, combining size with quality could form a strong core equity strategy which offers a degree of risk mitigation against low-quality stocks due to the poor portfolio and index construction.

A lot of this should primarily be driven by an investment process to sort through the stock universe with various sizes to identify the highest quality, undervalued stocks with attractive growth prospects. Similar exposures in value and small-caps can result from very different stocks and very different weighting schemes, discussed in Chap. 3. Then it comes down to the discipline to wait and be patient for the trees to bear fruits—adjustment of any market mispricing and reward for patience.

Investors with a specialisation in specific sectors or regions can encounter large swings in performance when those are out of fashion with the market. Hence, the investment process is essential to ensure consistency across all dimensions of the small and mid-cap universe, including countries, sectors, industries, and general strategy design. Smaller companies' limited product diversification and their common domestic focus imply that both good and bad news increases the volatility of size factor. This includes events like takeovers and bankruptcies, which are not uncommon in the space. However, diversifying stock bets may reduce the drawdown due to there being few losing positions in an index. For example, a global long-term average default rate is between 4–5% globally based on rating agency estimates (e.g. Moody's and others). That is not to say that there are 4.5% of companies in the small and mid-cap universe that run out of business. It is more on the broader corporates in the economy, including private companies.

Lower liquidity can increase bid-ask spreads and market impact on costs, which need to be considered when evaluating the return potential of investments. Investors may need to revisit the structure of their factor portfolios or adopt certain trading strategies (e.g. avoid trading during market volatility) to minimise these risks. With all these aspects in mind, the implementation of the small and mid-cap stocks, that could be illiquid, plays an important role in harvesting the size premium.

8.8 Concluding Remarks

This chapter provided an insight into the size factor, how it is constructed and drivers behind the size factor premium. This also completes our journey into single-factor investing for equities. The size factor, like other factors, requires patience. If you are investing in smaller stocks, you need to be able to stomach the volatility. Small-cap and to some extent mid-cap stocks have historically greater volatility and drawdown than the large-cap and broad market. So it is essential to understand the risk tolerance and where it is positioned in portfolios. As the Wall Street expression goes: "You don't know your risk tolerance until you live through a bear market."

At the same time, it has delivered an excess return for that risk. It is undeniable that the size factor has worked over the long-term despite some period of underperformance in history relative to the large-cap and broad market. In sum, it is important to reflect and analyse how the size factor is embedded in the overall portfolio and in conjunction with other factors.

9

Equity Multi-Factor Investing

A successful football team is often about the composition of the team rather than the individual star player or manager, although star players tend to sell more shirts with their name on them. Ultimately, it is the team's results that matter. The relationship between single-factor and multi-factor strategies is no different in this regard—the team is the combination of the factors into one strategy. In previous chapters, we addressed the five well-established factors and discussed how to think about and construct them in the most simplistic way. This chapter offers the final step on traditional equity "factor investing" with a focus on multi-factor strategies. The focus is on the academic and practitioners' thinking as to how factors can be combined into an investible strategy along with consideration when looking into multi-factors for short, medium and long-term investors.

A multi-factor approach is an evolution of single-factor investing from previous chapters, and similarly, has its root in academia with a few finesses by practitioners. In 1976 Ross described that stock market returns could be explained with macroeconomic influences, known as the "arbitrage pricing theory". This framework uses economic growth, inflation and exchange rates to explain differences in returns and to analyse portfolio sensitivities as a part of risk management framework or style factor positioning. Fama and French's iconic work in 1992 combined empirically, size and value with the market capitalisation portfolio in a model to show that the expected returns of a portfolio can be explained by the three factors. Later development extended the multi-factor allocation to momentum and others.

There is no right or wrong answer as to how many and which factors to include in a strategy. In reality, every investor has an asset allocation, and holding one factor is an asset allocation. However, this can be a painful venture, particularly when a factor undergoes prolonged underperformance, as discussed in previous chapters. Investors may run out of patience long before realising the benefit of a concentrated factor exposure. A multi-factor approach can offer diversification and less of a bumpy ride through the investment journey by harvesting multiple sources of returns without having to rely on a single source from a factor.

Knowing that multi-factor might be the right thing for you, the challenge remains to which factors to allocate, how many to include and what approach to take in the construction. This decision goes back to investors' preferences and objective. For example, an investor may decide to exclude momentum from the multi-factor allocation to keep turnover low or decide to include low volatility to reduce drawdown, or look to combine value and quality in an overall asset allocation framework. There is no right or wrong answer, and this decision is subjective.

Multi-factor strategies among index providers and asset managers vary to a great extent, and so does their complexity. The desired outcomes—in terms of risk, reward, factor intensity, the degree of factor timing—can guide investors in different schools of multi-factor strategy construction. These schools provide different outcomes for investors and are widely adopted among asset managers, with over 50 multi-factor index strategies implemented through ETFs and segregated portfolios in the market.

A strategic multi-factor investor, someone with a long-term view, aims to simultaneously capture factor characteristics of the stocks and not to obtain unintended exposure to one particular factor. As we established in previous chapters, a stock can be cheap and at the same time exhibit low quality and negative momentum features. Typically, strategic investors do not need to take a view on a particular factor but aim to achieve a balanced exposure to a set of factors—a one-stop shop if done reasonably. Some managers are interested and involved in financial markets on a day-to-day basis and prefer to adjust factor exposure—referred to as factor timing. This involves dynamic allocations to various factors through time. The active factor manager would dynamically allocate to a range of factors by over or under-weighting multi-factor strategy depending on valuation, market conditions and macroeconomic environment. This tends to lead to active management, which can involve quantitative and qualitative decision making through committees and asset allocation frameworks.

9.1 Factor Cyclicality and Diversification

Factors are cyclical. Due to the nature of the single-factor cyclicality over time, long-term investors aim to achieve a balanced factor exposure to a set of factors and not rely on factor timing, which will be discussed later in the chapter. Macroeconomic sensitivity of the factors indicates pro-cyclical (high beta) and counter-cyclical (defensive) features. Value, momentum and size are typically more sensitive to economic growth and tend to be high beta strategies—they underperform when markets fall and vice versa. However, low volatility and quality are typically considered counter-cyclical—they will do well during volatile market conditions but tend to underperform relative to the broad market during a market rally and economic recovery. Figure 9.1 provides an illustration.

The sensitivity of a factor to inflation, interest rates and other macro variables differ depending on the time horizon. Higher inflation generally has a negative impact on future long-term real GDP growth. Small capitalisation stocks may see short-term outperformance as inflation rises, but can be penalised more by inflation in the long-term, due to their greater sensitivity to real GDP growth.

Intuitively, momentum is expected to perform best in high growth regimes, while low volatility outperform in a stagnation environment (low growth and high inflation at the same time). Generally, in a slow-growth environment, the quality factor has generally outperformed (Fig. 9.1). Figure 9.2 illustrates the historical dynamics of single-factors and multi-factor through various economic and market regimes.

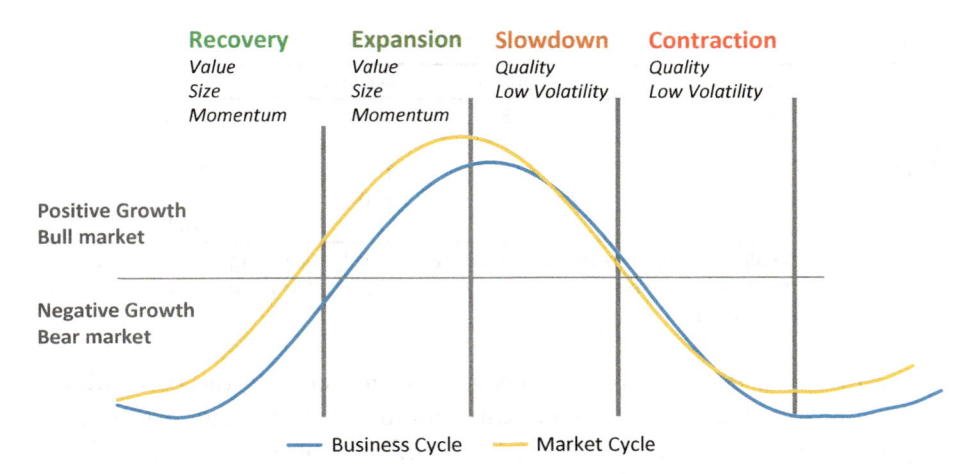

Fig. 9.1 The business, market cycle and factors. Note: For illustrative purposes only

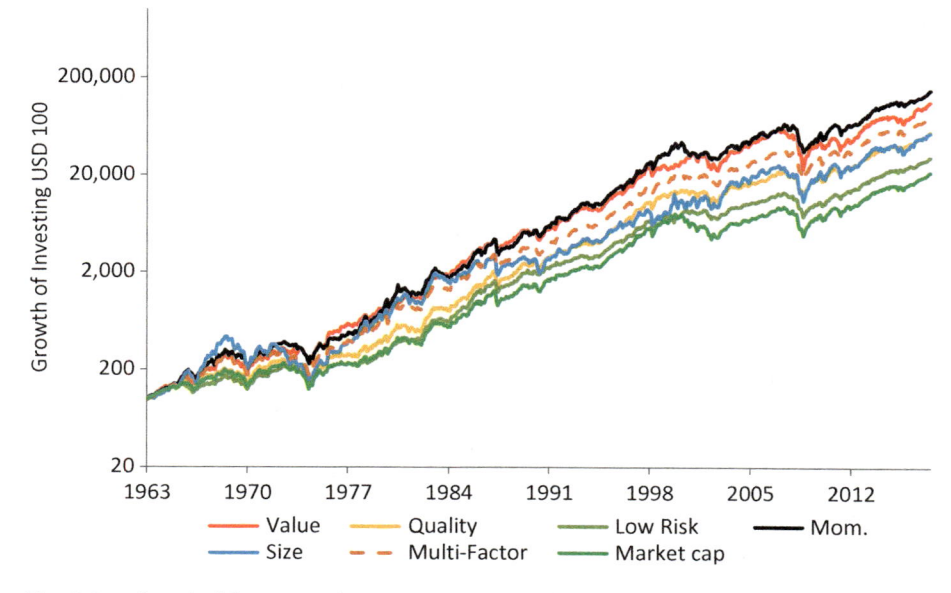

Fig. 9.2 Historical factor performance and multi-factor. Source: Author's calculations, Kenneth French database Jul. 1963–Dec. 2017 for the US. Note: The time series are logged and rebased to July 1963. The stocks are market capitalisation weighted after screening for the top 30th percentile for each factor. Factor definitions used are: value as high book-to-market (or low price-to-book), high quality as a combined definition of low investment and high operating profitability, size as the smallest 30% by market capitalisation in the stock universe, low volatility as the low beta definition as a proxy for low risk, and momentum as the monthly prior (2–12) returns. The multi-factor is just simply the average of the various building blocks for illustrative purposes. Historical returns are not a leading indicator of future performance

Table 9.1 Correlation (%) between various factor premia

	Size	Value	Quality	Momentum	Low beta
Size	100	33	−15	15	−43
Value		100	25	−7	16
Quality			100	10	51
Mom				100	−1
Low beta					100

Source: Author's calculations. Kenneth French database, Jul. 1963–Aug. 2018 for the U.S. Note: For factor definitions, see the note of Fig. 9.2. The factor premium is the excess return of the factor over the market cap

The historical diversification effects are also reflected in the correlations between factors. For example, the quality and momentum factor exhibit low negative correlation. Overall, the majority of the correlations range from about −30 to 30% (see Table 9.1).

Diversification across factors can mitigate the risks of individual factors, but cannot eliminate all risks completely. Correlations are time-varying between factors and the low long-term correlation can mask this, especially during crises where they often become positively correlated. On one hand, it may not be an issue for long term investors, and on the other, it can destroy the short-term benefits of diversification.

9.2 Blending the Factors into Multi-Factor Strategy

Establishing the historic relationship between factors might give some ideas about the long-term benefits of diversification. Though it is not the only thing that matters. Consideration for the "right mix" for a specific purpose and the way to construct the strategy are important too. Yet, it is better to guard against just looking at the simple comparison of the historical risk-return of each approach and take historical backtesting with a pinch of salt.

To investors' advantage, blending factors can provide transparency, which is similar to single-factor implementation. Also managing the turnover as a part of the construction approach does not necessarily make the implementation more expensive. For example, stocks can exhibit characteristics of many factors or may transition from value to momentum, creating a crossing that can reduce the turnover, assuming similar rebalancing dates for all the sleeves of the multi-factor components.

Given the increasing interest in multi-factor, a recurring question is about which approach to use to blend the factors. This section covers the main approaches to constructing a systematic multi-factor strategy. There are two main construction approaches for multi-factor: bottom-up and top-down. The top-down approach mixes different single factor portfolios and combines them into one—a simple allocation between various building blocks. The bottom-up approach combines factors at the level of the single security by evaluating multiple factors at once (also known as an integrated approach).

9.2.1 The Top-Down Approach

The top-down approach determines exposures to a set of individual factors at the outset of the strategy design. This method provides the benefit and flexibility to control the desired factors in the portfolio—weighting between factors, choice of implementation or asset managers for each factor. A way to think

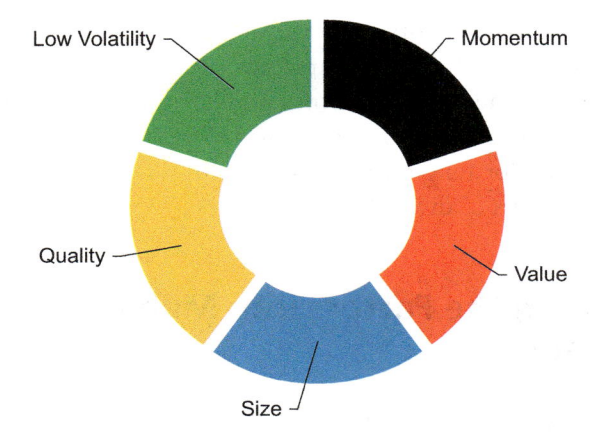

Fig. 9.3 Example of building blocks and equal weighted allocation. Note: For illustrative purposes only. This chart assumes that the single-factor sleeves are equally weighted. Each block—quality, value, low volatility and other factors—are filled with stocks that score the highest on each of the factors to create the multi-factor strategy

about it is as a modular approach with building blocks that can be structured in a way to achieve specific investment objectives—"index of indices" or "portfolio of portfolios". Figure 9.3 provides an illustration of a simple construction of single factors, representing a balanced exposure across five factors.

As the main advantage, the top-down approach provides investors with an opportunity to make explicit choices regarding the factor exposure in their portfolios. Therefore, it allows investors to choose the desired exposure to factor risks while diversifying away unwanted and unrewarded specific risks in the multi-factor portfolio. This can be achieved through weighting schemes that can help to control stock concentration and sectors in the single factor sleeve.

However, a simple combination of single-factor strategies could dilute desired factor exposures, if it is not controlled which is typically the case in the simplest form of top-down approaches. Individual stocks inevitably exhibit multiple factor characteristics at the same time. Combining single-factor strategies will inevitably create cross factor interaction. A value building block, for example, can contain low quality features and/or negative momentum. Hence, the cross factor interactions could dilute the factor exposure and create unintended risks.

9.2.2 The Bottom-Up Approach

The bottom-up approach allocates investments on an integrated basis by considering the factor attributes at a stock level. Each stock is simultaneously evaluated against all factors and essentially is seen as a combination of multiple factor characteristics (Fig. 9.4). Hence, it explicitly captures the characteristics of multiple factors at the construction level. This can offer insight as to how much value, quality, low volatility and other factor attribute are inherent in a stock. This approach can take into account cross-factor interactions and could create a more targeted factor exposure in a portfolio.

The bottom-up approach typically applies a scoring or ranking-based system on multiple factor characteristics. These scores are in turn combined to create a composite score or rank of the multiple characteristics (Table 9.2).

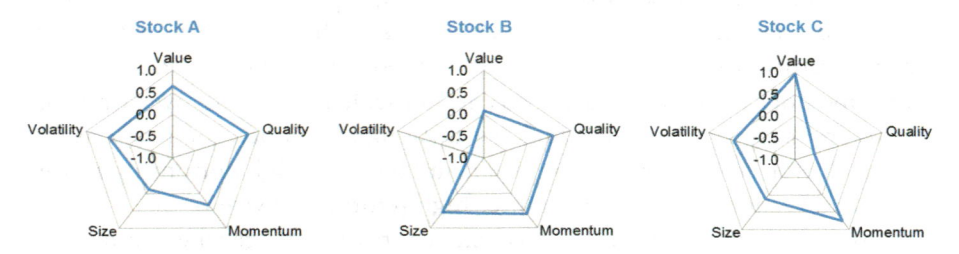

Fig. 9.4 Bottom-up approach illustration. Note: The scores are between −1 and +1 derived on the stock-specific characteristics described in previous chapters. The best score is +1, and the worst score is −1. For illustrative purposes only

Table 9.2 Bottom-up scores based on characteristics

	Value	Quality	Momentum	Size	Volatility	Combined Score Geometric Average	Combined Score Arithmetic Average
Stock A	0.65	0.75	0.33	−0.11	0.47	0.38	0.42
Stock B	0.09	0.6	0.6	0.54	−0.68	0.06	0.23
Stock C	0.97	−0.56	0.75	0.12	0.41	0.19	0.34
Stock D	−0.23	0.86	0.49	−0.33	−0.98	−0.52	−0.04
Stock E	−0.74	−0.35	0.22	−0.69	0.67	−0.36	−0.18
Stock F	−0.23	−0.56	−0.14	0.7	0.02	−0.13	−0.04

Notes: Author's calculations. The scores are between −1 and +1 derived on the stock-specific characteristics described in previous chapters. The best score is +1, and the worst score is −1. This example is for illustrative purposes only

Stocks with the highest composite scores would be chosen or tilted towards in the bottom-up multi-factor strategy. Alternatively, optimisation techniques can help maximise factor exposure subject to turnover limits, geographical, sector and stock constraints discussed in Chap. 3. However, optimisation techniques can lead to "model mining"—finding the right model to maximise factor scores that could impact the backtested performance but have limited robustness out of sample.

The bottom-up approach has some considerations of course. Depending on how the bottom-up multi-factor index is constructed, it may be more complicated than the top-down construction. Working with a broad and global stock universe requires a careful evaluation of each security and could lead to a more concentrated portfolio of stocks if not managed in the design process of the strategy.

As we know, stock level estimates are not always reliable—accounting and market price data can be noisy. The bottom-up approach assumes that the factor scores at the individual stock level are somehow proportional to the expected returns of security. It is well established, among both academics and many investors, that expected returns are difficult to estimate over time, as returns are noisy at individual stock level. Along these lines, the relationship between factors and returns is not linear, and having a high bottom-up factor exposure does not necessarily guarantee high returns and vice versa.

Furthermore, the relationship between factors can change when combined at stock score level—Cliff Asness established this observation in 1997. For example, value and momentum are not independent and are related as a value strategy tends to have a weak momentum. So that when designing bottom up multi-factor strategies, it might lead to unbalanced factor exposures, as stocks could have opposing factor exposure (such as value and momentum).

Scientific Beta further extended a pure top-down approach by capturing cross-factor interaction. Their approach retains factors with high factor exposure by removing stocks that score poorly on one or more factors (referred to as "factor losers"). Hence, stocks with low scores are less likely to be included in any multi-factor indices. This effectively captures cross-factor interaction and addresses the main criticism of the top-down approach.

As a result, this process still retains the main benefits of the original top-down approach such as transparency and ability to attribute performance at a factor level, while capturing cross-factor interaction. To sum up, the bottom-up tends to be more used by practitioners and has less of its foundation in the academic literature, although more research is emerging to back the approach. Arguably, investing is not an academic exercise and involves an element of art.

9.3 So Which Approach Is Best?

The debate about which approach is better or worse can be cumbersome. In general, both approaches, if properly calibrated, can generate the ultimate objective of smoothing out the investment journey for investors. Depending on the choice of factors and historical time horizon, one will outperform the other.

A study by Bender and Wang (2016) compares the historical performance of the two approaches using global stock universe for value, volatility, momentum and quality. Their results show that both multi-factor approaches exhibit less tracking error than the individual factors. The excess return of the top-down multi-factor approach roughly matches the average excess return of the individual equity factor tilt during the period (Fig. 9.5).

Bender and Wang show that the bottom-up approach earned an additional 1% per annum while increasing tracking error by 0.50% relative to the top-down approach. However, this does not imply that a bottom-up approach will always outperform the top-down method. It is arguable whether the difference on risk-adjust basis is materially significant to sway the decision of which construction approach to adopt.

Unless the investor accepts a very concentrated portfolio, both multi-factor approaches (top-down and bottom-up approaches) have a common issue. In

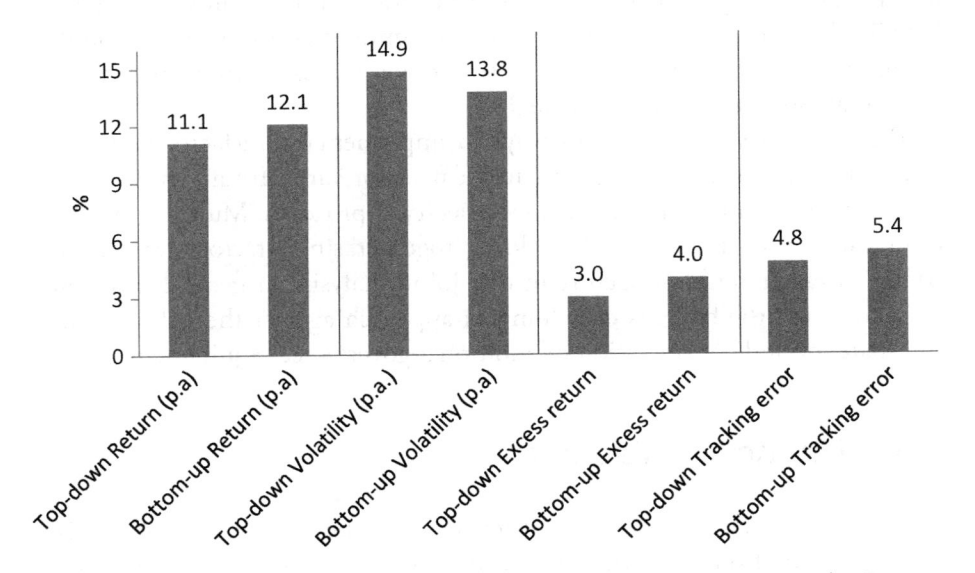

Fig. 9.5 Comparison between the top-down and bottom-up approach. Source: Author's recreation of Bender and Wang (2016), Exhibit 8, Jan. 1993–Mar. 2015. Note: Results are based on a historical simulation of an equally-weighted combination of value, volatility, quality, and momentum factor for developed markets. The excess return and tracking error is against a broad developed market capitalisation index

general, factors inter-dependencies are hard to overcome, as factors are not always independent of each other. It is widely known that smaller companies can appear as value stocks. Both approaches require fine-tuning and enhancement to minimise unintended stock-specific risk, and this can be done through constraints with weighting schemes (risk-weight, equal-weight or others) mentioned in Chap. 3.

The bottom line is: there is no better or worse approach, although the returns may vary for the period of the study. It is important to be mindful that, while a factor construction often works at a global level, the multi-factor can face issues when specific regional or country strategies are constructed. In the latter case, few listed stocks may lead to concentration (e.g. South Korea or Sweden). The concentration tends to get more exaggerated where the universe is limited to large mid-capitalised stocks. In such instance, countries like the U.K. with a rich stock universe could also end up in a quite concentrated portfolio within the mid-capitalised stocks.

9.4 Multi-Factor Indices in the Market

Multi-factor continues to gain traction among asset managers, and many multi-factor strategies are coming out of the doors of index providers such as MSCI, FTSE, RAFI and Scientific Beta. The multi-factor indices vary on the factor choice, construction approach (top-down versus bottom-up), weightings of factors and securities (Table 9.3).

There is a broad spectrum of ways to implement multi-factor strategies. The way index providers target a particular factor varies from simple, transparent styles to more sophisticated proprietary approaches. Multi-factor solutions can simply be created by adding together single-factor strategies or trying to target multiple factors in one joint analysis. In general, investors need to weigh the benefits of a complex approach against the risk of losing transparency and consideration of additional governance requirements.

9.5 Timing the Factors

"It's difficult to make predictions, especially about the future", said the Danish physicist Niels Bohr. Timing some factors is possible, but neither perfectly nor easily. For a tactical investor with a short-to-medium-term horizon, the legwork is based on the expectation of what may or may not happen in the market and the economy. A strategic (medium to long-term) factor allocator

Table 9.3 Comparison of various multi-factor indices

	FTSE developed diversified index	MSCI ACWI diversified multi-strategy index	EDHEC scientific beta—Multi-beta multi-strategy equity weighting index	RAFI-multi-factor
Value	✓	✓	✓	✓
Quality		✓	✓	✓
Momentum	✓	✓	✓	✓
Low volatility	✓		✓	✓
Size	✓	✓	✓ [a]	✓ [b]
Construction approach	Bottom-up	Bottom-up	Top-down with bottom-up features	Bottom-up
Factor allocation	Combined based on risk contribution of each factor	Combined based on risk contribution of each factor	Equal weighting	Equal weighting
Stock weighting	Market cap weighting with tilt based on factor scores	Optimisation	Combination of weighting schemes: Risk-based, equal-weighting and others[c]	Fundamental weighting

Source: Author's compilation from index methodology documents and factsheets from various index providers
[a]Scientific Beta stock universe is based on mid and large capitalisation firms
[b]RAFI size portfolio is an equal weighting between small value, small quality, small momentum and small low volatility
[c]Risk-weighting is typical the inverse of the stock volatility. High volatility stocks tend to have lower weight and vice versa

is less concerned about the rotations and predictions—the winners offset the losers over time by harnessing factor premium from multiple sources.

In factor timing, managing the allocation depends on market views and convictions, and there is no prescribed way of doing this. Instead, it all comes down to beliefs. In a world with perfect "foresight", a manager would hold only one factor and pick the winner at all times without any risk, but no one has a crystal ball. Instead, factor timing is based on forming expectations either through a systematic framework, investment process or discretionary investment decisions. This typically involves some thinking and analysis of stock valuation, factor valuation, market sentiment, potential market volatility, earnings expectations, central bank policies and factor sensitivities to market and economic conditions—the list is long. However, the most common approaches to time the factors are: (i) valuation of the factors, (ii) market sentiment, and (iii) economic cycles. These three ways of factor timing will be discussed in this section.

Arnott et al. in 2016 argue that it is possible to time the factors in their research. They provide a contrarian timing approach as a form of value investing. It focuses on segmenting cheap and expensive factors relative to the individual factor's own historical norm. Cheap factors relative to their historical levels are likely to do well in the future—and whatever is today expensive is likely to have two attributes: wonderful past and disappointing future returns.

In general, the basic construction approach described in the previous section is often used in strategic factor allocation. This section provides an overview and some fundamental thoughts on factor timing—an important part of managing portfolios. Of course, timing the factor is not dissimilar to timing the market, with a full spectrum of research out there and strategies, often proprietary, at various asset management houses. This section is limited to the underlying sensitivities of the factors, with key considerations around factor timing. In particular, the discussion is about which factors are likely to do better or worse during various economic and market cycles.

As established earlier, factor cycles are driven by reward for risk, market behaviour and structures. These tend to create the factor premia over time. These drivers have their own dynamics over time. This leads to different thinking of how to best time factors. Tactical or dynamic factor allocation, known as factor timing, aims to profit and manage risk due to the cyclicality of the factors. This approach is more active compared to a pure "balanced" multifactor strategy and tends to have higher turnover and could sacrifice diversification benefits.

9.5.1 Factor Sensitivities and Factor Dynamics

Based on the history since the global financial crisis, the economy and central bank policies have had a significant impact on the stock market and other asset classes. Historically, we have seen companies earnings fall because of economic slowdown pushing down earnings and equity valuations. That is not to say that all stocks and factors react in the same way at various stages of the market and economic cycle—expansion or contraction. Therefore, investors often choose one or combine a set of factors to express their view in various market conditions.

A substantial literature on the market and economic activity has been generated over decades, predicting aggregate equity returns and guiding asset and factor allocation based on future expectations. This is often part of an investment process to form market expectations and understanding sensitivities of factors to macroeconomic conditions. This is particularly important since

Table 9.4 Factor premia in various market and economic conditions

	Phase	Value	Growth	Momentum	Low volatility	Size	Quality
Market cycles	Bullish	+	+		−		+
	Bearish	−			+	+	+
	Recovery period	+	+		−	−	+
Business cycles	Expansion	+	+		−		+
	Contraction	−	−	−	+	+	+
Investor sentiment	Neutral and bullish	+	+	+	−	+	+
	Bearish	−	−		+	−	+

Source: Author's reconstruction from S&P Dow Jones Indices, 1994–2014. For illustrative purposes only. "+" indicates positive factor premia, "−" indicates a negative factor premium versus the broad market (market capitalisation benchmark). The blank section in the table indicates inconclusive results for the period

business cycles are not all identical. Expansions and contractions of the economic activity (total output, income and employment) can usually last for 2–10 years and differ in nature—with either investment-led and/or and consumption-led growth. However, the market cycle can contain three market environments: bear market, recovery and bull market (see Table 9.4).

Historically, economic slowdown tends to have had an impact on the stock market, although there are exceptions. Jeremy Siegel showed in 2002 that for the 42 recessions that have occurred since 1802, 39 were preceded by broad stock market declines of at least 8%. However, a bear stock market does not lead to recession—between 1946–1998, the Dow Jones industrial average fell by more than 10% without any direct impact on the economy within 12 months.

As we mentioned earlier in the chapter, during an expansion phase, momentum and value strategies tend to do well in developed market economies. Low volatility and quality often outperform other factors and the market capitalisation index during a slowdown and contraction in the economic activity (see Table 9.4). This reflects the nature of these stocks being relatively less risky than the general market and other factors. Value stocks tend to outperform growth stocks in the U.S. during the periods when the Federal Reserve is hiking rates.

Along the market cycle journey, market sentiment plays a role. It is increasingly a popular measure and typically based on market and survey data. The term is quite loose and is described in the press and news as the level of short-term risk aversion, optimism and greed and fear in the market. Few studies have evidenced the power of market sentiment in predicting factor premia. An example to a reference study is by Huang et al. in 2015 who showed the possibility of 1-month predictive power of sentiment.

Moreover, standard indicators used to gauge the market sentiment are based on the VIX (implied market volatility, a measure of the cost of buying equity insurance against the market) and economic survey indicators such as Purchase Manager Index, Institute for Supply Management (ISM) or composite scores from various banks and research houses. The market sentiment approach makes sense during extreme market events, especially when valuations are overall distorted during market volatility—e.g. dot-com crash, global financial crisis or the euro debt crisis, where investors' confidence was rattled beyond just a normal market correction. This allows managers to take a risk when others in the market are most uncomfortable and fearful.

Research Affiliates (RAFI) provides systematic factor timing strategies, particularly on the contrarian front—buying in contrast to the prevailing market sentiment. The RAFI Dynamic Multi-Factor weights its factor allocations by overweighting cheaper factors with positive recent price trends and underweighting expensive factors with negative price trends. Their multi-factor strategy maintains an allocation to each factor to avoid overconcentration in any individual factor for diversification purposes. Using a contrarian investing style can serve the purpose of gauging the market, being a contrarian can be painful, and you may have to stomach the pain for some time to gain the benefit.

9.6 Considerations When Timing the Factors

There are ways to structure a factor timing strategy and benefit from the ups and downs in the market by forming expectations and views on turning points in the market and business cycle as well as sentiment. However, success might be hard to come by as timing the market is challenging, even among many professional investors and economists. Regardless of the level of conviction, it is crucial to maintain a diversified factor portfolio even if the exposures are not perfectly balanced.

Even if history may repeat itself, it is a mistake to think that factor timing is perfectly feasible, unless the investor is sitting on correct information that no one else has. There are periods when factor timings based on valuations and fundamentals are more warranted—for example during the recovery or later business and market cycles. Of course, this assumes that the investors know where they are in the business cycle, which is a tall task in itself.

The investment process should reflect forward-looking economic views and active allocation between factors. There is a saying that God created the weatherman to make economists look good—many economists have historically failed to provide directions. Macroeconomic forecasting is a hard business with no holy grail. However, forecasting with "safety" without being perfectly precise is far more informative. In this case, deploying a macroeconomic scenario framework could potentially provide insight into portfolio sensitivities and assist in the asset allocation in portfolios.

When it comes to quantitative models for factor timing, challenging and reviewing the model's assumption is essential. Models are, by the end, based on assumption. They aim to describe the current and past state of the world with limited foresight of the future, although they might work perfectly on historical time series.

Finally, dynamic factor allocation may incur higher trading costs compared to a strategic balanced multi-factor exposure. Overtrading could undermine long-term factor performance, for some factor more than for others. Momentum already has a high turnover, often 2–4 times, compared to other factors. So if you are not successful in factor timing, you will at least be busy trading.

9.7 Multi-Factor Portfolio Analysis

A lot of academics and practitioners use the term "factor analysis" interchangeably with "style analysis". The next subsection includes an overview of the different thinking style analysis surrounding in the context of multi-factor strategies.

After finding the right set of factors that drive risks and returns, investors can assess their exposures on an on-going basis, ensure the best structure of the strategy and take advantage of the factors. Multi-factor style analysis is a way of "x-raying" the combined factor mix. The portfolio style analysis is useful in monitoring any systematic factor bets, communication, due diligence and understanding unintended style biases in the multi-factor portfolio construction. We know so far that factors overlap each other. Value factors constructed from the top percentile (e.g. 30th percentile) are likely to gravitate to small companies, or quality factors typically exhibit low volatility, which give an overlap with volatility factors.

Portfolio performance attribution gives a better understanding of specific investment decisions or helps in evaluating a fund manager skill (timing ability through asset allocation and security selection) and also can distinguish between luck and skill. Like portfolio performance attribution, we should also perform factor attribution on a regular basis to understand the performance drivers.

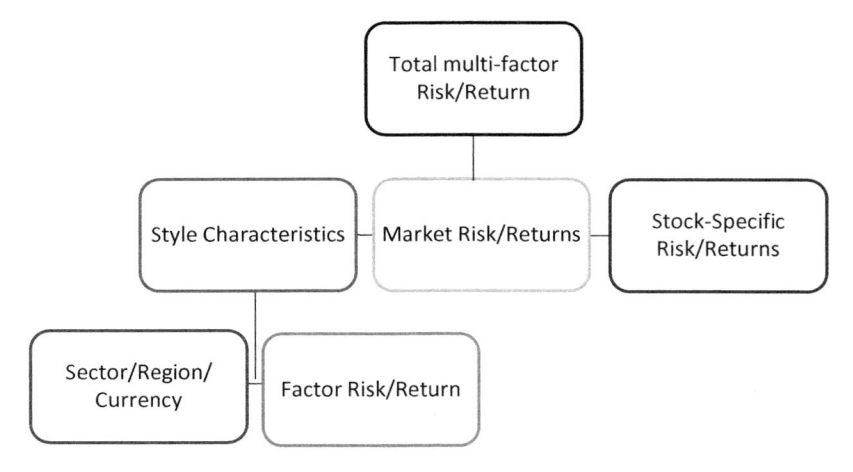

Fig. 9.6 Multi-factor risk and return attribution. Note: For illustrative purposes only

Factor attribution enables investors to identify the cause and effect of over or under-performance by disaggregating between the factor and portfolio allocation, weighting scheme, security selection. The process of factor attribution is all about decomposing overall performance into its components (Fig. 9.6). Broadly diversified balanced multi-factor portfolios with limited market timing tend to move proportionally to its factor style components over time.

Many managers build their internal factor attribution either as standalone tools or integrated within their portfolio management system. There are existing packages in the market such as Style Research, Axioma, Bloomberg, FTSE, MSCI-BARRA and others that can provide the style biases of portfolios, risk and return attributions that can do the job for the fund manager or the evaluator. Two ways of evaluating factor exposure are discussed in the following subsections.

9.7.1 Portfolio Return-Based Style Analysis

The first way to estimate a factor model is factor analysis (a statistical relationship between one variable to a set of other variables). A factor model implies that multi-factor returns are related, linearly or non-linearly, to the returns of a set of a single style or non-style factors (e.g. macro factors).

The idea is to estimate, based on past returns, how sensitive a multi-factor portfolio is to various factors, characteristics and/or general macroeconomic and market factors. Consequently, outcomes from the analysis indicate the style allocation (e.g. 25% exposure to quality, 25% value and 50% exposure to general market means the multi-factor fund is expected to move 25% whatever happens to quality stocks as well as 25% and 50% whatever happens to value and general market returns).[1] The return based approach can be illustrated as:

$$\text{Estimated Multi-Factor Returns} = B_1 \times F_1 + B_2 \times F_2 + \cdots + B_n \times F_n,$$

where the B is the sensitivity of the multi-factor portfolio to the F is factor style, and Factor is the return of the individual factor style.[2]

To analyse the factor premium alone, we can modify the regression above by deducting the Market Returns (MR) such that:

$$\left(\text{Estimated Multi-Factor Returns} - \text{MR}\right) = B_1 \times \left(F_1 - \text{MR}\right) + B_2 \times \left(F_2 - \text{MR}\right) \\ + \cdots + B_n \times \left(F_n - \text{MR}\right),$$

The advantage of this approach is simplicity—there is no need to estimate a factor model for every single security compared to a more sophisticated factor model. Security data is noisy, whereas portfolio-level analysis tends to reduce the noise due to the aggregation of securities at a portfolio level.

However, it takes a while to pick up significant changes in styles with analysis based on historical returns. Hence, a security-specific approach is likely to capture style changes a lot quicker. In addition, the return-based approach could face some challenges when analysed on concentrated investment strategies, leading to a spurious view of what is driving the underlying returns. This is especially the case in times when factors have a significant overlap between securities and when specific single factors are highly correlated.

---

[1] Return-based analysis was applied in the 1992 study of mutual fund performance by William Sharpe, showing through the analysis that 92% of variation in return could be explained by the funds' allocations to Treasury bills, bonds and stocks. Later studies show that 97% of the variation in return could be explained by the funds' allocation to a broader range of asset classes. Although the Fama-French model was originally developed as an asset-pricing model, it has become popular as a form of returns-based style analysis.

[2] To measure sensitivity the B sums to one larger or equal to zero. Some variation of the regression deducts the risk-free rate from the factor returns.

9.7.2 Security-Based Style Analysis

Variation of the security-based approach could include individual regression on the security returns against the underlying single-factor (similar regression analysis to the portfolio return based). The idea of this approach is to decompose the factor returns from the aggregate multi-factor portfolio attributed to the individual stock. The starting point is to calculate the excess returns between the multi-factor and the average single-factor (the simple single-factor).

The security-based approach uses characteristics of the underlying factor (e.g. price-to-book, leverage or volatility) in the multi-factor index. While this approach requires underlying securities data and information, the analysis is transparent and can assist in assessing how each holding contributes to the portfolio style. The distribution of the characteristics in the portfolio provides the attribution analysis to the specific factor. For example, a weighted Z-score (or another scoring mechanism) of an individual stock in the portfolio for value (say based on price-to-book) indicates how the portfolio is positioned in relation to the average stock. Below is a construction example based on value characteristic such as price-to-book (P/B):

$$\text{Security Z} - \text{score} = \text{Security Weight} \times \begin{bmatrix} \text{Security P/B} \\ -\text{Average}(P/B) \text{ in the universe} \end{bmatrix}$$
$$/ \text{ Standard Deviation}(P/B) \text{ in the universe}.$$

If the score is negative, then the security is better value than average. The scores are aggregated to provide an overall value-score. The same exercise can be repeated for other securities. As a disadvantage, the security-based approach requires access to the portfolio holdings' data. Where data is available, it is ideal to use both approaches to complete their strengths and weakness.

9.8 Concluding Remarks

Multi-factor investing diversifies investment exposure, reducing reliance on any single factor. Yet it would be a mistake to say that multi-factor strategies are always a better choice than single-factor strategies. Multi-factor strategies reduce an investor's reliance on timing the market or making the "right" call. They will most likely underperform the strongest factor of the year but should offer some insulation against the weaker ones. Choosing multi-factor over single-factor is all about the investor's conviction in their specific views.

Certain factors have historically outperformed market-cap based indices. But investors who do not wish to be the authors of their own misfortune should not view these factors' outperformance as an incontrovertible truth at all times. Performance may not be repeatable, either because the investment strategy is not diversified across styles or because of a prolonged period of underperformance of one or few factors. Individual factor strategies designed now may be skewed by hindsight ("selection bias"), and future returns will likely be lower than any backtest suggests. In general, combining factors, just like individual factors, can also experience lengthy and sizeable drawdowns.

It is human to want to hang on to certainties; this is part of the reason why *ex-post* (historical) return measures, such as back-tests, loom large in the minds of investors. But *ex-ante* (future) measures may be at least as good a predictor of what is going to happen. These build in market expectations, looking at the facts on the ground today. In some cases, it is more of a risk to focus on the certainty (what has happened) than the uncertainty (what will happen).

In sum, irrespective of design choice, tactical or dynamic management, it is all about achieving the desired outcome of investors and understanding the overall portfolio strategy. There is no silver bullet for a multi-factor combination or approach, and there are many advocates for one over another. The bottom line, multi-factor today is an evolving art and not just a precise exercise.

Part III

Fixed Income and Multi-Asset Factor Investing

This part introduces factor strategies to assets other than equities, with a focus on fixed income, currencies and commodities. The two chapters in the last part of the book introduce the common fixed income long-only factors among academics and professionals. The last chapter concludes with the so-called alternative risk premia, extending into currencies, commodities as well as various long and short factor strategies in fixed income and equities.

10

Fixed Income Factor Investing

In previous chapters, we addressed the five major equity factors—value, quality, momentum, size and low volatility—and showed how they could be combined into a multi-factor strategy. This chapter focuses on fixed income factor strategies, a less conventional way of thinking of factors in a portfolio. The topic has its controversy, particularly around the debate of developing and managing fixed income factor funds. Similar to equities, traditional fixed income benchmarks are concentrated in nature and tend to include the most indebted issuers. Factor investing could come to the rescue and alter the inherent biases in the traditional benchmarks.

This chapter presents examples of factor strategies to assist in extending the horizon into government and corporate bonds. There is no prescribed route of doing this other than going back to basic principles of bond characteristics and what drives their risks and returns. Ultimately bond factor strategies aim to provide investors with an improved risk-adjusted return over the long term or serve a particular objective. The main focus here is still on long-only bond portfolios without any involvement of derivatives, which will be covered in the next chapter.

Bond factors tend to be lost in translation and investors often confuse them with active investment decisions and timing the market. Being invested in short-dated versus long-dated bonds, for example, is a choice based on risk appetite, and being invested in short-dated bonds is likely to do relatively well compared to long-dated bonds when interest rates are rising. Instead, what is classified as a factor or style is a strategy based on a specific view. The objective of such a strategy is to improve risk-adjusted returns versus benchmarks.

Of course, everyone wants to beat their benchmark with higher returns and lower risk. But that does not come easily. Systematic factor strategies are data

© The Author(s) 2019
F. Zaher, *Index Fund Management*, https://doi.org/10.1007/978-3-030-19400-0_10

intensive and require greater computation power and resources. A traditional bond benchmark contains far more constituents than an equity index—often two to four times more for a global index, although many of them are from the same issuer. This is simply due to the fact that a company can have many bonds outstanding, perhaps over 100 bonds with different maturities across the capital structure of a corporate balance sheet. Also, new bonds come to the market every day that could be eligible to the index benchmark, as old bonds mature and cease to exist.

However, over the years, improvements in computational efficiency have driven calculation times from hours to few minutes. The age of technology, the ability to record, store and access data is increasingly making it possible to evaluate and develop factor strategies at a fast pace. The size of the global fixed income market amounts to over USD 100 trillion at the end of 2017 according to PIMCO—about 38% of this is the U.S. alone. The depth of the market creates many opportunities to deploy factor strategies and move away from traditionally weighted bond indices.

10.1 Why Factor Investing in Fixed Income?

The bond market exceeds the size of most asset classes in the capital markets. Investors lend their capital to a company with the expectation of earning periodic income and receiving the principal at a future date. However, many things can happen along that journey. This is different from equity investment, which is a title to ownership, no maturity date and no obligation for the company to pay or fix a dividend. In addition, if a company goes into liquidation, creditors and bond investors are paid first from the remaining asset value, but there are no guarantees that anything will be left for the owners (the shareholders).

The global financial and euro debt crisis prompted investors to search for more diversified bond indices compared to the traditional debt-weighted ones (bonds weighted by the size of the outstanding debt)—often heavily weighted to the debt addicts. Companies or governments with most debt tended to have the highest representation in the index and did not translate into sustainable long-term investment. The significance of asset-backed securities in bond indices in 2008 came as a surprise to many investors and as did their impact on performance. The Greek debt restructuring and the contagion to other peripheral countries (Ireland, Portugal, Italy, and Spain) drew further attention to the weakness of existing debt-weighted benchmark indices. These events, among many, challenged the investment thesis of traditional bond indices.

One of the key messages to take from the book is that, factor investing, and alternatively-weighted strategies are moving away from traditionally debt-weighted benchmarks and could provide more a disciplined investment approach. The alternative weighting breaks the link between total debt and index weights, in traditional bond indices where over-indebted issuers could be overrepresented for the wrong reason. Conceptually as a borrower's debt level increases, its cash flow coverage drops, at least temporarily, and its credit quality would deteriorate. In this case, a debt-weighted index could progressively increase the exposure to issuers even if they become riskier.

The bottom line is that bond factors look at the risk and return characteristics systematically, in the same way as for equities, and assist in shaping a diversified and targeted investment approach. It is important, even here, that the horizon of measuring performance for bond factor styles is not shorter than the investment period of intended objectives. Misjudgement in this regard will often bring more pain than joy. The next few sections will define the different styles in government and corporate bonds and how they can be constructed in a systematic way.

10.2 Drivers of Bond Risk and Return

The two common premia in bonds, displayed in Fig. 10.1, are typically linked to interest rate risk (duration risk) and credit risk. These are similar to the traditional equity risk premium (i.e. excess returns of the market over a risk-free rate) and reflect the reward for taking exposure to either high credit risk or to longer-dated bonds, for example. The reward for risk is mostly linked to interest rate and credit cycles, often a reflection of market and economic conditions. Investors are expected to win or lose for taking risks in various market conditions.

Bond factor premia exist for similar reasons to equities as we discussed in earlier chapters—behavioural, market structures and reward for risk. This section provides the debate on three underlying drivers and structures that create the factor premia (Fig. 10.1).

It is no surprise by now to readers that we can over-react or under-react to new information and news. It is human nature to be over-pessimistic about recent losers and optimistic about the prospect of recent winners. We can also be overconfident about our ability to take risks, which sometimes gets us into

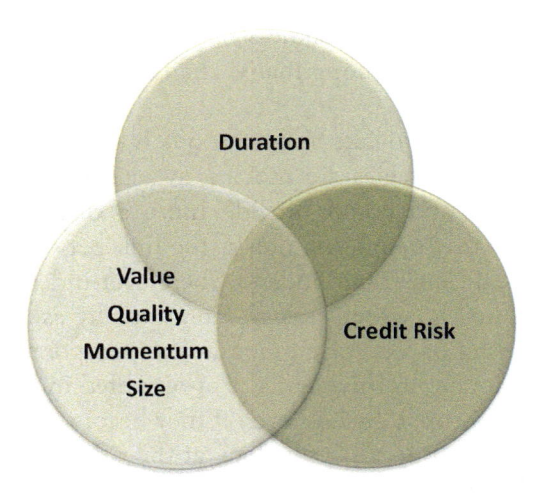

Fig. 10.1 Bond risk premia. Note: For illustrative purposes only

trouble. These behaviours are recurring and deeply ingrained in the investor's decision making.

Also, market structures are at play in the bond market—the way bond markets operate from trading to how assets are managed. Typical examples are stop-loss mechanism when yields and credit spreads rise sharply or simple hurdles to access to markets (local debt markets) or ability to execute trades at competitive prices. Other market structure considerations involve various covenants (collateral or protection to investors) that could reflect various risk and return profiles—senior secured versus senior unsecured or subordinated bonds. Yet, the market risk for bonds tends to vary based on interest rates and the credit cycle.

Interest rate changes are perhaps the centre of gravity for most bond risks. The business cycle tends to produce pro-cyclical interest rates and impacts the supply and demand for bonds as they usually rise during economic expansions and fall during recessions (Fig. 10.2).

The supply of debt is impacted by changes in the borrowing needs of governments, general economic conditions, and inflation expectations. The state of government finances, for example, is just one of the many factors that drive government bond yields: the economic climate and investors' collective risk appetite is important too—often more so. The fact that German inflation is high relative to German yields may not matter to an investor based in Japan,

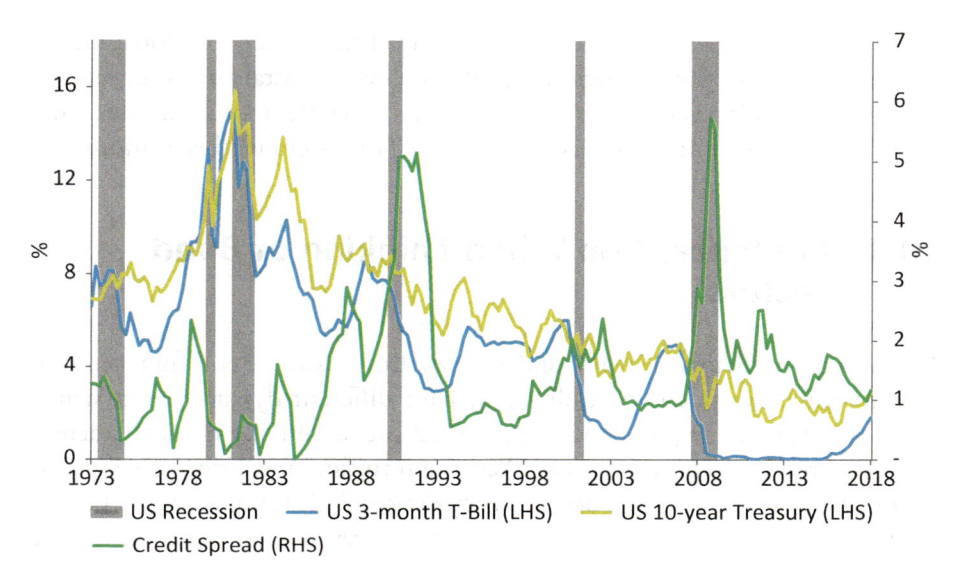

Fig. 10.2 U.S. interest rates, credit spread and recession. Source: The U.S. Federal Reserve Bank of St. Louis, BofAML for U.S. Corporate Index from 1996, NBER, and Author's compilation of historical credit spreads between 1973–1996, Full time period Jan. 1973–Apr. 2018. Note: The 3-month T-bill is a proxy to illustrate the short-term interest rate and the 10-year is a proxy for long-term interest rate in the U.S.

for whom those nominal German yields look attractive relative to local Japanese inflation (assuming the low cost for hedging the currency risk). That said, the prolonged period of low inflationary and deflationary environments in Japan helps explain why Japanese bonds are able to yield 1% in the face of one of the largest debt/GDP ratios in the developed world: the Japanese bond market itself is mostly held by local investors.

The other source of risk and return is the credit cycle. The credit cycle can reflect the ease of access to credit by borrowers and the general condition of the credit market. It is a key driver of bond factor premia across all segments of the fixed income market. The economy goes through an expansionary phase when capital is easily available—with lower interest rates and lending requirements, which are generally supportive for credit markets. Periods of expansion are followed by a contraction phase of credit and capital—often driven by higher interest rates and stricter lending rules. This process continues until lenders revive their confidence to supply capital to borrowers.

Credit cycles are not mutually exclusive from interest rate and business cycles. In the past, downturns in the U.S. was due to either Federal Reserve tightening policy too much, a market crash or both. In all cases the credit cycle downturns were accompanied by business cycle downturns, pushing default rates and credit spreads higher (see Fig. 10.2). Since the global financial crisis, the traditional relationship of the global central banks' monetary policy and credit cycle, by no surprise, has become more complex and erratic—even the central bankers at times struggle to decipher this relationship.

10.3 Misconception When Thinking of Bond Factors

Not all equity factors mirror bond factors. Both asset classes fulfil various objectives in investment portfolios and have different dynamics and structures. Bond factors require tailoring to reflect the underlying bond characteristics (interest rate and credit risk). Yet, the intuition and principles for any factor premium are still valid here—structuring an index strategy according to desired characteristics that are expected to be rewarding or reducing risk over time.

It is important to highlight that no two bonds (even from the same issuer) have the same exposure to interest or credit risk, and this has an impact on the choice and performance of factor strategies. Government bonds are often referred to as "rates products", and rates-based factors may be more applicable in that space. Corporate bonds have a "hybrid" exposure to credit and interest rate risk and are often referred to as "credit products". Corporate bonds are further split into Investment Grade (IG) and High Yield (HY), the latter of which has a higher credit component. Therefore, when considering factors, it is essential to segment the bond market into specific sectors such as developed government bonds, corporate IG, HY and emerging markets or even sub-segments of these markets.

There are grey areas as to whether some strategies in the market constitute a factor. A so-called tax premium (i.e. different tax treatment for different bonds) is not necessarily a factor as the underlying bond characteristics are different to begin with—e.g. municipal bonds versus Treasury in the U.S. or inflation-linked bonds in the U.K. versus conventional bonds. Furthermore, low-interest rate risk (low duration) and "safe haven" (particularly AAA securities or high-quality government bond) bond strategies are not persistent factors and are instead are driven by prevailing market conditions. However, I am yet to be convinced by the argument among many practitioners and researchers that some of the attributes are actually factor related rather than just constituting an asset allocation decision. Neither is the argument that these characteristics are similar to the low volatility factor in equities (in Chap. 6).

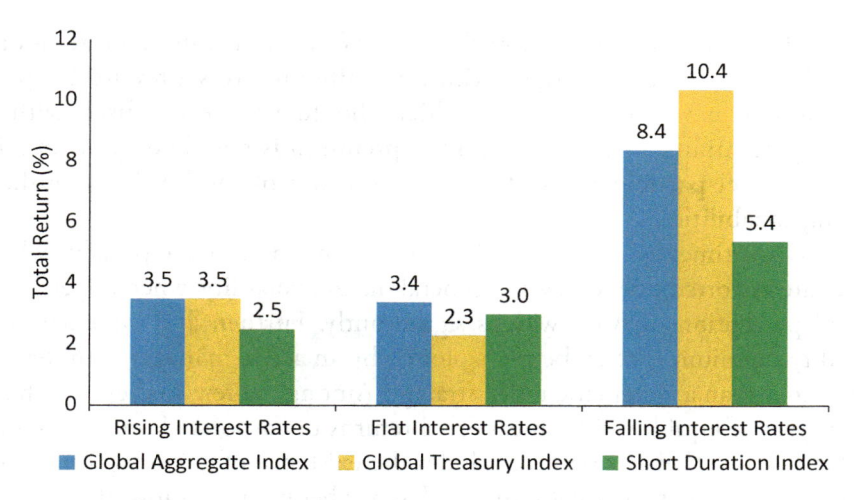

Fig. 10.3 Performance of bond indices in various interest rate environments. Source: Author's calculation, U.S. Federal Reserve, Bloomberg, Bloomberg-Barclays Indices, Mar. 2003–Dec. 2017. Note: The global aggregate, treasury and short duration (1–3 years) are based on Bloomberg-Barclays indices' total returns

In the short-term, low duration will do relatively well when interest rate expectations rise and "safe haven" will do relatively well in a risk-off market environment. Although they may work for a small period of time, in the long-run, this has not necessarily been the case. Also, risk aversion amongst some investors does not make low risk segment a factor, but an asset allocation decision (Fig. 10.3).

Similarly, the difference between long and short-dated bond yields (also referred to as the term spread) has historically been more positive than negative. Long-term interest rates normally offer a high compensation or premium for taking long-term investment risk. This tends to be used interchangeably with the so-called term premium, which is the compensation that investors require for bearing the risk that future short-term Treasury yields do not evolve as they expected. Once again, it is out of scope for this chapter as it fits better under asset allocation, market timing decisions or alternative risk premia, which is covered in the next chapter.

Furthermore, another challenging area revolves around the availability and implementation of liquidity premium in the bond market. In theory, liquidity premium arises due to the lack of availability of pricing information, supply-demand imbalance or small size bond issue. The liquidity can be extended to the price differential between older vintage bonds (off the run) and newly issued bonds (on the run). New bonds can be more liquid than old ones. Investors, large institutions, often receives a reward for participation in new bond issuance, which should not be confused with a liquidity premium. In general, liquidity premium is mainly only accessible to few market participants and requires considerable and well-established trading capabilities.

There are times when the liquidity premium increases, especially when prices are distorted due to news or general market volatility, when buyers' and sellers' perception of price widens significantly. Further, any evidence of a liquidity premium is often better exploited by an active manager with discretion rather than a systematic index strategy. Among the few studies that show the impact of liquidity risk on expected returns of corporate bonds is by Lin et al. in 2011. Their research concludes the existence of a 4% liquidity premium (measured as the total return difference between the most illiquid and liquid bonds) for global corporate bonds over a sample period of 15 years. On paper, it makes sense, but it is far more complicated to trade and implement systematically unless the manager is deeply engaged in trading with robust capabilities and scale. The remaining part of this chapter will give an overview of what we define as a factor and its characteristics.

10.4 What Are the Factors in Bonds?

This section provides an overview of the factor styles in the fixed income space. Fixed income style investing is rich enough to keep researchers and practitioners busy. Many of the styles adopted in the bond factor arena emerged from traditional active management. The typical style in fixed income includes size, quality, value and momentum (see Table 10.1). Some of them received attention in the academic literature—Fama and French in 1992.

In the corporate bond space, not dissimilar to equities, accounting figures are useful measures to reweight a traditional index in order to shift the exposure to the desired characteristics (the ingredients of the factor). Corporate profitability-weighted indices, for example, can be constructed by using each company's profit as a percentage of the total profit from all companies in the index. The forthcoming section provides further insights into the factor styles and the construction of the factor strategies for government and corporate bonds.

Table 10.1 Typical styles strategies in fixed income

	Government bonds	Corporate bonds
Value	Cheap bonds based on fair value or relative value to similar bonds	Cheap bonds based on fair value or relative value to similar bonds
Quality	Credit quality based on government finances and the health of an economy	Credit quality based on corporate finance and creditworthiness
Size	Larger economies based on Gross Domestic Product or low debt	Small bond issues or issuers
Momentum	Short term trends in bonds yields or total returns	Short term trends in bonds yield, spread or total return
Low volatility	Combination of government bond duration and yield to measure risk	Combination of corporate bond duration and credit spread to measure risk

10.5 Government Bond Style Factors

The focus here is on established factors that have been observed by academics and practitioners with logic and economic intuition without going into the art of bond mathematics. Again, to repeat one of this book's messages, the aim is to avoid going down the perils of factors that are coincidental or subject to data mining—transparency, simplicity and common sense are equally valid for implementation and understanding of the underlying drivers of the factor risk and returns. Asness et al. provides an example of this and showed in 2013 that value and momentum are significant factors in government bonds.

The bond factor styles are not new and acknowledged among pure passive and active investment managers. These factors include value, quality, momentum, size and low volatility. The factor styles in government bonds can provide some insight into a country's fundamentals and whether a bond is fairly valued. It can also offer information on the risk and reward. This is particularly useful during volatile markets or uncertainties around credit risk.

During the euro debt crisis from 2010 and years after, bond yields of major European countries, particularly France, Italy and Spain jumped significantly. On a risk-reward basis, these looked attractive. In this particular case, applying a size, quality, value and momentum screen would have given investors a tool to manage their exposure to various risks and potential opportunities that a traditional index may or may not have provided.

10.5.1 Size Factor for Government Bonds

There are many ways of evaluating and alternatively weighting a government bond index instead of using a simple debt-weighting. An intuitive way of deploying a size factor could be through an alternatively-weighted index using the size of the economy. A popular measure of the size factor for government bonds is the Gross Domestic Product (GDP), often used as a measure of economic activity. GDP tells you how much value everyone generated in a country in a given time period—from employees who sell their time to businesses who sell products or services. It adds up the value of all final goods and services. Historically GDP has been used in the events of debt restructuring via so-called GDP-linked warrants by providing investors with income based GDP growth goals. Examples include Costa Rica, Bulgaria, and Bosnia and Herzegovina in the 1980s and 1990s, and later Argentina, Greece, Ukraine and Portugal. A typical bond will adjust its coupon based on GDP growth. Suppose a country has a GDP growth threshold of 3% linked to a bond with coupon ("base coupon") of 5%. If the GDP growth is 4% the following year, then the bond shall pay a coupon of 6% (base coupon plus the excess growth percentage over target). If the GDP growth rate was 2%, then the bond would have paid a coupon of 4% instead.

Suppose a country has been growing in the last few years at an average rate of 4% and is expected to do so in the coming years. Suppose also that this country can issue debt using a bond with a coupon of 8%. This country can issue a GDP-linked bond that pays 8% when growth at the end of the year is exactly 4% it can pay the investors based on its economic performance. For example, if the country grows 1% instead of 4%, then the GDP-linked bond will pay a coupon of 5% instead of 8%. In a scenario of an unusually better economic performance, where the country grows at 6% instead of 4%, then the GDP-linked bond would pay a coupon of 10%.

In this section, we are focusing on the allocation between countries based on GDP, rather than between bond maturities and specific debt instruments in a sovereign bond index. The idea behind GDP weighting is to systematically capture a borrowing country's capacity to repay its debt instead of just weighting the constituents based on the market value of the debt.

The issue of highly leveraged sovereigns and corporates in bond indices came into the spotlight during the global financial and euro area debt crises. Icelandic banks, Greece, Portugal and few other banks and countries were at the epicentre of these crises. It triggered the quest for alternative indexing to manage risk more effectively. Barclays developed benchmark bond indices based on GDP weighing in 2009 followed by Merrill-Lynch. GDP weighting can play an important role for some segments of the sovereign bond space by reducing exposure to smaller economies within a region or globally. However, it does not remove concentration completely to larger developed economies with sizeable GDP such as the U.S., which is about 25% of the world economy.

A typical construction of the nominal GDP-weighted index, similar to Bloomberg-Barclays GDP weighted index uses trailing weighted-average nominal GDP over three years for each country, described in the following steps:

- Calculate as weighted GDP = (1/2) × GDP (t) + (1/3) × GDP (t-1) + (1/6) × GDP (t-2), where t is the most recent observation, and t-1 is the previous year's GDP, and t-2 is the two previous year's GDP.
- Determine the weight of each country using the weighted GDP as a percentage of total weighted GDP of all index members (e.g. weighted GDP for the U.S. / Total Weighted GDP of all countries).
- Rebalanced these target GDP weights on a monthly or quarterly basis (depending on the GDP reporting frequency) throughout the year.

For illustrative purposes, Fig. 10.4 shows the dynamics between debt-weighted and traditional global treasury index. The duration difference as a result of the alternative weighting ranges from 0.5 to 1 year. Although we argue that historical performance is not always a leading indicator of the future, the difference in performance during the sample period is in favour of the GDP-weighted index.

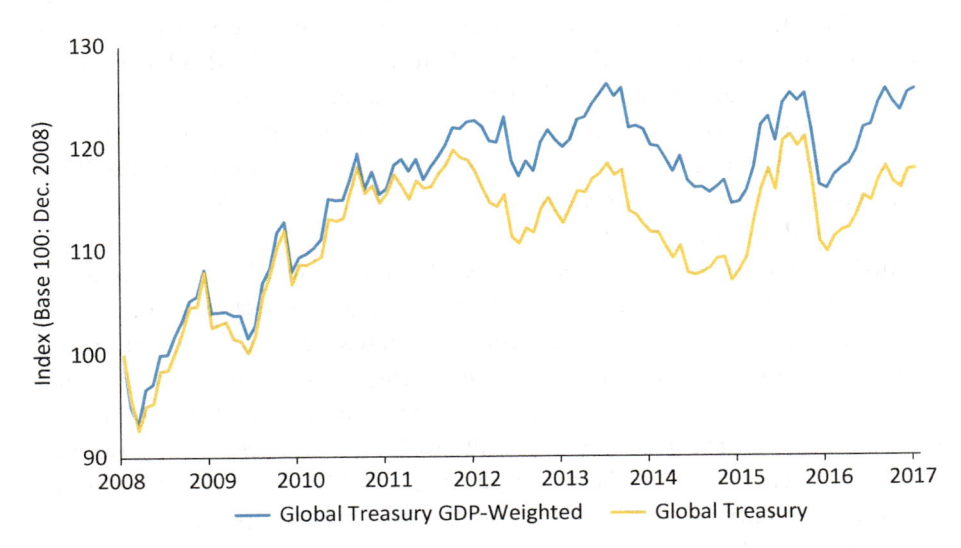

Fig. 10.4 GDP versus debt-weighted global treasuries. Source: Author's calculations, Bloomberg-Barclays index, Dec. 2008–Dec. 2017

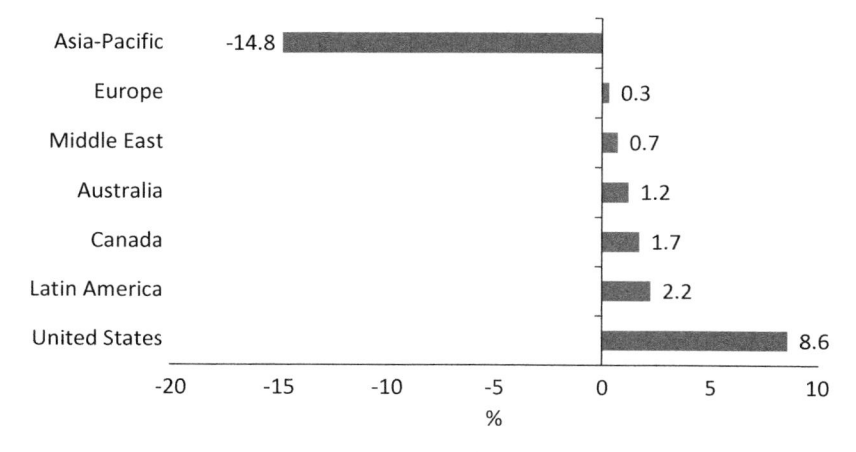

Region	%
Asia-Pacific	-14.8
Europe	0.3
Middle East	0.7
Australia	1.2
Canada	1.7
Latin America	2.2
United States	8.6

Fig. 10.5 Regional difference between GDP and debt-weighted index. Source: Bloomberg-Barclays as at Dec. 2017

The GDP-weighted index presented in Fig. 10.4 increases the allocation to sovereigns with the largest nominal GDP over time. This can help to capture opportunities in regions with an increasing share of the world's growth and vice versa.

The GDP tilt tends to underweight some regions in a global index. Figure 10.5 shows that the Asia Pacific has significant underweight of 15% from the original weight of 32%. The U.S. gains an overweight of 9% from 28%. The increasing concentration would require attention in a GDP-weighted index and often managed through capping the maximum weights to a borrower.

There are some short-falls to GDP-weighting. Generally, the major emerging markets have relatively low debts compared to the size of their economies—Russia's sovereign debt is now below 7% of GDP. Hence, in a debt-weighted index Russia would have a small allocation. However, if the world switched from debt-weighted to GDP-weighted indices, it would increase the demand for countries in emerging markets by the index fund managers aiming to replicate the indices. This can create artificially low yields on these markets in the future.

Further challenges are brought to GDP-weighting. A GDP-weighting scheme may alter the risk-return profile from the benchmark beyond the size factor, for example, through unintended currency exposure and duration. Positive economic growth typically results in higher government bond yields (bond prices lower) and higher inflation expectations—at least in theory. Debt-weighted index strategies, especially in G10 countries, tend to do well in a risk-off environment. At the same time, a GDP-weighted index could increase the relative weight of countries that are enjoying positive economic growth when yields are rising.

Yet, despite the biases that may emerge from GDP-weighting, it can be an effective indexation tool, particularly during debt crisis or for emerging markets, where growth has been a signal of healthier economies which could bring some confidence around the creditworthiness of these countries. While GDP can assist in providing some insight into the health of an economy, a deeper dive into the quality of the borrower can also be meaningful.

10.5.2 Quality Factor for Government Bonds

This section focuses on quality factor characteristics of borrowers in order to capture more current and forward-looking measures of quality. Unlike GDP-weighting, the quality screen provides an overlay or relative metrics to existing credit ratings in the market implemented in an index.

As we mentioned throughout the book, when alternatively weighting a government bond strategy, it is essential to take into account the investment thesis and the reason to deviate from the debt-weighting approach. The keys to the long-term sustainability of government balance sheets are the credibility of fiscal policy and economic growth. In the short-term, these objectives can be in conflict, as higher taxes and lower public spending bite into aggregate demand and impact the perception of the borrowing country.

The primary distinction between bonds and equity is made on the basis of borrowers' credit quality. Sovereigns do not default as frequently as corporates on their debt, but when they do, it grabs the headline news and TV shows. Fresh examples that come to mind are Argentina as a serial defaulter and Greece that restructured its debt. The aim of a sovereign quality screen is to look at the fundamental characteristics to gauge the financial strength to create a rules-based index.

Currently, most investors derive country credit quality assessment from credit ratings set by Standard & Poor's or Moody's and Fitch. In some cases, at least historically, credit rating agencies were either too slow or too fast in reacting to the market and economic developments. For example, some of the rating agencies were too slow to react to the full-blown debt crisis in peripheral Europe in 2010. Later on in 2011, S&P jumped the gun by downgrading the U.S. At that time, even nervous investors felt that a downgraded government as an issuer is still worth investing in even with the fear of a double-dip recession. Instead, the U.S. downgrade hit equity markets, but not the government bonds. That is not to say that rating agencies are the root of all evil. It is simply that both financial markets and rating agencies incorporate information differently when they establish credit risk assessments at various points in time. This has led to some alternatively weighted indices that focus on the fiscal strength of sovereigns.

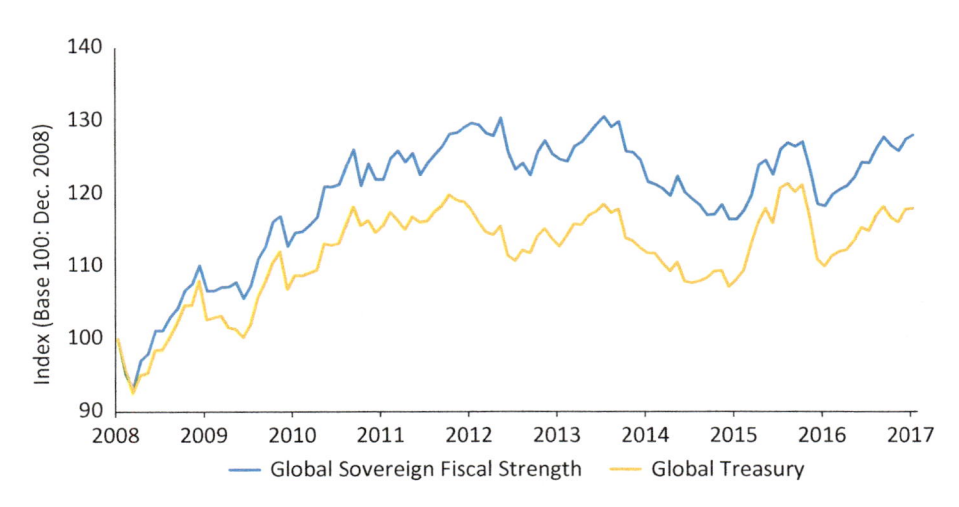

Fig. 10.6 Fiscal strength versus debt-weighted index. Source: Author's calculations, Bloomberg-Barclays index, Dec. 2008–Dec. 2017. Note: The strategies are adjusted for USD market value and duration basis

The Bloomberg-Barclays Fiscal Strength Weighted Indices, for example, further expanded from GDP weighting by tilting to countries with healthy finances in a global index, illustrated in Fig. 10.6. The new index uses measures of financial solvency (debt as a percentage of GDP, the deficit as a percentage of GDP), dependence on external financing (current account balance as a percentage of GDP), and governance to adjust market value weights at the country level. The scores are updated annually. The index is rebalanced monthly to reflect changes in eligible securities for the index.

There is a frequent discussion about whether simply weighting on the basis of debt-to-GDP is a form of quality, and if it is a bad idea on a stand-alone basis. Although this factor strategy did well during the euro debt crisis, it has its limitations. Countries with similar debt-to-GDP can have similar weights although they have different problems. Spain and France are examples. Spain is running a close to 100% debt-to-GDP ratio and is still battling chronically high unemployment, while France is struggling with weak productivity and low wages. Japan is another example which is running a debt-to-GDP ratio in excess of 200%, but a lot of this is internal debt. Of course, this does not consider the high national wealth of Japan and it is still considered a safe haven asset. Hence, it is essential to make additional considerations in the development of weighting schemes for sovereign quality index strategies, which can reduce these biases through a combination of economic indicators.

A quality factor based on government financial and economic characteristics can be integrated into a score-based approach. The score-based approach ranks each country based on its fundamentals, which in turn is used to adjust or "tilt" a debt-weighted index. For example, such scores could be based on fiscal balance (deficit or surplus), level of debt, net foreign assets, GDP growth expectations, debt to GDP and credit default spread. The aim of the scoring approach is to adjust or completely reallocate more or less exposure to the debt of stronger or weaker economies. This approach helps to generate scores that can be used to tilt or optimise an index for a given yield target to capture the quality characteristics in the portfolio construction. A popular example of an index that uses a score-based system is Barclays Financial Strength Index that follows an approach as described below:

1. Calculate the following ratios over 12-month rolling period: (1) Debt/GDP, (2) Deficit/GDP, (3) Current Account/GDP and (4) Country Governance score. The Governance is defined by six pillars: voice and accountability, political stability and absence of violence, government effectiveness, and regulatory quality, the rule of law and control of corruption published by the World Bank.
2. Calculate a composite score (0–10) by averaging across the four characteristics in step 1.
3. Multiply the scores by the market parent index weight (debt-weighted index) to create the fiscal strength index

Arnott et al. at Research Affiliate in 2010 provided more extensive analysis for sovereign emerging market bonds by analysing population, land area (a proxy for resources), GDP, energy consumption (oil, gas, coal and others) to drive a fundamental assessment of the issuers. In their sample period, they achieved a tracking error of 4–7% versus the debt-weighted Merrill Lynch EM Sovereign Index but outperformed on a risk-adjusted basis in the sample period 1997 to 2009.

Another measure of quality in the market is the Credit Default Swap (CDS) spread—the cost of buying insurance against the sovereign default and reflects the market expectations of credit risk. However, CDS are subject to market sentiment and technical factors which do not always synchronise well with the fundamentals of a borrower. A prominent example of this is when the CDS market attributed higher default risk to the U.S. government versus McDonald's in 2008. In reality, it is unlikely that more people would have eaten more burgers if the U.S. had defaulted on its debt back then.

10.5.3 Value Factor for Government Bonds

We discussed the quality of the borrowers in the previous section and its importance. This section extends to value investing for sovereigns. Value investing in fixed income is slightly different as we know it from equities—price-to-earnings and price-to-book do not exist, although the principles to buy outright cheap or relatively cheap bonds is similar here.

Yet, it is not straightforward to pinpoint what constitutes a good measure of value for sovereign bonds in the context of a systematic index strategy unless quality is also taken into consideration. If the global government bond market rewards investors efficiently for the level of risk they take, then in theory, it should factor in high debt levels. Value investing style comes in variations. One way is either through exploiting price dislocation in the market or another based on the concept of mean-reversion (bond yields revert to historical long-term tendency). The general idea here is to form an index strategy that points to whether a specific market is undervalued, fairly valued or over-valued. That is easier said than done due to some challenges.

Developed market government bonds are among the most efficiently traded securities, and any price anomalies tend to be arbitraged away swiftly, often quicker than equities. It is hard, if not challenging to find, inefficiencies in the over USD 9 trillion U.S. Treasury market—the most liquid bond market in the world and the price of the bond reflects the available information.

Typically it is harder to extract pricing anomalies for U.S. Treasuries compared to smaller and less liquid government bonds in developed and emerging markets. Yet, attractive valuations in government bonds can be visible, at least in the short term, simply due to the general market sentiment and geopolitical risks that can distort valuations. Many of the euro area bonds looked attractive, for example, in France due to its banks' exposure to Greece and other peripheral countries in 2012. At that time, even the Italian and Spanish government bonds featured value characteristics on a risk-reward basis. Both markets traded at elevated yields even after the debate moved on from a potential debt restructuring and the implementation of rescue measures.

There are few statistical approaches to construct value factor strategies. The objective of such approaches is to calculate fair-value yield (nominal or real) for a given maturity based on government financials and economic indicators (such as economic growth, inflation and short-term interest rates) to determine what the market is pricing in. The concept is similar to the quality factor but directly linked to the valuation of the bonds with various maturities.

Other simple methods introduced by De Bondt and Thaler in 1985 aims to identify over and undervalued securities by looking at long-term averages. Research by Asness et al. in 2013 suggest using the 5-year change in the 10-year yields, 10-year real yield and term spread (the difference between 10-year and short-dated bonds). In this study, three portfolios were constructed (expensive, fair and cheap) using data from 1982 to 2011 and found the persistence of value in the developed government bond markets. The return from a cheap portfolio in the study outperformed the expensive one by 1.1% per annum and also on a risk-adjusted basis. Their study supported momentum as well, which is the discussion for the next section.

10.5.4 Momentum Factor for Government Bonds

Momentum is the most common factor across all asset classes and segments of the markets as it is mainly focused on price behaviour. Asness et al. 2013 demonstrated the presence of momentum in developed government bonds using 12-month cumulative raw return on the asset. High momentum portfolios outperformed on a risk-adjusted basis over a 29 years sample period for treasuries in the study by Asness et al. in 2013. However, as discussed in the previous chapters on equity markets, momentum tends to have a high portfolio turnover and could erode returns in more illiquid markets due to higher trading activity.

The strategy construction can be done on total return momentum or yields over a formation period of t-6 or t-12 and skip the latest month to avoid price reversal effect. This can be applied for a given maturity bucket. The maturity buckets with yearly intervals can be defined as: 0–3, 3–5, 5–7, 7–10 or 10y+, or with fewer buckets depending on the bond universe and tolerance for duration risk. Other considerations may involve regional, rating buckets and currency denomination.

The selection of the bonds in the index can be based on the 30% of the bonds that exhibit positive momentum or exclude those with negative momentum. Further modification to the approach can be conducted by using alternative weighted schemes (such as equal weighting) discussed in Chap. 3.[1] Momentum will also be discussed in the next section for corporate bond factors as we complete the journey of fixed income factors.

---

[1] Some construction may involve nominal or real yield (nominal yield net of the inflation). The disadvantage of using the nominal yield is that it does not adjust for the inflation rate. However, nominal yield is what investor receives without adjusting for purchasing power. For simplicity, I will focus on the nominal yield momentum as the construction and principle of looking at momentum is similar to real yield.

10.5.5 Low Volatility Factor for Government Bonds

The primary bond risks for high quality issuers emerge through the time to maturity of the bond, which is a known, and the yield. The concept of low volatility is similar to the equity low risk factor that we discussed in Chap. 6 although the approach to constructing the strategies differs. Simple price and return volatility are inefficient for two reasons. First, a bonds' risk (interest rate and default risk) vary over time and often decreases as it approaches maturity. Second, new bonds are issued regularly and are almost immediately included in indices. Obviously, newly issued bonds will not have sufficient historical prices to calculate the risk accurately.

Although the literature is thin on the bond low volatility factor, a studies by Carvalho and his colleagues at BNP Paribas in 2014 uses a measure that does not require historical data to estimate the risk. The risk metrics is Duration-Times-Yield (DTY) defined by Fisher in 2006 as:

$$\text{Modified Duration} \times \text{Yield to Maturity},$$

where modified duration measures the sensitivity of the bond price to changes in the yield to maturity. Fisher showed that DTY is a better representation of bond risk than modified duration and yield to maturity on a standalone basis. Carvalho et al. segments and rank bonds based on DTY in various global sovereign and quasi-sovereign bond markets (U.S. Euro, Japan U.K.). Each bond universe is sliced into quintile and then they apply the market-value weighting for each bucket. An alternative approach is to overweight the market-value weight of the low DTY quintiles and underweight the high DTY quintile by a given basis point deviation tolerance, while the middle quintile maintains its market-value weight (i.e. neutral) in the parent index. Carvalho shows that the low volatility bond factor outperformed the traditional market-value weighted indices between 1997–2012 for major developed bond markets.

The segmentation approach of indices by DTY could provide similar results to segmentation by duration in normal market conditions. However, the difference between DTY and duration ranking is more apparent during volatile market conditions such as equity market corrections and elevated corporate credit spreads.

Investors in the low volatility factor are simply just allocating to short-dated bonds if it is not controlled in the construction process of the portfolio, where the DTY is applied within various maturity buckets. Still, the low volatility strategy may have tracking error to the broad debt-weighted bond benchmark even with maturity bucketing. The next section extends the factor investing strategies into the corporate bond space.

10.6 Corporate Bond Style Factors

In 1992, Fama and French identified key bond factors such as term spread (long versus short-dated bonds), credit spread (high risk versus low risk) and liquidity premium. The style factors for corporate bonds are quite similar to government bonds, although credit risk plays a prominent role, as corporate bonds are generally priced with reference to government bonds. The credit spread of an issuer is in itself a measure of risk premium (or compensation for risk) as it measures the expected return over a government bond of similar maturity. The credit risk and spread of non-IG issuers are higher than for IG issuers.

Credit spread should reflect the price of risk in an efficient market. However, this is not necessarily the case in corporate bond markets as credit spreads are noisy and do not always reflect the "true" default risk of a borrower. Investor behaviour and market structure are often catalysts for this distortion, as well as the depth and size of the market—over USD 35 billion of corporate debt was traded per day in January 2018 alone according to the Securities Industry and Financial Markets Association in an over USD nine trillion corporate bond market size.

This section focuses mainly on the most common and well-understood factors and investment styles among academics and practitioners in the corporate bond space. Similar to government bonds this involves size, quality, value, low volatility and momentum factors. However, the number of fixed income factors is increasing in the literature. Some argue that low volatility in fixed income is a factor through low duration and safe havens. We mentioned earlier that this is very much driven by the sample period, economic cycle and investor's risk appetite. Arguably, this is different from targeting a factor premium within the short duration segment.

Furthermore, it is important to pinpoint that investors are rewarded differently in different market conditions—high-interest rate (long-dated bonds) risk is rewarded during economic slow-down as we established in the government bond section—credit risk is rewarded in benign market conditions, where rates of corporate defaults are close to or below their long-term average. The remaining sections of this chapter look at various factors and how they can be constructed.

10.6.1 Quality Factor for Corporate Bonds

As a general principle, quality aims to measure a borrower's creditworthiness or risk of default and is often deployed as a defensive strategy in bond portfolios. A quality factor targets issuers with quality characteristics to reduce potential market price volatility or loss of the initial investment during the life of a bond.

Once again, the common market standards of quality indicator of corporates are credit ratings from various rating agencies. While credit ratings can provide valuable information, they can be slow to react to market developments and news. That is understandable as the construction of a corporate rating aims to represent less cyclical views of a corporate's credit risk when compared to the market. Yet, changes in credit ratings and outlooks (positive or negative) do impact the market price of the bonds, at least in the short term, and remains a reference of credit quality among many market actors. Typically, downgrade from IG to HY tends to have a short-term impact of price behaviour, which will be discussed in a later section.

Historically, good quality bonds tend to provide a good "store of value" or diversifier during times of market stress. In addition, the quality factor in corporate bonds is often linked to the individual bonds of an issuer compared to equities. Bonds simply have a different risk profile and dynamics due to the capital structures, convents and maturities. Bender and Samanta in 2017 showed a low correlation, about 20% between quality bond and equity.

So what are the characteristics of a quality factor for corporate bonds? Some characteristics include asset and liability measures, profitability and other accounting figures. Again, the scoring framework can be constructed to rank and measure the quality of the borrower using accounting figures (**accounting-based approach**). An alternative way also incorporates market data to estimate the probability of default (**market-based approach**) over the life of the bond.

First, the accounting-based default prediction framework takes into consideration the firm's past performance as a base for predicting the firm's future likelihood of survival. A popular framework and research go back to Edward Altman in 1968, often referred to as Altman Z-score and originally applied on manufacturing companies. Altman's framework has been extended and is still looked at by many in the market, despite its critics of poor predictive power in the current age.

For simplicity, we will focus on the original framework by Altman. The initial research analysed a sample of 33 non-failed and 33 failed U.S. firms listed between 1946–1965 and applied statistical analysis to choose from a basket of 22 accounting ratios, where five of them helped to distinguish between non-failure and failure. The framework classifies a company in one of the following category:

- **Distressed zone** indicated a high risk of bankruptcy and defined by Altman's Z-score < 1.81;
- **Grey zone** indicate neutral on both the risk of bankruptcy or healthy corporate defined as
- 1.81 < Z–score < 2.99;
- **Safe zone (low risk zone)** indicate a healthy corporate with Z-score > 2.99.

The Z-score formula is applied as:

$$\begin{aligned}Z-\text{Score} = &\ 1.2\times\left(\text{Working Capital / Total Assets}\right)\\&+1.4\times\left(\text{Retained Earnings / Total Assets}\right)+3.3\times\left(\text{EBIT / Total Assets}\right)\\&+0.6\times\left(\text{Market Value of Equity / Book Value of Total Liabilities}\right)\\&+1.0\times\left(\text{Sales / Total Assets}\right)\end{aligned}$$

This is one version of Altman's Z-score. There are versions of the formula that are specific to some industries (non-manufacturers), private companies and emerging markets.

To put these approaches into an index strategy, the Altman Z-score can be used to: exclude bond issuers in the "distressed zone", reduce the weight of bonds in the "grey zone" (e.g. by 50%) and increase the weights of the in the "safe zone". For the fundamental-weighted strategies, tilting or the optimisation approach can be applied in the same way as for equities. However, it is essential to ensure that these are applied within similar rating and maturity buckets in order to avoid unintended exposures and risks.

Along the line of Altman's Z-score, a more recent accounting-based application alternatively weights a market benchmark using fundamental characteristics similar to equities—total assets, dividend, cash flow and sales. Arnott et al. in 2010 applied these characteristics on IG and HY. The study showed that a fundamentally weighted strategy on these criteria outperforms the Merrill Lynch indices, but at the cost of tracking error of 1% for IG and 7% for HY.

Moreover, the RAFI quality fixed income index for U.S. HY is more defensive than the general HY market—a beta of 0.8–0.9 compared debt-weighted USD HY index illustrated in Fig. 10.7. During the market volatility in the fourth quarter of 2015, the quality strategy fell by 5% compared to a benchmark such as the Bloomberg Barclays U.S. HY of 6%. The difference in the

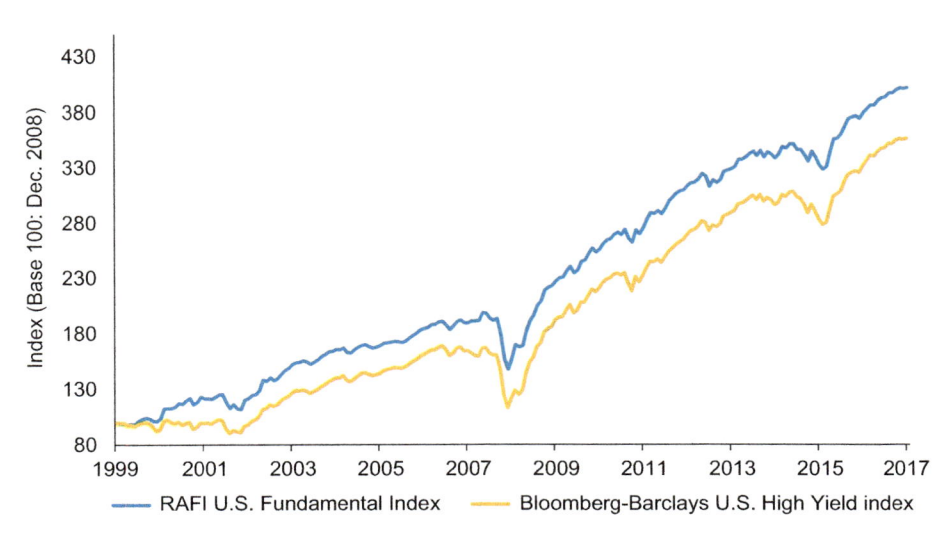

Fig. 10.7 RAFI-HY US versus Bloomberg Barclays U.S. high yield. Source: FTSE-RAFI, Bloomberg-Barclays. The RAFI index focuses on bonds with up to 10-year maturities

drawdowns was more pronounced in 2008—the index fell by 28% against the market benchmark of 37%. By construction, this strategy is expected to act defensively during risk-off market environment and underperform during risk-on market environment.

Second, the **market-based approach** aims to estimate the probability of default of issuers over various future time periods. This approach goes back to Black, Scholes and Merton in the early 1970s, now widely used as a measurement of the risk of debt. Versions of this approach are commercialised today and supplied by Moody's as a measure for expected default frequency, known as Moody's Kealhofer, McQuown, and Vasicek (KMV).

In simple terms, Moody's KMV model estimate how far a company's assets are from its liabilities which provide a distance-to-default estimate. Under this model, a default occurs when the market value of a firm's assets falls below the liabilities as illustrated in Fig. 10.8.

Typical criticism of the distance-to-default approach is the lack of predictive power for companies in the financial sector. This is due to the difference in the importance of liabilities between financial and non-financial institutions. A bank's business model is built on leverage (through borrowing and lending). On the asset value side, the bank's assets are restricted from moving freely as the regulators have minimum regulatory capital standards linked to the bank's equity. However, empirical studies have shown that the distance-to-

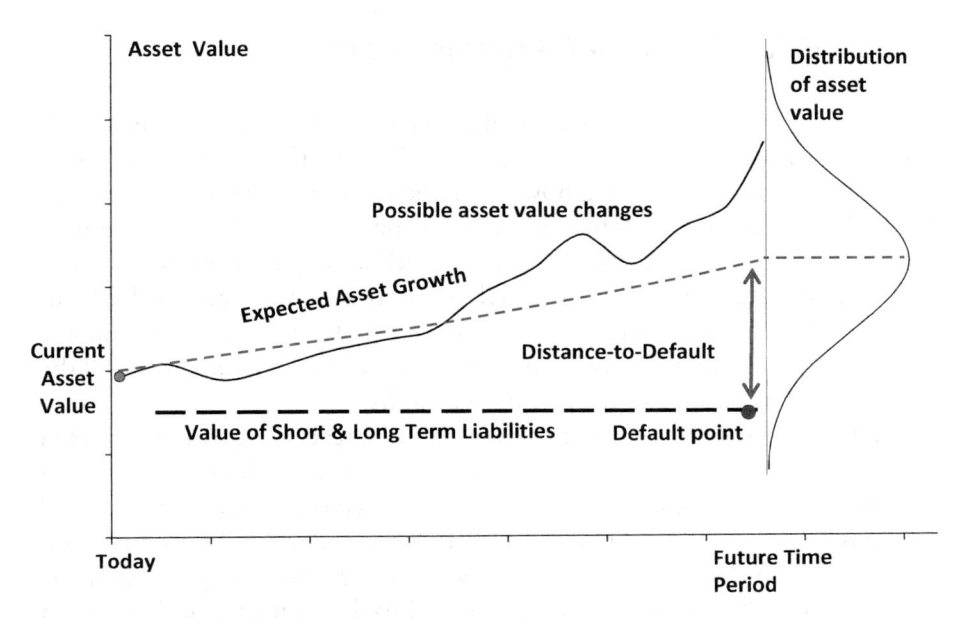

Fig. 10.8 Distance-to-default approach. Note: For illustrative purposes only, Default point is often defined as a combination of short term and long term liabilities (e.g. the total value of short term and half the long term liabilities)

default method can predict the rating downgrades of banks in developed countries and in emerging market countries.

In general, the market-based approach is quicker to react to the changes in a corporation's financial position compared to the accounting-based approach. Whereas the accounting based model only presents lagged financial information and in some instances it may have less predictive power as witnessed during the financial market meltdown in 2008. The academic literature is divided as to which framework works best and how to proceed. Again, even the sun has its spots, and there is no perfect framework. Most approaches have weaknesses and may be ineffective from time to time.

Credit quality prediction assumes that the ratios used are general enough to be applied to various sectors (e.g. the difference between banks and utilities) and markets (developed and emerging markets). However, it is important to keep in mind that predicting default, which is the holy grail of bond investing is difficult. Hence, a common sense approach to investment and construction of the quality factor is often a safer bet.

10.6.2 Value Factor for Corporate Bonds

Buying value means that you are buying a bond at a discount or at least "fair price" with the expectation of being paid during the life of the bond. Credit spreads are a way of measuring how the market perceives credit risk (implied probability of default) today for a particular issuer or bond. They reflect investors' attitudes toward risk over time and could be subject to overreaction to market news. If investors are collectively more risk-averse than usual, like in 2008/2009, they require higher spreads due to a higher risk of default and loss of principal investment. However, market credit spreads do not always tell the "true" credit risk and lag expected future defaults.

The idea is to simply estimate a Fair Value Spread (FVS) from expected default rates using a market-based approach (from the previous section). FVS is then compared to the market credit spreads, which reflect investors' required compensation for taking on the credit risk on particular issuer or bond. Correia et al. in 2012 showed, among other things, that the global market-based approach by Moody's KMV performed well in out-of-sample between 1980–2010. Also, a study by Li et al. in 2012 shows the benefit of a similar approach for IG and HY universe. Figure 10.9 provides a summary of the risk-return of the analysis.

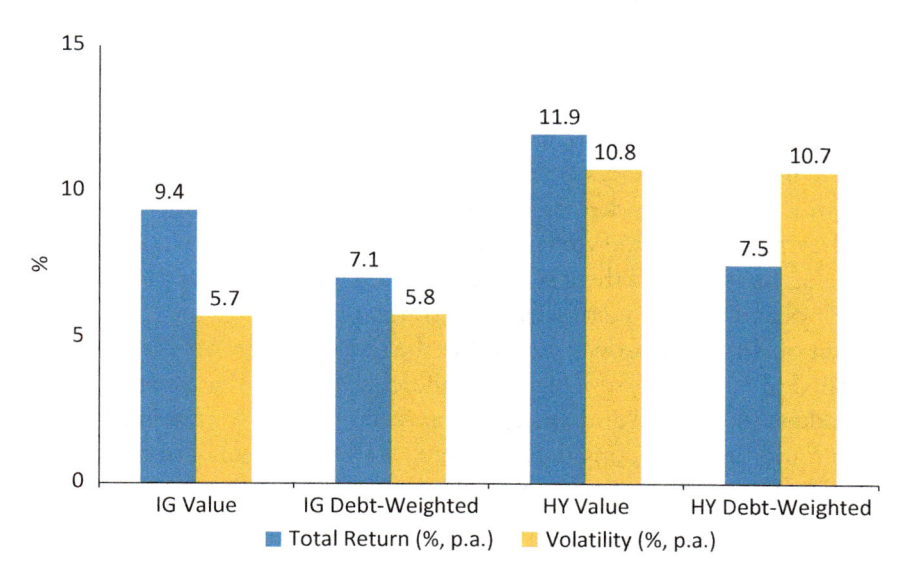

Fig. 10.9 Corporate bond value factor versus debt-weighted bonds. Source: Author's reading from Li et al. (2012), Aug. 1999–Feb. 2012

A market index that adopts a FVS approach was launched by Solactive-Moody's Analytics in 2017. The index intended to reflect the total return performance of a selection of 100 bonds from a debt-weighted index.[2] The bond selection is based on bonds that appear to be undervalued and have relatively low predicted probabilities of default, among a liquid subset of the benchmark. To remove market risk mismatches from the selection, the weights of the interest rate and sector (financial and non-financial) exposure are matched to the benchmark using buckets of maturities and sectors.

Another approach for FVS involves statistical regression using leading indicators such as fundamentals. The idea is to link the company fundamentals to the bond credit spreads. In general, the fair value spread approach has been supported by research and practitioners. Irrespective of the approach, capturing the value premium is more distinguished in HY compared to the IG space. If a value factor is deployed in the IG space, it is essential to make sure that unintended duration and credit risks emerge as not all value bonds are quality. It goes back to the value trap debate from the equity section.

Another method is the relative value analysis, where bonds that are identified as cheap (higher credit spread) or expensive (lower credit spread) relative to other bonds belonging to the same issuer or credit risk profile, taking into account duration or other risks which may justify the pricing difference. The bonds which are cheap are then given a higher weight relative to those that are expensive, with the expectation that the differences will mean revert. In practice this requires specialist knowledge, to investigate whether these are genuine mispricings, and the opportunities may be too ephemeral in order to implement into a rules-based strategy.

Other dimensions of particular value strategies are related to credit downgrades of companies, particularly fallen angels. In theological terms, a fallen angel is one who has rebelled and been exiled from heaven. In financial markets, it is a bond or issuer that has been expelled from the IG universe. Historical examples are General Motor's, Tesco or Telecom Italia.

When a bond is downgraded by a major rating agency, it often implies that the business is suffering in some shape or form, either from a weakening financial position, or a loss in revenues and/or market share that could have an impact on the issuer's ability to service their debt. When a company's debt is downgraded below IG, it no longer remains a constituent of IG benchmarks.

Over the medium-to-long term, the fallen angel issuer has the opportunity to recover from the downgrade, by regaining financial strength and being upgraded. The fallen angel may improve its ability to navigate balance sheet

---

[2] The value-quality index is called Solactive Moody's Analytics IG EUR Select Credit Index.

challenges, or its assets may become more valuable. The bottom line is that these issuers have a high incentive to regain their IG status in order to maintain a low cost of capital over the longer term.

Prior to a fallen angel downgrade, the bond or the issuer may be placed on negative "credit watch". As individual rating agencies issue downgrades, this can lead to selling pressure that makes the underlying bond prices fall. Historically, the price of a fallen angel bond starts to underperform the IG universe in the months before the downgrade. The price behaviour is illustrated in Fig. 10.10. A lot of investors cannot hold the bonds following a downgrade, typically due to investment policy restriction and are often selling where prices are artificially low.

As selling pressure dissipates, the price of the fallen angels typically recovers partially or entirely within 3–6 months after the downgrade. Thus, by continuing to hold fallen angel bonds after the downgrade, investors have the opportunity to benefit from price reversion and outperformance versus the investment grade universe.

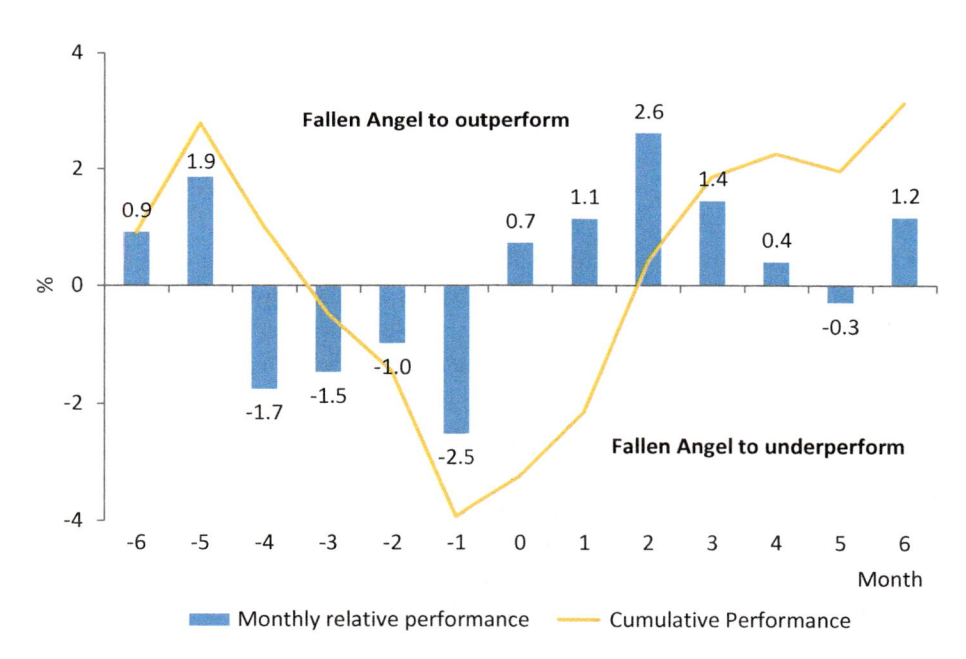

Fig. 10.10 Fallen angel performance relative to investment grade. Source: King and Zaher (2017), LGIM, Markit, iBoxx, Bloomberg, Jan. 2012–Feb. 2012. Note: Price changes are calculated based on the average of all prices for 64 GBP fallen angels that entered the index during the sample period

The increased demand for high yield bonds and the supply of fallen angels have had a pronounced effect on the fallen angel premium globally. Yet the evidence is still there for GBP, EUR and USD corporate bonds.

10.6.3 Momentum Factor for Corporate Bonds

Momentum in IG and HY bonds is gaining interest among practitioners. Studies and evidence point to the existence of momentum premium in the corporate bond space, more so in the HY segment. In principle, behavioural driver, market structures as well as a reward for risk sit at the heart of the momentum factor—not dissimilar to what was described in the equity section about herd bias and inclination to follow the herd. Hong and Stein (1999) attribute momentum to "information frictions" (i.e. imperfect information) related to the gradual diffusion of information particularly in the high-risk spectrum of the bond market where information may be harder to interpret.

In terms of construction, corporate bond momentum is similar to government bond construction, where a formation period can be used on total returns. For example, each month, bonds are sorted into deciles or quartiles of the winners based on their cumulative returns from the past six or 12 months excluding the last month to avoid potential biases from short-term price reversal.

A study by Jostava et al. in 2013 shows the significance of momentum in a comprehensive sample of 81,491 for U.S. corporate bonds with both transaction and dealer-quote data from 1973 to 2011. The study shows that momentum is driven by HY bonds. The role of momentum has increased over time along with the growth of the HY market (Fig. 10.11).[3] From 1991 to 2011, the high momentum outperformed the low momentum by 10 basis points per month for IG bonds and 192 basis points for HY bonds (defined as non-IG in Jostova et al.). Momentum persisted even after adjusting for the duration in the sample. However, in a subsample (between 1973–1990) momentum performance was driven mainly by IG bonds. Hence, the strength of the momentum may vary over time between segments in the corporate bond market.

In addition, the study shows that: momentum performance is persistent even after transactions costs with a turnover of 10–20% per months. The turnover tends to increase for HY bonds, which is more volatile than the IG

---

[3] Over 1973–1990, only 10% of bonds are non-investment grade versus 22% over 1991–2011.

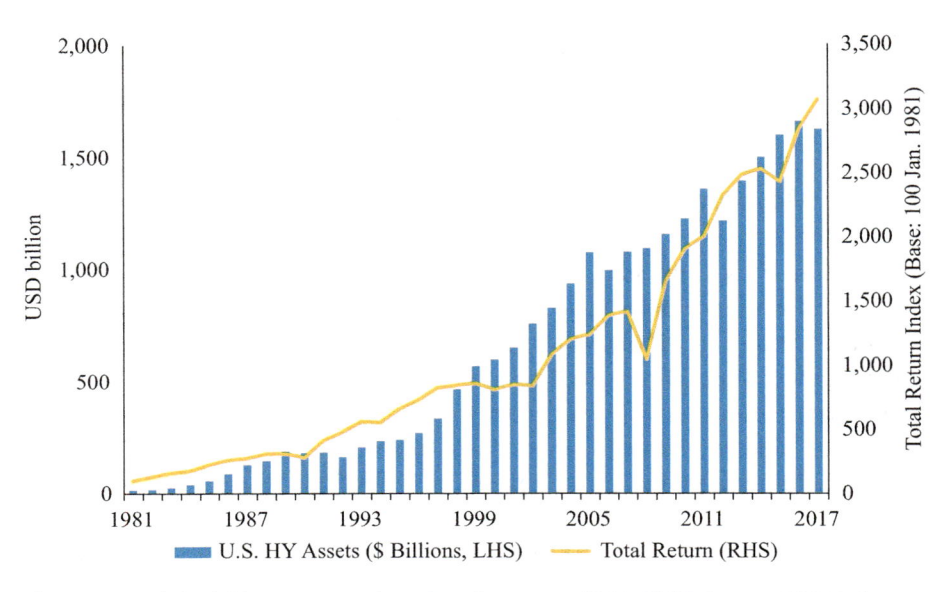

Fig. 10.11 High yield asset growth and performance 1981–2017. Source: NYU Salomon Center estimates, Credit Suisse, Citi Bank, Barclays data, 1981–2017

siblings. Interestingly, the correlation between general corporate bonds (IG and HY) and equity momentum is low—about 34% during the sample period.

10.6.4 Size Factor in Corporate Bonds

In Chap. 8 we looked at the market capitalisation of stocks as a measure to gain exposure to the size factors, while in the corporate bonds space it is simply looking at the smallest debt issuers in the bond universe. The rationale for the existence of such premium is not dissimilar to equities—companies with lower debt levels are likely to outperform the more leveraged ones.

A simple way to construct the size factor for corporate bond portfolios is to increase allocations to bonds from the same issuer with smaller issue size (outstanding amount), by reducing allocations to bonds with higher issue size—i.e. issuer-neutral. Alternatively, we can re-weight the bond universe by the outstanding amount irrespective of the issuer.

Houweling and Zundert in 2017, among the few academic studies, shows that the size premium exists for corporate bonds. In their study they showed that smaller corporates debt issuers tend to do better than those with higher debt on a risk-adjusted basis—both within the IG and HY universe during the sample period of just over 21 years of data sampling (Fig. 10.12).

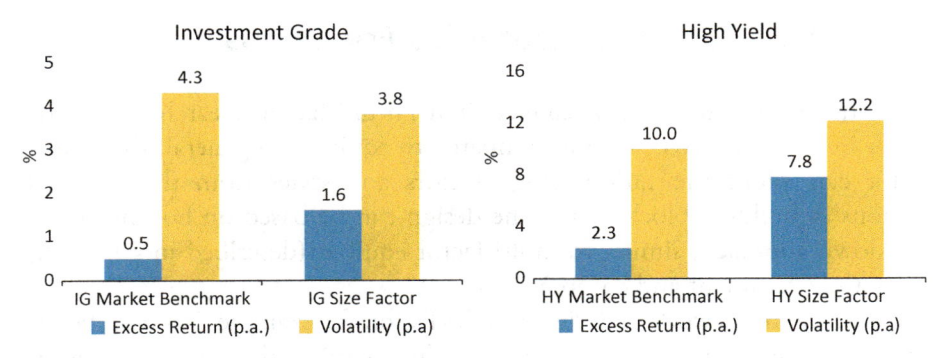

Fig. 10.12 Size factor for investment grade and high yield between 1994–2015. Source: Houweling and Zundert in 2017, Table 3 in the research paper, Jan. 1994–Jun. 2015. Note: The excess return is the size factor return over duration-matched Treasury bonds

The result from the study is consistent even when adjusting for sectors, ratings and maturity. However, it is important to note that risks and returns are partly influenced by the fact that smaller bonds tend to be less liquid relative to the largest bond issues.

10.6.5 Low Volatility Factor for Corporate Bonds

The logic for the low volatility factor corporate bonds is similar to government bonds that we discussed earlier in Sect. 10.5.5, with a minor difference. Instead of using DTY, it uses Duration-Times-Spread (DTS), which is similar. DTS takes into account the sensitivity of the bond price to credit risk and defined as follows:

$$\text{Spread duration} \times \text{Option} - \text{Adjusted Spread},$$

where the spread duration measures the bond price sensitivity to changes in credit spread and option-adjusted spread is the credit spread adjusted for any optionality embedded in the bonds in an index. DTS could imply that low credit spread and long-dated bonds have as much credit risk as high credit spread and short-dated bonds.

Similar to DTY, the segmentation approach of indices by DTS could provide similar results to segmentation by spread duration in normal market conditions, but differently when corporate credit spreads widen during market volatility. Carvalho et al. in 2014 showed the relative outperformance of using DTS characteristics in the low volatility factor strategy for major developed corporate bond markets (IG, HY and emerging markets) between 1997–2012.

10.7 Multi-Factors Strategies For Bonds

Very little development has taken place in the multi-factor research and multi-factor investing in fixed income compared to equities. In general, the multi-factor can adopt the various single-factors and styles from the previous sections as building blocks. Also, the design can be based on bottom-up or top-down approach, similar to multi-factor equities (described in Chap. 9), for both government and corporate bonds.

A starting framework to design a multi-factor, for example, is a dual-factor approach which combines quality and value as value alone may not mean much in fixed income. Good value might not mean high quality. Hence, combining quality and value can help to ensure that bonds that appear as value are not distressed as well as evaluate how the market is pricing the bonds relative to their underlying fundamentals.

A common way of combining quality and value for corporates is to compare a quality-based credit spread (fair-value spread based on a model) with market credit spread (what the market is pricing in). In this case, a quality score or a fair value spread is estimated using fundamentals, which is compared to the market pricing. The quality aspect can be used to remove poor quality issuers—e.g. remove issuers with the highest probability of default, using the approach mentioned in the previous section.

Some fund managers combine value and low volatility (a strategy by Quoniam) or momentum and quality (a strategy by Deka). Among the few strategies in the market that combines more than two factors is the Robeco QI Global Multi-Factor Credits strategy which focuses on value, momentum and low-volatility with at least BB-rating or better aiming to provide a balanced factor exposure. More are likely to follow as multi-factor is yet to make it into the mainstream market as more single factors are developed.

10.8 Considerations When Building Bond Factors

Bond factor strategies are typically more expensive for investors due to the nature of the implementation complexity, higher transaction costs on the back of lower liquidity and the lack of a broad short market, aside from government bonds. When it comes to the implementation of factor strategies, returns need to be scrutinised to ensure that the cost does not eat too much into the returns and the benefit that the investor is achieving from the strategy.

Factor-based ETFs tend to have higher implicit fees than ETFs tracking a debt-weighted index since they have more complex strategies to execute and often experience higher turnover, as they deviate from the bond market benchmarks. These funds must overcome these cost differences to outperform their passively managed counterparts, which can be a high hurdle to surmount in an increasingly efficient bond marketplace. Hence, investors should always be cognisant of these fees when comparing their fund options.

Additionally, consideration needs to be given to unintended exposure to currency, interest rate or credit risk as part of the design of the bond factor strategy. Alternatively-weighted indices are prone to this. For example, when weighting bonds or issuer by GDP or another fundamental method, the exposure to duration may be significantly different from the benchmark. One method to alleviate this is to use a tilted or optimised approach, where the market value weight of a bond is adjusted based on its exposure to a factor.

Investing in fragmented bond markets is another major challenge. The level of expertise required to deliver factor or alternatively-weighted strategies successfully is unlikely to change anytime soon. Long only portfolios are the most common ways to gain factor exposures in fixed income, especially in the corporate bond space.

Today, the majority of the corporate bond market still trades over the counter. Limited liquidity in some markets and lack of readily available data are few reasons for slower asset growth in the bond alternatively-weighted space. While liquidity may be low in some segments of the fixed income market, the improved bond market transparency brought on by Trade Reporting and Compliance Engine introduced by the Financial Industry Regulatory Authority, the digital age and electronic trading is likely to help the future evolution of the bond market and fixed income factor investing.

10.9 Concluding Remarks

A factor strategy does not need to have the kitchen sink thrown at—it can be kept simple and meaningful, as I hope we showed in this chapter. We discussed a common set of factor styles in fixed income and showed how they: can serve different purposes; can be used as a tool to understand borrower trends; and characteristics that drive their risk and return profile.

Research has been complemented by the efforts of the investor community to translate factor investing into investable and implementable fixed income strategies. However, the same factors that produce factor premia in one market may not work in another (e.g. developed versus emerging markets or government versus investment grade and high yield).

Readers must be familiar by now with the fact that factors are cyclical even for bonds. It makes sense for a strategic fixed income investor to combine these various factors—similar to equity multi-factor. This could be the third generation type of development in the fixed income factor space. But the second generation is yet to come on the single-factor front. It will simply become more accessible and available on the shelves for investors to implement in the coming years.

11

Multi-Asset: Alternative Risk Premia

Previous chapters discussed factor investing and associated risk premia in long-only equity and bond portfolios. As an extension of the traditional Factor-Based investing, more sophisticated strategies would historically serve as a foundation to hedge funds. In the late 1990s, research showed that some hedge fund returns could be systematically captured through the approach known today as Alternative Risk Premia (ARP), or alternative beta. By now, over USD 300 billion are invested in ARP globally as we understand and practice these strategies more efficiently.[1]

ARP is a development from long-only factor investing in bonds and equities. It branches out to commodities and currencies among other areas of financial markets. There is no clear definition of ARP in the literature and among practitioners. Simply speaking, it is a collection of a broad range of non-traditional risk premia.[2] Similar to traditional market risk and factor premia, ARP is also a compensation for taking systematic risks in financial markets (Fig. 11.1). The premia can be driven by economics, market anomalies, behavioural biases, general market structures. The widely used investment techniques to extract these premia involve long and short trading between two securities, indices or markets. The ARP strategies often involve a degree of leverage through a range of derivatives (e.g. futures and options or swaps).

In the past decade, the relationship between traditional asset classes got distorted by crises, low-interest rate environment and central bank policies

---

[1] Based on a survey of 200 institutional investors by The Economist Intelligence Unit on behalf of BlackRock in January 2016.
[2] Arguably, there are plenty of ARP strategies (e.g. in equities) that are "alternative" simply by taking a traditional style premia and implementing it in a market neutral way.

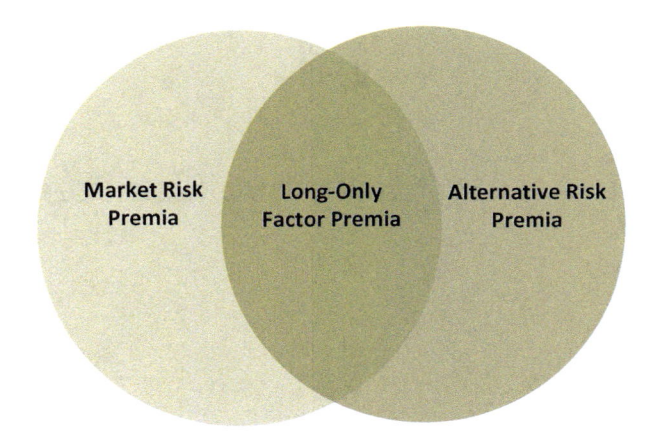

Fig. 11.1 The commonality of risk premia. Note: For illustrative purposes only

globally. Asset classes became more (positively) correlated, posing challenges in finding liquid, diversified strategies. Faced with this challenge, ARP can assist in providing uncorrelated sources of return to traditional asset classes and general markets.

However, the ARP may still have a degree of exposure to macro risk factors as well as style-specific risks (e.g. value, momentum or carry), and they are subject to behavioural biases and investment constraints such as leverage. For example, the term spread premium (the long-dated versus short-dated bond spread) can be explained by investors demanding higher compensation for exposure to inflation risk and long investment horizon. Similarly, investors in corporate bonds expect to be compensated for taking higher credit risk when allocating between bonds with various credit quality (IG versus HY).

The ARP is a very broad concept and provides exposure to many risk factors and asset classes. It is important to recognise that not all premia are easy to harvest, especially in areas where the strategy is specialised, discretionary and proprietary to the managers. These types of strategies are often discretionary and proprietary and not generally available in an index or transparent fund vehicles due to the inherent degree of complexity. For the benefit of this chapter, the selection of the presented premia is transparent and straightforward, without enforcing unnecessary complexity on the subject. Of course, some simplifications are more challenging than others, depending on the area of application.

This chapter aims to provide insight into the theory and practicality behind ARP strategies. The focus is narrowed to the segment of ARP strategies that have academic roots and allow for systematic implementation in portfolios.

This chapter further bridges the different worlds of financial theory and practical experience, while offering an interdisciplinary framework in risk premia across multiple asset classes. Some of it has been covered in previous chapters but linked into one piece here.

11.1 Why Are We Thinking of ARP?

The increasing adaptation of ARP is driven partly by the opportunity of systematically harvesting the returns of hedge funds through long/short style investments—e.g. carry trades are among the most important alternative beta strategies that can now be accessed through ARP funds. This does not require a "black box" and allows assessing the sources of returns of hedge fund and Commodity Trading Advisor (CTA) strategies in portfolios. CTAs are systematic trend-following funds that rely on derivatives for implementation.

Hedge funds typically have more complex structures and exposures than a traditional long-only mutual fund. In a study by Hasanhodzic and Lo in 2007 and more recent ones showed that a significant fraction of hedge fund returns could be explained by various risk factors for 1610 funds between 1986–2005. While the performance of linear clones is often inferior to their hedge-fund counterparts, they perform well enough to warrant consideration as a simple index—a transparent, scalable, and lower-cost alternative to hedge funds.

Over time, interest in ARP strategies with a focus on systematic rules-based implementation has grown. Adopters of ARP include various institutions such as pension funds, sovereign wealth funds, endowments, insurers, asset allocators and lately wealth managers. Surveys indicate the increasing interest in these strategies. The 2017 survey from bFinance suggests that ARP have been the area of greatest investor interest.[3] Deutsche Bank reported survey results showing that the percentage of respondents who allocate to ARP increased to 26% in 2017, up from 20% in 2015.[4] Nearly half of all pension fund respondents reported allocating to ARP, which is nearly double the proportion observed in the prior year's survey. A recent survey from Morgan Stanley Prime Brokerage reports that 79% of investors with more than USD 5 billion in alternative investments such as hedge funds are currently allocated to, or considering an investment.[5] This growth is expected to continue as the

---

[3] "15th Annual Alternative Investment Survey," Deutsche Bank (March 2017).
[4] "Manager Intelligence and Market Trends," bFinance (February 2017).
[5] "Recent Hedge Fund Trends," Morgan Stanley Prime Brokerage-Strategic Content Group (July 2017).

strategies are becoming increasingly available through systematic implementation in a cost-efficient manner.

It is important to keep in mind that ARP is not just about alpha. Alpha is still defined and derived from the skills and ability of the manager to generate returns over the index benchmark strategies. Some hedge funds are specialised (e.g. sector specific, illiquid securities) and are able to extract alpha in specific markets that cannot be harvested systematically.

The ARP debate among researchers and professionals is around the ability to reduce exposure to market directions as a backdrop of slowdown in economic activity. Market volatility remained low on average through the bull market post the 2008 financial crisis. Concerns over a potential slowdown of economic activity and stretched valuations are fuelling the search for flexible and diversified investment strategies that can adapt to changing markets. Today more investors are looking for a systematic way to capture a premium regardless of market directions. ARP strategies can assist in this objective, as we will discuss later in this chapter.

Many ARP strategies (e.g. long and short-based strategies), especially the ones that tend to reduce exposure to market direction, have historically exhibited low correlation with the traditional asset classes, For example, a value-tilted portfolio will often consider a single security (bond or equity) with the best scores that best meets defined value characteristics. A long-only value factor portfolio will most likely be correlated with a traditional market value-weighted index as the underlying assets are heading in the same direction. However, many ARP strategies have historically displayed a low correlation to traditional asset classes (Table 11.1). The benefit of ARP lies in its ability to reduce market exposure and still provide investment returns. This is a valuable feature in adverse market conditions.

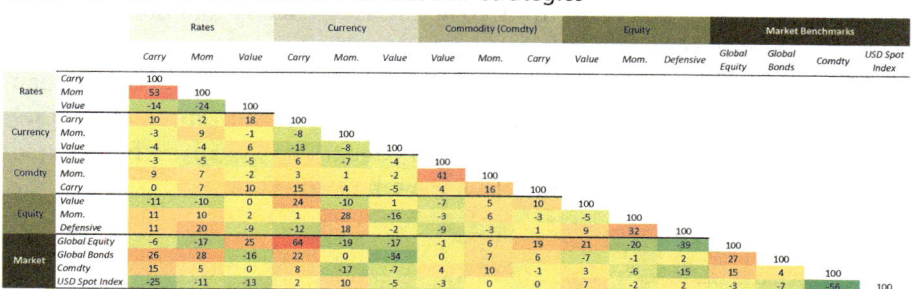

Table 11.1 Correlation between various ARP strategies

		Rates			Currency			Commodity (Comdty)			Equity			Market Benchmarks			
		Carry	Mom	Value	Carry	Mom.	Value	Value	Mom.	Carry	Value	Mom.	Defensive	Global Equity	Global Bonds	Comdty	USD Spot Index
Rates	Carry	100															
	Mom	53	100														
	Value	-14	-24	100													
Currency	Carry	10	-2	18	100												
	Mom.	-3	9	-1	-8	100											
	Value	-4	-4	6	-13	-8	100										
Comdty	Value	-3	-5	-5	6	-7	-4	100									
	Mom.	9	7	-2	3	1	-2	41	100								
	Carry	0	7	10	15	4	-5	4	16	100							
Equity	Value	-11	-10	0	24	-10	1	-7	5	10	100						
	Mom.	11	10	2	1	28	-16	-3	6	-3	-5	100					
	Defensive	11	20	-9	-12	18	-2	-9	-3	1	9	32	100				
Market	Global Equity	-6	-17	25	64	-19	-17	-1	6	19	21	-20	-39	100			
	Global Bonds	26	28	-16	22	0	-34	0	7	6	-7	-1	2	27	100		
	Comdty	15	5	0	8	-17	-7	4	10	-1	3	-6	-15	15	4	100	
	USD Spot Index	-25	-11	-13	2	10	-5	-3	0	0	7	-2	2	-3	-7	-56	100

Source: Author's calculation based on data from Kenneth French database, Jan. 2001–Dec. 2017, and various ARP indices from investment banks and Bloomberg, author's construction, Jan. 2001–Dec. 2017

With the growing interest in these strategies, the implementation part in the portfolios has become increasingly important. Historically, ARP was mainly considered for constructing specific hedges but is now regarded as an asset allocation tool. Due to some benefits of these strategies (e.g. low correlation to various markets), ARP offers a new way of thinking about diversification in portfolios, particularly since traditional asset classes have exhibited high correlation levels since the global financial crisis. With this in mind, the ARP is increasingly used as a part of asset allocation to provide diversification in multi-asset portfolios and to blend in new sources of returns beyond the traditional market risk premium.

This extends to portfolio construction in asset and liability management where ARP is used as a building block to meet long-term liabilities through growth and optimal asset allocation. This brings a new tool, for example, to "target date" funds (a type of retirement fund with decaying investment risk profile as members approaches retirement age) in the growth and de-risking investment phase.

Not surprisingly, while moving more towards indexed solutions (ETFs and mutual funds), ARP strategies are likely to serve as building blocks among asset allocators and wealth managers who are increasingly looking for cost-effective solutions and aim to stay competitive and relevant to their client base.

11.2 Fund Manager Types in ARP

Traditional long/short strategies in factors have been established academically and are transparent and straightforward in nature. In the ARP domain, the long and short exposure of factors intersects falls within equities and extends to other asset classes. Unlike cash strategies (physical assets) these are often implemented via derivatives: on an index, bespoke portfolio or single-line securities. There are various types of ARP managers in the market. For simplicity, they can be categorised as follows:

Traditional asset managers (factor long/short): Focus on well-established academic factors (value, momentum, size) in equity and extended into other asset classes such as fixed income as a main source of returns. The stock selection is based on factors such as value, momentum, size or quality characteristics, where the manager goes long one security versus another.

Macro managers: Focus on momentum and trend-following across asset classes as the main source of returns. Macro managers aim to source their returns through long or short trades and dynamic asset allocation and fundamental economic data. A typical trade within macro managers is trend-following strategies across asset classes or a currency value trade.

Commodity Trade Advisor (CTA) managers: May include features of macro fund strategies that follow a trend while reducing or maintaining low exposure to market direction. The difference from Macro fund managers is the way CTAs exploit and identify the trends by using computer algorithms. Other CTA trades may include pair-trading (long-short positions to benefit from the convergence between two securities).

The list of common strategies among various types of managers is broad: momentum (long securities with rising trends and short the falling ones); value (long cheap securities and short expensive ones); carry (long high yielding assets and short low yielding ones); and finally, low volatility (aims to harvest premiums from implied and realised volatility differential). In the next sections, we will focus on ARP strategies emerging in the traditional asset management bucket and implemented systematically in a transparent and liquid fashion.

11.3 Taxonomy of ARP Strategies

As mentioned earlier, risk premia are distinct from traditional sources of market exposure (e.g. equity and bond beta) and different from "true" alpha (e.g. market timing and security selection skills). Figure 11.2 provides a high-level map of ARP strategies. Some are more established than others among academics and practitioners. The list is not exhaustive, but a few of these will be central to the remaining sections of the chapter.

This section groups the risk premia based on their styles across asset classes to facilitate portfolio construction and target specific objectives (low risk or income).[6] The increasing availability and complexity of ARP strategies, which extend beyond bonds and equities, bring some challenges. It is important to keep in mind that different strategies provide different outcomes in portfolios. Under the presumption that an ARP strategy is well-designed and implementable, the allocation to ARP comes down to investors' beliefs and the portfolio fit.

---

[6] For a more insight into ARP strategies and technical treatment, see Hamdan et al. from 2016.

11 Multi-Asset: Alternative Risk Premia

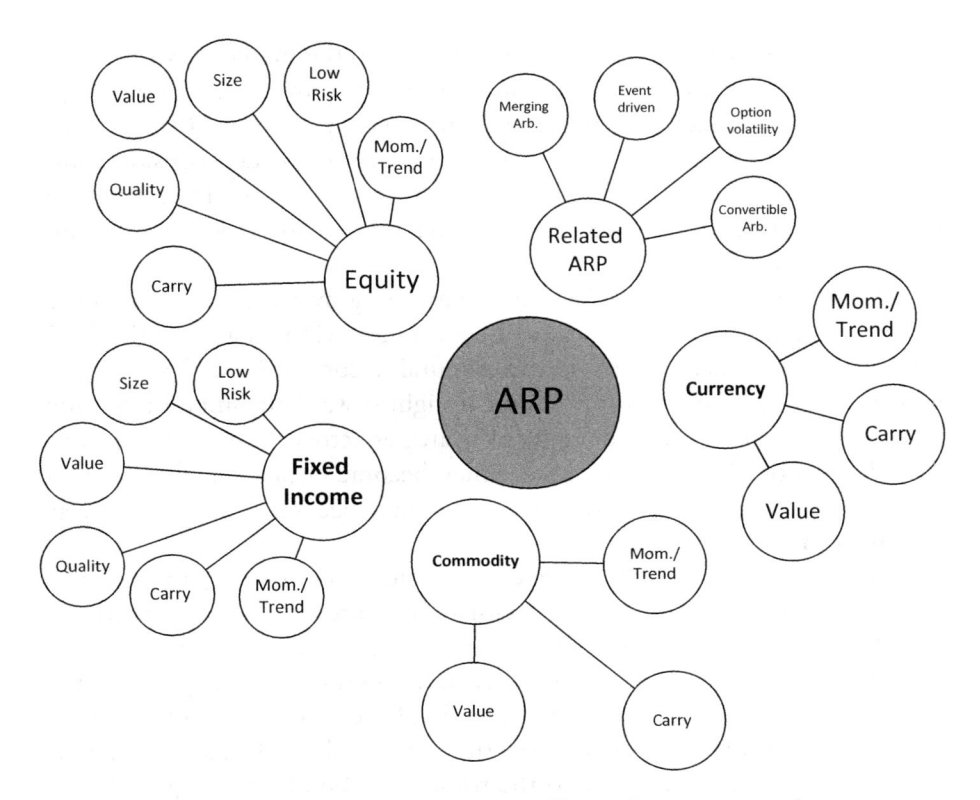

Fig. 11.2 Branches of ARP strategies. Note: For illustrative purposes only

Some ARP strategies may involve complex implementation through options, which can sometimes be hard to extract systematically or may require high leverage. Some other strategies (such as merger arbitrate or specific EM strategies) are also difficult to extract and may require a discretionary oversight for efficient implementation. Historically, the majority of the available rules-based indices in the ARP space are designed and implemented through investment banks that tend to provide access to derivatives implementation.

One of the objectives of the book is to focus on simple, transparent and well-established risk premia strategies. These premia are well-researched by economic intuitions in currencies, commodities and fixed income market. Many of the equities and physical bond strategies are left out from this chapter as we discussed them in previous chapters. The factor equity and bond premia effectively imply going long the factors that investors are expected to be rewarding over time and short those that are not (e.g. bottom 30% securities subject to poor factor characteristics).

By design, many of the strategies are agnostic to the market environment, and some involve directional views (such as momentum or trend following). The exact impact is likely to depend on the manager's positioning (e.g. amount of net long or short) at a different point in time. An important consideration in this chapter is to, again, focus on medium to long-term strategies (three years or longer). Short-term strategies for ARP that involve market timing are not part of this chapter.

The systematic ARP strategies can be rewarding over time, similar to the physical (long-only) factor strategies discussed in previous chapters. The ARP across various asset classes exists for behavioural reasons and imbalances in the markets. Nevertheless, it is not always straightforward to pinpoint specific drivers common to the entire family of strategies across the asset classes. For example, equities in a specific market may become cheaper in the short to medium-term while the underlying currency may become more expensive at the same time.

Within these areas, ARP strategies are segmented in value, momentum (trend-following), carry, size and defensive. This provides a combination of some ARP strategies that can be deployed on a stand-alone basis or as a combination into portfolios. Some currency and commodity strategies are discussed in later sections, particularly those that have theoretical and empirical foundations. The intent is not to repeat the equity and bond factor discussion, as it should be self-explanatory to the reader that building an equity factor strategy involves a long and short position. This could, for example, be either by shorting a market capitalisation or debt-weighted index versus a specific factor, or shorting the most expensive stocks versus the cheapest stocks.

Similarly, we discussed low volatility and quality premia in previous chapters. In an ARP context, the idea is to go long defensive stocks such as low volatility and high-quality stocks versus a representative broad market portfolio, high beta or poor quality stocks. These strategies can be labelled as defensive strategies in the ARP context for stocks and bonds. Currencies and commodities are not covered within the defensive strategies and may not be as obvious and intuitive as for the other main asset classes.

To ensure complete transparency and simplicity, I have focused on robust and well-understood factors and ARP strategies in the investment community. These strategies can be implemented in a straightforward and transparent manner without overfitting, data mining, complex derivatives and avoiding any "black boxes".

The next section discusses some of these ARP strategies that are widely adopted as a part of systematic and index strategies. Carry trades that extend across various securities—currencies, commodities and fixed income, are among the most popular strategies. In sum, the ARP is simply a long-short of a combination of the factors presented in previous chapters. The list is not exhaustive and only aims to provide an idea of the type of indices that are available. The selected index strategies are quite similar to the strategies that we have discussed in previous sections.

11.4 Carry Premia Across Assets

This section will provide discussion on central carry trade premia among macro managers across asset classes. A carry trade strategy buys (or goes long) higher-yielding assets and sells (goes short) a lower yielding asset in the expectation that those yields will persist without too much price depreciation of the high yielding asset or any significant change in that market conditions. This type of strategy is common across asset classes and initially adopted by currency speculators. We will focus on well-established carry strategies in the ARP index domain and limit our discussion to currencies, commodities and fixed income.

The research dedicated to carry strategies goes back to the early 1980s by Robert Shiller, Lars-Peter Hansen, and Eugene Fama. Up until today, the academics still disagree on the ultimate drivers of a carry premium, despite sharing the Nobel Prize in 2013. The collective explanations for the driving forces of the carry trade premia are: investor behavior (over-extrapolating or under-reacting to information), efficient markets but with varying risk premium (reward for risk) and the fact that the fundamental finance theory is not sufficient to describe the real world (the "known unknown" true theoretical model).

11.4.1 Currency Carry Premium

The currency carry trade is one of the most well-known trading strategies in the global macro and ARP space. The practical concept of the carry trade is that currency forward price (a fixed price at which one currency can be exchanged for another at a future date) are not a good predictor of expected spot rates. The strategy aims to trade on the difference in interest rates linked to two or a basket of currencies. An investor would buy (long) the currency which carries high-interest rate—investment currency in the money market—and sells (short) the currency with low-interest rate (known as the funding currency).

Practically, when establishing a currency position, the investor is simultaneously holding and selling funds from different countries using derivatives such as futures and forward contracts. The funds which the investor has bought and sold have different interest rates either by receiving or paying on those funds (i.e. receiving an interest payment on a currency position). A positive carry occurs when the trader is holding a long position in the higher interest rate currency and short position in lower interest rate currency.

The existence of the currency carry premium is determined by the interest differential. As we know, the interest rate in a country is determined by the economic conditions in the country or market-specific risk factors. Developed economies generally have lower interest rates due to their lower risk nature. At the same time, emerging markets have higher interest rates compared to the developed economies, which reflects a higher compensation for risk through higher interest rates.

This premium is attributed to the limitation of the so-called Uncovered Interest Rate Parity (UIP) hypothesis. Uncovered interest rate parity says that the difference in interest rates between two countries should be equal to the potential change in exchange rates. Higher yield currencies should depreciate and low yielding should appreciate in value. For example, an investor in Japanese yen (JPY) has two options—either buying JPY 1,000,000 of government debt with 1% yield after a year the investor would have JPY 1,010,000; or invests in an Australian government bond at 4% yield. In this case, if there is uncovered interest rate parity between the two investments, then the Australian dollar would depreciate against the Japanese yen by about 3%. In this case, the expected change in the exchange rate is equal to the difference between the two interest rates. However, the UIP hypothesis has not always been successful historically and a reflection of the real world.

The interest rate differential between the Australian dollar and Japanese yen rates is in positive carry of 3%. Although 3% may seem like a small return, when leveraged, it can provide a generous interest income in addition to the interest on funds. However, it is not always rosy for the carry trade. The carry trade can lose if the Australian dollar depreciates against the Japanese yen.

Historically, the carry trade has gone in four episodes, almost the same number of recessions in the U.S.

- The first episode is linked to the yen as a low yielding currency and the higher yielding European currencies in the late 1980s. The yen carry trade was a success until the Japanese institutions, as net creditors to the world,

were forced to repatriate their capital from overseas, which led to the collapse of the yen carry trade.
- The second episode involved the yen, other G10 currencies and emerging markets. It started mid-1995 and finished end-1998 when the yen appreciated by 15% in a matter of a week due to panic in the financial market, the Asian financial crisis, Russian default and the collapse of the hedge fund Long-Term Capital Management.
- The third episode emerged after the 1998 financial crisis and lasted through the dot-com bubble, healthy market conditions and depreciation of the yen until 2007. The yen, again, was the perfect target currencies for funding due to loose monetary policy by the Bank of Japan to combat deflation for many years. At the same time, the U.S. and many developed markets were running with high inflations and offered higher interest rate, making it the ideal carry trade.
- The fourth episode was post the global financial crisis in 2008. The low-interest rates in developed markets and divergence of monetary policy created another thrilling environment for carry trades. The U.S. and Euro became funding currencies due to nearly zero interest rates. At the same time, emerging market currencies and Australian dollar remained attractive investment currencies by offering 3–10% money market interest rates.

History tells us that the currency carry goes in cycles, often attributed to fundamental economic structures. It tends to do well for years before collapsing. There is no crystal ball for when carry trade may collapse other than staying diversified and imposing volatility target, stop-loss and profit-taking targets.

Construction of a rules-based strategy can be devised as follows:

- Select a set of currencies G10 and emerging markets;
- Rank each currency pair by 1- or 3-month money market interest rate such as Libor or equivalent interest rates in the respective market;
- Long currencies with the highest interest rate and short currencies with the lowest interest rates;
- Apply a weight to each currency pair—often equal weighting between the long and short currency positions;
- Rebalance every three months within the roll date of the futures contract;
- Implement via 3-month forwards or other derivatives such as swaps.

In general, to implement a currency carry trade requires some sophistication and market access to global financial markets and instruments. Moreover, the limitation on borrowing and leverage may discourage some from exploring these strategies.

11.4.2 The Commodity Carry Premium

The commodity carry strategies (or curve premium or cash-and-carry) typically sit with traditional and macro fund managers. These are often different from the currency carry in the ARP family. The carry trade in commodities aims to exploit premium from current and future commodity prices—also known as the commodity term structure. In this section, we will go through the basic of the commodity carry trade and how it can be harvested systematically.

The commodity carry premium goes back to John Maynard Keynes' theory of "normal backwardation" in 1930—commodity producers sell long-dated futures contracts at a discount to hedge their production and consumers often buy short-dated contracts at a premium to access near-term consumption need. Again, the existence of the premium is due to the fact that the futures curve systematically misjudges the expected spot movements due to supply-demand imbalances and risk appetite among speculators in the market.

In practice, one of the main risks for a farmer or commodity producer is the disruption to the production that could impact the output levels. A farmer is faced with production risks from adverse weather conditions or failure of equipment to meet full capacity. The suppliers of a commodity have "naturally" undiversified exposure to prices. This exposure is managed through commodity futures to reduce this risk. A wheat farmer, for example, may hedge the price per bushels before the harvest season by taking a short position in wheat futures in the market. An airline, as a consumer of jet fuel, may "proxy" hedge with long positions in oil futures. The investors are on the other side of the commodity transaction to the farmer and the airline. That is where the commodity carry trade comes into the picture and provides insight into the mechanics of the term structure of commodity prices. Hence, investors who buy from the farmer and sell to consumers can often capture a risk premium in the form of excess return between changes in the futures price and changes in the spot prices—also known as the roll yield.

The roll yield is the return a trader receives by rolling a near-term into the longer-term futures contract. Assume an investor holds a January WTI oil futures contract that is trading at USD 50 (an obligation to buy at that price), March oil futures is at USD 45, and the spot price of oil is at USD 50/barrel on the day of January expiration. Suppose you decide to roll the January contract into the March contract. If the spot price on the January expiration date is unchanged at USD 50/barrel, then the roll yield would be USD 5, calculated as futures price of USD 5 (USD 50–45) and change in spot price USD 0 (USD 50–50). So the carry trade here aims to benefit from the price differential between futures contracts of various maturities, often determined by the shape of the commodity term structure curve. This is not an arbitrage as it not risk-free since the carry trade takes a long position where the roll yield is positive and takes a short position where the roll yield is negative.

The shape of the curve is determined by whether the nearest month(s) prices are cheaper or more expensive than the longer-dated prices. The shape of the curve provides insight into the current and future expectations of the supply-demand balance for a given commodity. There are two types of common shapes—contango and backwardation (Fig. 11.3).

The shape of the commodities curve can be used to construct a rules-based carry strategy. When a commodity is in **contango,** the nearest futures price is lower than the longer dated futures price (Fig. 11.3a). This curve structure is normal for a non-perishable commodity like crude oil and products with actual costs of carry (that involves the cost of storage and maintaining the commodity over time). This means that if you were to buy the non-perishable commodity and store it for sale later, investors would incur costs such as transportation, storage fees and interest forgone on money that is tied up in inventory. Intuitively, one would expect a higher sales price in the future to recoup these costs. A steep contango curve can also suggest that there is currently pressure on the short-dated futures contract due to oversupply, lack of demand

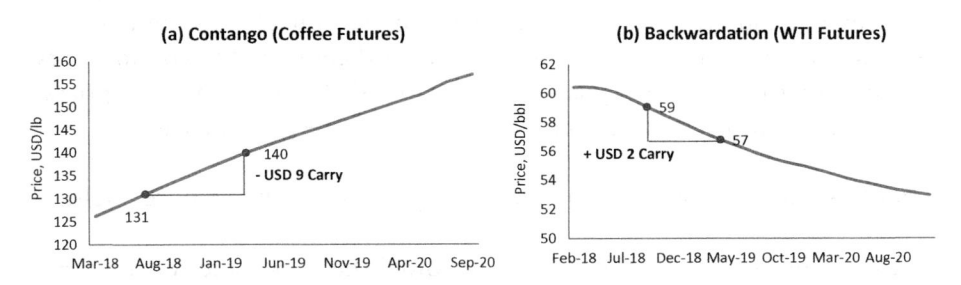

Fig. 11.3 Contango and backwardation. Source: Author's construction and Bloomberg, Dec. 2017. For illustrative purposes only

or some combination of the two in the market. In this case, the carry trade consists of taking a short position in the commodities in which the market is expected to decline.

On the other hand, **backwardation** is a negatively sloped curve, where there is a premium on current commodity prices (short-dated futures contracts) over the longer-dated future since the current price is higher than the future expected price (Fig. 11.3b). This typically occurs when there is increased demand for a commodity today, which can be associated with expanding global economy or uncertainties about the supply due to geopolitical risks. A market that is in backwardation often indicates perception of current shortage in the commodity and will encourage owners of the commodity to pull it out of storage. Hence, in a backwardated market a long position in a future position and short the "nearest" futures contract (a proxy for the spot price) on the expectations that futures commodity prices are expected to rise.

A way to implement this strategy systematically in an index is through long and short futures based on quantitative signals such as roll yield and other indicators (macro or simple momentum on underlying commodities). This index would be designed to provide long exposure to commodities with positive roll yield (backwardated curve) and shorting commodities with a negative roll yield (contangoed curve). This carry strategy would aim to target yield from the "natural" carry of commodity futures prices. The return for a fully collateralised long-only commodities future can be defined as:

$$\text{Total return} = \text{Spot Return} + \text{Roll return} + \text{Collateral Return}.$$

The theory of storage is a key driver of the shape of the commodity curve. The difference between the futures and spot prices can be explained by the cost of storage and so-called convenience yield of holding it in inventory. For example, commodities that are expensive or more difficult to store (e.g. live cattle or live hogs) have higher convenience yield compared to commodities that are easier to store (e.g. grains). The relationship between futures prices, spot prices, storage costs and convenience yield can be presented as:

$$\text{Futures price} = \text{Spot Price} + \text{Direct Storage Costs} - \text{Convenience Yield}.$$

A study by Basu and Miffre in 2013 showed the importance of the commodity carry premium. They constructed long and short portfolios by buying backwardated and selling contangoed commodities. Their results showed that consideration to the shape of the curve to harvest a risk factor premium improves the risk-adjusted returns over simple long-only strategies.

It is not all rosy, and it is important to be aware that the physical supply and demand situation can become disconnected from what the futures market is telling us, leading to an unprofitable trade. Moreover, various commodities have different characteristics and are inherently more volatile, making the carry premium more effective in some markets segment such as metals, agricultural or energy. Hence, the correlation between various types of commodities can vary and offer a various degree of diversification. To put it more into perspective, the annual average correlation between various commodities is 15% based on daily data from CME.

11.4.3 The Bond Carry Premium

By now the readers are familiar with the spirit of the carry trade. There is another potential source of return that arises from trading the yield curve or credit spreads in the fixed income market. There are many variations of the fixed income carry trade within the ARP context with the objective to provide low correlated sources of returns to the direction of interest rates and credit spreads—market neutral strategies. This section will focus on a few of them.

Carry here can be defined as the net financing cost of a trade measured as the difference between the yield to maturity of a bond and the cost of financing another through a short position or borrowing. A position, for example, has a positive carry when the yield is greater than the financing cost of the short trade. This is typically the case when the yield curve is positively sloped—yield of long-dated bonds is higher than the one of the short-dated maturities (Fig. 11.4). Positive carry is similar to currencies and commodities. It can provide as a cushion against losses if bond prices fall, while negative carry could still be a losing position even if bond prices rise.

There are also different versions of carry trade within the fixed income—rates carry (including government bond futures) and credit carry (often corporate bonds and emerging markets). Rates carry can be constructed, for example, by looking at the relative yield between two bond futures' contracts such as the yield spread between the 2-year and 10-year Treasury notes (known as the Treasury spread).

For example, a simple strategy for a positively sloped curve could entail the following steps:

- Buy a long-dated bond futures contract (e.g. 10-year), yielding 3%
- Sell a short-dated bond futures contract (e.g. money market or 2-year), yielding 1%

- The carry is 2% (3–1%). The cost of financing the trade is 1% (i.e. the yield on the short positions)
- Variation of this carry trade may involve a reduction in duration risk by applying a so-called hedging ratio. The hedging ratio aims to provide how many short-dated bond futures are required (based on so-called Dollar Basis Point value) to proxy the interest rate sensitivity of a long-dated bond. The ultimate objective is to be duration neutral, leaving the investor exposed to changes in curve shape but insulating against changes in level of interest rates.

The influencing factor for a Treasury spread trade is the shape of the yield curve (Fig. 11.4). There are times where investors, for example, will demand higher yields on long-dated bonds due to high inflation expectations and general market conditions. Hence, the most common carry trade takes a long position in bond futures with the highest yield and short those with the lowest yield of the bonds referencing the futures contracts. This type of rules-based approach takes advantage of a positive and steep yield curve in various bond markets to imply the "carry". This can apply across markets where the strategy could rank the bond futures based on their Treasury spreads.

There are more advanced versions of this rates strategy, but out of the scope of this chapter, where the strategy could involve some hedging of the interest rate risk to resemble "market neutral" (also known as duration neutral). This is often managed by investing more in one futures bond contract and less in another. More dynamic bond strategies in the government bond space which follow the same principle as the yield curve trade involve multiple markets.

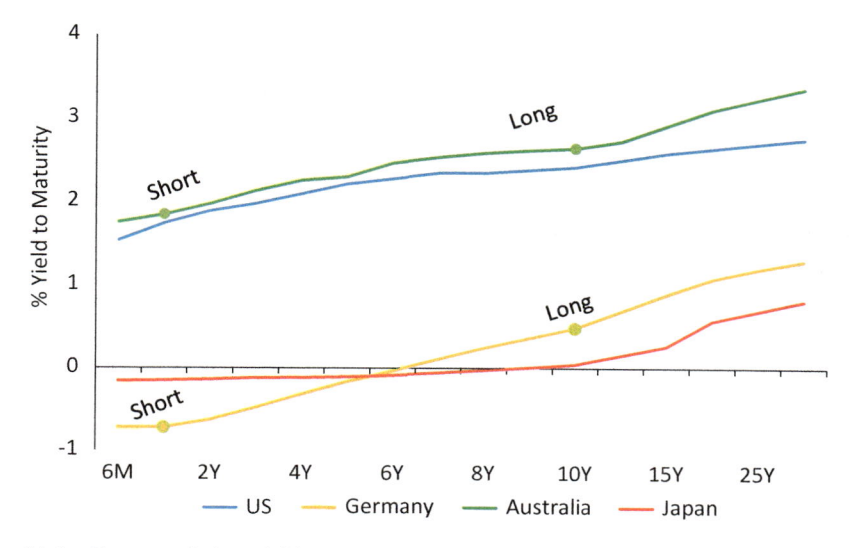

Fig. 11.4 Shapes of the yield curve in some developed markets. Source: Author's construction and Bloomberg, Dec. 2017. For illustrative purposes only

11.4.4 Other Carry Premia

Other fixed income carry trades are played between high yield and investment grades through liquid index strategies in Credit Default Swap (CDS) space for North America and Europe. Known CDS index strategies are Markit CDX for North America and Markit iTraxx for European credit, where CDX-based CDS tend to be the most liquid contracts. In a risk-on environment, an investor could consider selling a CDS contract on the high yield CDS index and buy CDS on the investment grade CDS index for specific or combined regions. The credit carry trade is often attractive when the credit spreads are elevated within and across the segment of the corporate bond market. The limitation of just having CDX and iTraxx available in the market for carry trade means that investors have narrow liquid securities to choose from across two currencies (USD and Euro). This can pose some challenges for construction and implementation.

In general, the success of the fixed income carry trade, like other carry trades in other assets classes, depends a lot on the liquidity environment of the underlying bond market. Most execution in the market is often through derivatives (forwards, futures or swaps in U.S. Treasuries, Eurodollar or other short-dated government bonds).

Equity carry premia are sometimes discussed in equities, but less common due to the absence of a well-established term structure. There are dividend futures contracts in the market that could allow for some implementation of the equity carry trade. Another aspect of equity carry is that high dividend yielding stocks may outperform low dividend yielding stocks over the long-term. This can be implemented through a long and short portfolio of high dividend versus a broad market index or the bottom low dividend yielding stocks in an index. Equity carry may require a forward-looking measure of dividend yields, which can be challenging for a systematic based index strategy—see Koijen et al. (2016) discussions.

Moreover, volatility carry premium can be extracted through option strategies by trading the implied volatility markets which are often higher than realised volatility over time, which is out of the scope of this chapter. However, the reason for this is that selling volatility corresponds to say selling hedges or insurance-like contracts against downside movements in the equity market—often seen as volatility carry trade across assets. There is typically an imbalance between the supply and the demand for volatility-linked instruments in a market. This phenomenon could emerge from investment banks or brokers who are selling volatility whereas most investors will want to buy volatility as insurance against downside risk. This supply and demand imbalance historically led to a premium being placed on the implied volatility markets.

In sum, carry trades touch on many asset classes. They can be rewarding if the risk from leverage is managed and the strategies are switched on and off depending on the market environment (even without perfect timing). Still, the success to any carry trade requires stable or low market volatility as well as harmony between high and low-yielding assets.

11.5 Value ARP Strategies

We discussed value strategies for bonds and equities in previous chapters as long-only strategies. In the ARP context, the most straightforward value trades in equities involves a long and short portfolio of stocks or bonds based on value characteristics (e.g. price-to-book or price-to-earnings) as defined in previous chapters. Cheap stocks (based on value factor metrics) could outperform growth or expensive stocks. A value equity strategy would go long value and short growth stocks or long the top percentile (e.g. 30%) and short the bottom percentile (e.g. 30%) or just the broad market capitalisation index. The amount of investment in each of the long and short leg of the trade can be adjusted (known as beta-adjustment) to achieve a market neutral position. In the bond universe, it is more about pricing a fair value of securities or the default risk versus the market expectations. This is implemented through long undervalue and short overvalued bonds or a broad index representative of the market. This section introduces currency, commodity and fixed income rules-based value ARP strategies.

11.5.1 Currency Value Premium

Value strategies for currencies are about establishing whether a currency pair or basket is overvalued or undervalued. A common way to establish a value trade in the currencies market is to gain exposure to undervalued currencies relative to fair value. Two approaches can be deployed to create a rules-based approach for currency value investing: the theory of Purchasing Power Parity (PPP) in economics or a simple long-term average as a so-called mean-reversion level.

The long-term average is a simple framework. It can be estimated using 5-year Moving Average (5-year MA) of spot rates, which is common in the literature and among professionals. Figure 11.5 provides an example of a Euro, Japanese yen, Swedish krona and Pound sterling against the USD. It illustrates the cyclicality of the USD and how it goes through a period of being over-and undervalued. A market neutral strategy would go long undervalued currencies and short overvalued currencies with equal exposure on the short and long positions.

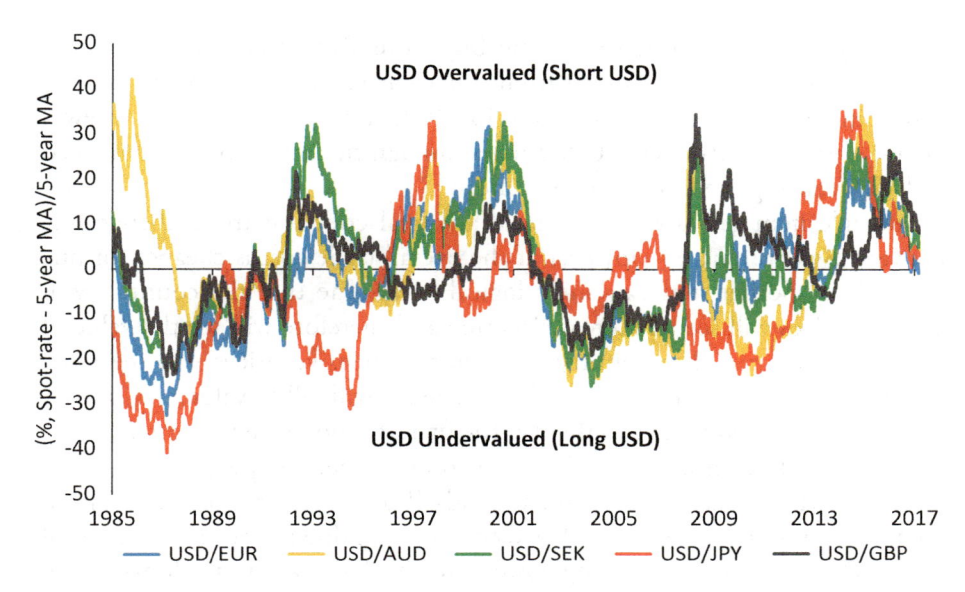

Fig. 11.5 Mean-reversion of spot rates versus USD of few G10 currencies. Source: Author's calculation and Bloomberg, Oct. 1985–Dec. 2017. For illustrative purposes only. Historical returns are not a leading indicator of future performance

An alternative measure with economic meaning is PPP—also known as the law of one price. The PPP compares the price of trade between two countries using a basket of goods and services, which is a group of similar items that are frequently purchased by consumers—OECD PPP index is a commonly used one. By comparing the prices of a basket of items, theoretically, we can determine if prices or currencies are too high or too low in a country. If prices are lower in a country, then the currency could rise in value as money flows into the country from countries with higher prices. If prices are higher in a country, then the currency could drop in value as money flows out of the country into countries with lower prices.

There are several versions of purchase power parity. Some models take into account not only real price differences but also income levels, inflation levels, and cost-of-living. The goal is to try to compare not only the baskets of items with cost in real conversion rates but what costs are compared to what people can really afford to buy. For example, let's say the exchange rate is JPY 90 per 1 USD. Let's also say that an iPad costs USD 20 in the U.S. but in Japan, it costs JPY 900. This means in U.S. dollars the iPad costs USD 20 in the U.S., but it costs only USD 10 in Japan. Since the iPad is half the price in Japan than in the U.S., people would rather buy the iPad from Japan. This means that the demand for goods for iPad would rise in Japan causing the price of iPad to rise in Japan. This also means the demand for iPads from the U.S. would fall causing the price of iPad in the U.S. to drop. More demand for iPads in Japan would mean that people buy more iPads in Japan. This leads to more currency being exchanged from other currencies into yen causing the yen to increase in value. Less demand for iPads in the U.S. means that fewer people are buying iPad in the U.S. and less foreign currency is being exchanged to USD, causing the USD to depreciate.

A single item probably has little, if any, real effect on the exchange rate between two currencies. However, if the overall trade cost is cheaper for one place than another it is extremely logical to assume that the country with cheaper prices will see an increase in trade and therefore will see the value of their currency rise. The country with more expensive prices will see trade decline and therefore the value of their currency will fall in value.[7]

There are challenges to this theory. The first, it is not a trivial matter to find a set of items to compare prices between countries because people in different countries typically consume different goods. The second, it can be difficult to compare real purchasing power between countries due to the vast number of factors that affect real purchasing power. The third, is that this is a longer-term view that could take several years for the currency to react to price differences in the shorter term.

11.5.2 Commodities Value Premium

Similar to currencies, commodity value strategy aims to monetise divergence from a "fair value" driven by fundamental analysis or a medium to the long-term mean of the price. The fundamental analysis evaluates the supply and demand of a commodity. The supply-demand imbalance often creates the prices divergence from fair value due to geopolitical risk, weather conditions, and business cycle. In theory, a commodity price should be fair when the long-term supply and demand are in "equilibrium". The idea is that distorted prices are expected to converge to the fair value. However, fundamental analysis tends to be costly and quite resource intensive to conduct.

Most systematic strategies tend to use a long-term average (often adjusted for inflation) to gauge a mean-reversion level for a commodity, often described as the marginal cost of the product in literature. Geman and Nguyen provided

---

[7] There are several variations of the purchasing power parity including the Big Mac index instead of a basket of goods the Big Mac index compares the price of a Big Mac from country to country as an indicator of the level of cost per country. If the Big Mac costs more in a country theoretically the prices and then in turn the currencies are overpriced and the currencies should drop in value over time. If the price of a Big Mac cost less in a country theoretically the prices and in turn the currency is undervalued and the currency should rise in value over time. It is interesting to note that when comparing the Big Mac index to the actual purchasing price parity chart they are strikingly similar. Like all economic theories, the purchasing power parity has its problems.

evidence for it in 2005 for agricultural commodities and Pindyck in 2001 for energy commodities. The overall concept is that commodities are mean-reverting (i.e. prices are expected to gravitate to its fair value or the long-term average such 5–7 years). For example, a spot price, which is above the long-term equilibrium level, is expected to fall. This expectation will lead to a negative slope of the term structure of futures prices. The argument holds the other way around.

Moreover, an ARP value strategy can also be devised based on relative value of two commodities. Figure 11.6 illustrated a trade between short-dated soybean and corn futures. In this particular example, a relative price ratio is created with volatility bands around the long-term average. If the ratio is within the volatility band, then the investor would not trade. A buy and sell signal is extracted often when the ratio is trading outside the one-standard deviation band as an example.

Many agricultural commodities inherit the feature of mean-reversion in production costs to long-term fair value. It suggests that spot prices will eventually revert to this cost because of supply response. For example, when prices are high for grains, supply could increase. Consequently, it may put downward pressure on prices. On the demand side, when prices are high, the quantity demanded will decrease, which push the price down. In some commodities,

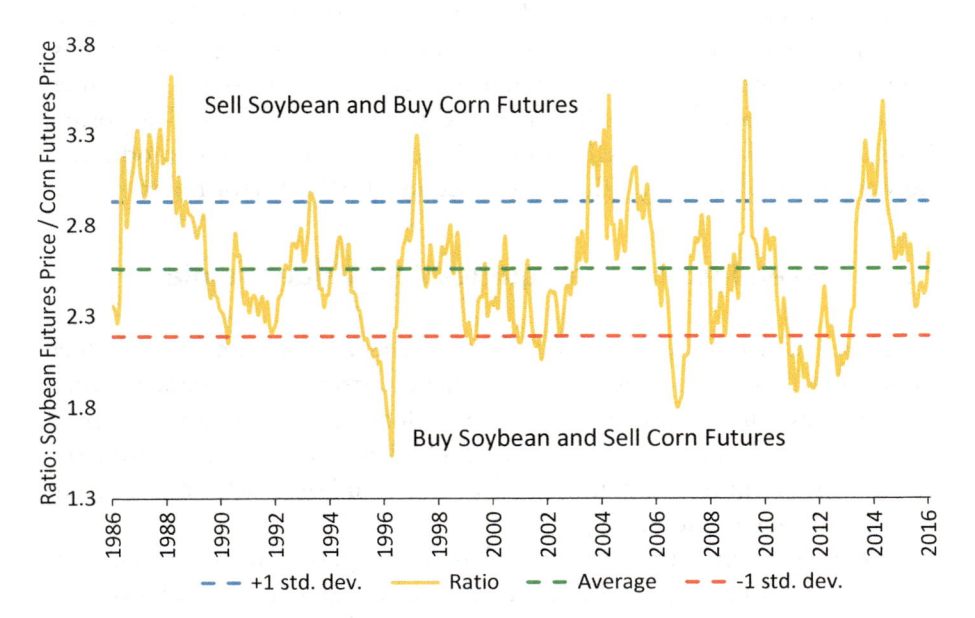

Fig. 11.6 Relative value trade example between soybean and corn futures. Source: Author's construction. Bloomberg, Dec. 1986–Dec. 2017. Note: +1/−1 std. dev. stands for one standard deviation of the price ratio. The ratio is based on the shortest maturity futures contracts. For illustrative purposes only. Historical returns are not a leading indicator of future performance

mean-reversion is mainly induced by so-called convenience yields. The convenience yield is the value of owning the physical commodity instead of a futures contract on the underlying commodity. Hence, more scarcity of a commodity tends to imply a higher convenience yield.

Mean-reversion has important implications for index strategy construction in commodities, and less so in equities. Some index strategies incorporate the mean-reversion—e.g. Deutsche Bank Liquid Commodity Index-Mean-reversion (DBLCI-MR). DBLC-MR contains crude oil, heating oil, gold, aluminium, corn and wheat. Unlike a traditional commodity index, the mean-reversion strategy would use a "trigger event", where the distance between the 1-year Moving Average (MA) and 5-year MA to generate trading signals—"cheap", "fair" or "expensive". If the 1-year, for example, is above the 5-year, then it is an "expensive" commodity. This indexing strategy can be deployed as a long-only or a long-short trade by tilting away from the base index with the trading signal scores. In sum, most mean-reversion strategies look great with hindsight. Hence, it is important to understand that it takes time for a trade to reverse to its long-term mean, and the strategy requires patience to pay off.

There are alternative value strategies that implement a rules-based approach by using the shape of the term structure of the commodities curves—contango and backwardation discussed in the previous section. The idea is to trade the relative value between various commodities by going long the most backwardated and short the most contangoed commodities. To reduce market risk, the long and short positions of the trade can have equal exposure. Deutsche Bank has developed a similar index based on 14 commodities—known as the Commodity Value (Cross-Sectional) Risk Factor Index.

11.5.3 Fixed Income and Equities ARP Value Premia

For government bonds, going long futures, which are deemed undervalued and short the overvalued ones is a market neutral strategy. The market neutral value strategy can be implemented using a long-term average of the price returns of an index, or the bond yields of a basket of securities. The underlying assumption, in this case, is that price levels and bond yields mean-revert, as discussed for commodities,

Alternatively, value strategies can be based on a statistical approach or economic theory. A strategy would aim to create a fair value for the yields of various maturities. In particular, the economic-based approach uses a general equilibrium between the economy and the natural long-term interest rate, assuming that long-term interest rates are equal to real economic growth and inflation (i.e. nominal growth). A rules-based strategy such as the Barclays Rates Value Factor Index defines value as the difference between the 10-year

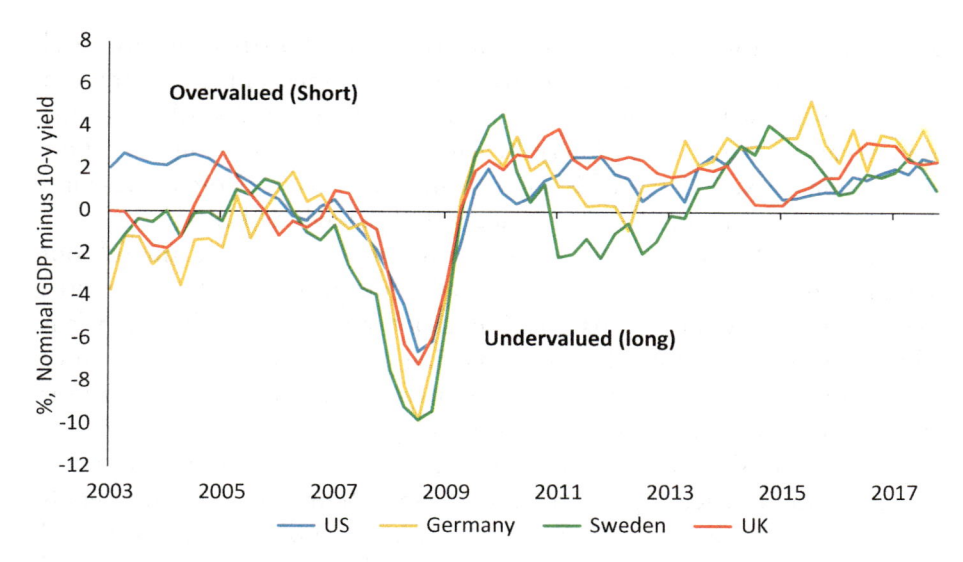

Fig. 11.7 Rules-based value strategy for rates. Source: Author's calculations. IMF database, Bloomberg, Dec. 2010–Dec. 2017. For illustrative purposes only. Notes: The overvalued and undervalued rate is defined based on the difference between nominal GDP (g) growth and 10-year interest rates (r) for each economy. If the g > r, then the 10-year bond is overvalued and vice versa. Historical returns are not a leading indicator of future performance

nominal yield and the most recent nominal GDP annual growth rate, where the positive difference indicates overvalued securities and the other way around. The strategy takes a long position in the most undervalued government bonds futures and goes short for the most overvalued ones by taking an equal nominal position for the long and short exposures (Fig. 11.7).

This approach shows that the majority of the developed market government bond rates are overvalued as nominal growth has exceeded the nominal long-term interest rates in the past years. This makes it harder to create a long-short strategy. One way to apply this is to go long the least expensive bond futures and short the most expensive ones. However, it is important to make sure that the currency risk is hedged, and the cost of hedging does not erode the potential future value of the trade.

11.6 Momentum and Trend-Following Strategies

Momentum and trend following are often associated with CTA funds, although other types of funds deploy momentum too. Chapter 7 presented two types of momentum: cross-sectional (relative) momentum or time series momentum (trend following). The former compares the best and worst performing securities, and the latter creates a portfolio based on historical winners and losers. Unlike the cross-sectional momentum, this approach includes stocks with positive stock returns for winners and stocks with the most negative returns for the losers. In general, a simultaneous long and short momentum of various types is more market neutral and often generates sources of returns that are less correlated to the general market.

A rules-based index with a trend-following strategy tends to smooth out trading signals to capture the trends instead of just using actual price returns changes, which are noisy in nature. The smoothness of the trading signals is often implemented with a historical moving average of returns (e.g. three months or 12 months). A trend follower may benefit more in a bull or bear market due to the potential of being net long or short but exposed to the general market risk—i.e. not market neutral. However, CTA strategies tend to struggle in the absence of price trends in the market or sudden trend reversals in the market. Many studies, including Baltas and Kosowski in 2013 showed that monetary and sovereign fiscal uncertainties between 2009–2011 caused asset price trends to reverse more frequently than in the past. This is among the reasons that are attributed to the lacklustre performance of CTA funds during that period.

When it comes to construction of these strategies, they can be designed in a quite simple way for a rules-based index. A currency time-series momentum, for example, ranks currency returns against a defined base currency, either using the spot or forward foreign exchange first. Then, it applies a weighting to each long (winners) and short position (losers) using a lookback period of 12 months and excluding the latest month. This can be typically rebalanced monthly or quarterly within the roll date of the forward or futures contract.

For commodities, both types of momentum are commonly used in a long and short fashion. The idea is to earn a premium by going long commodities with the highest relative momentum and short commodities with the lowest relative momentum. An example is the Deutsche bank Commodity Momentum Risk Factor Index, which targets 14 commodities by going long seven commodity futures and short seven others.

A fixed income and equities momentum strategy goes long outperforming bond futures and short underperforming ones either on a relative or time series basis using a 12-month lookback period with monthly rebalancing. Barclays has a similar index (the Barclays Momentum Factor Index) with a focus on developed market government bonds. The rates index strategy can be implemented through futures or swaps (on 2, 5 or 10-year bonds), CDS indices for corporate bonds (investment grade and high yield) and for equities by using long and short factor indices.[8]

So far we have discussed some of the nuances of rules-based ARP strategies. We did not discuss some of them here, particularly the ones in the equity space (for example, defensive strategies that can be devised through long-short trading using the factors from previous chapters on quality and low-risk factors). We hardly touched on the variation of momentum in the ARP context in this chapter. However, we have seen proliferation of momentum strategies across asset classes because of the high number of combinations of moving average rules to determine momentum. Those rules can be used in combination to extract short and long-term signals. The next section looks at the impact of ARP strategies on asset allocation.

11.7 Portfolio Construction of ARP Strategies

The starting point is to understand the dynamics of the ARP strategies and how they interact between each other and with other traditional asset classes that provide pure market exposure. As we already know the correlation between these strategies and traditional market value weighted strategies (e.g. market capitalisation and debt-weighting) is low. The correlation with the traditional equities and bonds, as expected, is low as well.

Despite the low long-term correlations between the various premia, these correlations can change as some strategies may work better in different environments. For example, carry trades thrive during a steady market and economic environment, while the market neutral momentum strategy may fair better in a downturn.

The next question is how to allocate between the various premiums. This can be achieved through various weighting mechanism and risk budget thinking around each premium. This helps to create more robust implementation into portfolios through various market conditions. The simplest weighting is an equal weighting or risk-weighting or other weighting to create a multi-factor ARP across assets (Table 11.2). An alternative and more sophisticated approach involves an optimisation to achieve a balanced risk-contribution weighting, similar to the weighting that we discussed in Chap. 3.

---

[8] Barclays Rates Momentum Factor Index use the average of the past 6-month, 12-month and 18-month futures return.

Table 11.2 Comparison of various ARP strategies

	FX carry	FX momentum	FX value
Return (% p.a.)	2.2	1.7	2.9
Excess return (% p.a.)	1.0	0.4	1.7
Volatility (% p.a.)	9.0	8.3	7.7
Maximum drawdown (%)	−35.2	−25.3	−15.7
Sharpe ratio	0.1	0.1	0.2
Beta	−0.4	0.1	0.4
	Rates carry	**Rates momentum**	**Rates value**
Return (% p.a.)	2.7	3.3	0.4
Excess return (% p.a.)	1.5	2.1	−0.9
Volatility (% p.a.)	3.4	4.7	3.4
Maximum drawdown (%)	−6.4	−7.0	−11.8
Sharpe ratio	0.4	0.4	−0.3
Beta	0.0	0.0	0.0
	Commodity carry	**Commodity momentum**	**Commodity value**
Return (% p.a.)	4.0	9.5	11.0
Excess return (% p.a.)	2.7	8.2	9.8
Volatility (% p.a.)	2.7	17.5	14.0
Maximum drawdown (%)	−2.7	−38.4	−24.8
Sharpe ratio	1.0	0.5	0.7
Beta	0.0	0.0	−0.1
	Quality	**Momentum**	**Value**
Return (% p.a.)	2.5	2.6	2.7
Excess return (% p.a.)	1.2	1.3	1.5
Volatility (% p.a.)	2.8	7.3	8.5
Maximum drawdown (%)	−2.8	−20.5	−26.9
Sharpe ratio	0.4	0.2	0.2
Beta	−0.1	−0.1	0.1

Source: Author's construction and calculations. The commodity indices are from Deutsche bank and Rates indices are from Barclays, between Jan. 2001–Dec. 2017

The allocation between these can either be strategic or dynamic depending on the investment objectives—Fig. 11.8 provides an illustrative blend of factors in an asset allocation context. A risk budget for ARP is more suitable than trying to time these premia in general. Individual ARP strategies by construction have low correlation with traditional asset classes as the market direction is often taken out through a short leg of the trade. Moreover, these strategies have a low correlation with each other as well. This can make it a difficult exercise to time risk premia.

Of course, more specialised and dedicated strategies may be attractive where asset prices dislocate significantly from their long-term value or high yielding carry assets becomes more high-yielding while market fundamentals remain unchanged. Despite the cyclicality of these premia, investors need to observe ARP strategies over a full market cycle before forming conclusions about their performance.

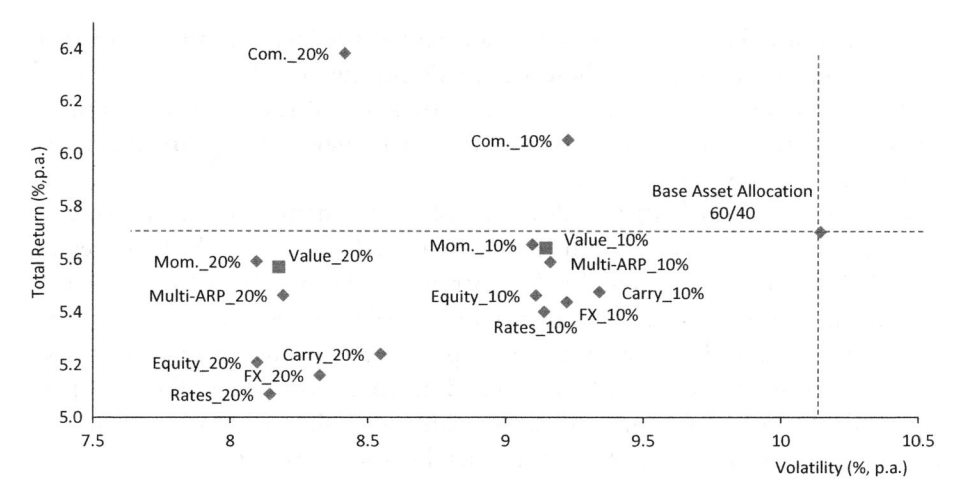

Fig. 11.8 60/40 portfolios and ARP strategies. Source: Author's calculations, Bloomberg, Barclays, Kenneth French database, Deutsche bank, Jan. 2001–Dec. 2017. Note: The base asset allocation (Base AA_60/40) of 60% equity and 40% bonds is based on a representative market cap and Bloomberg-Barclays Global Aggregate. FX denotes currency ARP for (carry, momentum and value) with the percentage allocation of ARP in a modified 60/40 asset allocation, Com. denotes commodities with similar factors to currencies; Multi-ARP is equally weighted ARP strategies across asset classes and styles

11.8 Access to ARP Strategies

Today, ARP strategies are accessible in a transparent, liquid and cost-efficient way through index building blocks, bespoke indices designed by investment banks and some ETFs. An investor can implement alternative risk premia in various ways: by buying a fund that provides exposure to an individual or multiple strategies. Historically, these premia have been accessed through hedge funds. An increasing number of asset management houses offer dedicated ARP strategies where structuring, risk management and selection techniques are provided on a customised basis. A dedicated alternative risk premia fund owns the investment risk and responsibility for the selection and performance.

With the increasing access to ARP strategies, they are often placed into the alternative bucket in a multi-asset allocation framework for wealth managers and institutional investors. In some instances, depending on the objective and expected outcomes, ARP strategies can be a direct replacement of hedge funds, CTAs or complement to a hedge fund allocation. ARP adds value through cost-effectiveness, transparency and diversification to the overall investor portfolio. However, these aspects do not justify a full replacement of hedge funds adequately without full consideration of the investment objectives, risk and reward dimensions as the ARP may not capture the non-systematic alpha opportunities.

Historically, many hedge funds use a cash plus benchmark to gauge or display their performance. Currently, the characteristics of the ARP strategies and their availability makes the ARP strategies the benchmarks that many hedge funds need to beat. The transparency of ARP strategies allows the investors to monitor and understand their exposure to various investment styles, "true exposures" to various risk premia and the sources of return. For example, it is difficult for a hedge fund manager to justify its high fees if the returns are generated from traditional ARP and general market exposure.

11.9 A Consideration When Selecting ARP

We have discussed the concept of a handful of ARP strategies. While the rules-based strategies may work in the real world, it is as important to be able to implement them efficiently. For a successful ARP implementation the investor needs to consider some questions related to underlying strategies and execution of the trades. Here are a few considerations, although the list is not exhaustive:

- **Systematic approach:** One of the key aspects around ARP is the ability to generate the strategy systematically as well as understanding where it may succeed and fail;
- **Transparency:** The level of transparency of the strategy can help to perform due diligence on the ARP strategy in portfolios;
- **Rationale of the strategy:** There are many ARP strategies and it is essential to understand and challenge the rationale for the existence of the premium (economic, behavioural, market structures, or temporary and if they are specific to segments of the market);
- **Exposure and leverage:** Market neutral trades require both long and short positions, which is not a bad thing but needs fine-tuning to balance the exposure on the long and short side of a trade. Imbalanced exposure, if unintended, by the fund manager could create permanent losses that are hard to justify;
- **Trading efficiency:** Ability of the asset manager to trade efficiently, access bank derivatives and the futures market on a cost-effective basis as well as

with a suitable margin requirement. This will ensure the scale of the investment strategy and the ability to meet the execution in a cost-effective manner;
- **Methodology review:** Ability to review and adjust the investment strategy for structural shifts in the market that could impede capturing risk premia efficiently over mid- to long-term. An example could be low and decreasing oil prices over time due to oversupply.

Investment risk measures may require more than just a simple standard deviation measure. Volatility is too simple a measure of risk for many ARP strategies, particularly for those with asymmetric return distributions. Complementary measures such as maximum drawdown and tail-risk assessment through various techniques may help. Of course, it is not the full picture as risk management is common sense, not just numbers.

Last but not least, it is important to keep the strategies close to the "real world" and understand the relevance of the drivers of their returns—the reward for risk, market structure and behaviour. Failure to take these into account can be illustrated by the famous collapse of Long-Term Capital Management (LTCM) in 1998. LTCM was a hedge fund led by the king of arbitrage in fixed income, John Meriwether, and two Nobel Prize winners, Robert Merton and Myron Scholes. The strategies employed by LTCM were sophisticated back then but were implemented in a way that failed to adapt to market dynamics and behaviour.

11.10 Concluding Remarks

Alternative risk premia are not new and with the digital age they are becoming increasingly systemised investment strategies. They have been known by academics and exploited by hedge funds and Commodity Trading Advisors for many years.

By construction, the sources of returns have low correlation with the traditional asset classes and can offer a dose of diversification in portfolio construction. However, with the increasing number of available strategies, investors should be mindful about allocating to different ARP strategies and their implementation in portfolios. In some cases, these are not a full replacement of alpha strategies. As an argument in favour of sticking to hedge funds and not switching to ARP strategies, in some cases the capacity of a strategy is low, and the fund manager has a specialised skill in extracting a risk premium in specific markets, sector or region in a non-systematic way.

Last but not least, there are no universal rules that govern the ARP world. The choice and design of the underlying strategies may provide different outcomes over time, as we established earlier for the factor in previous chapters. On this note, we complete our journey into the risk premia and factor-based investing, which are more likely to become a norm than just a new term in the coming years.

Bibliography

Alpert, M., & Raiffa, H. (1982). A progress report on the training of probability assessors. In D. Kahneman, P. Slavic, & A. Tversky (Eds.), *Judgment under uncertainty: Heuristics and biases* (pp. 294–305). Cambridge: Cambridge University Press.

Altman, E. I. (1968). Financial ratios, discriminant analysis and the prediction of corporate bankruptcy. *Journal of Finance, 23*(4), 189–209.

Ang, A. (2014). *Asset management a systematic approach to factor investing*. Oxford University Press, Chap. 14.

Antonacci, G. (2014). *Dual momentum investing: An innovative strategy for higher returns with lower risk*. McGraw-Hill.

Arnott, R., Beck, N., & Kalesnik, V. (2016). Timing 'smart beta' strategies? Of course! Buy low, Sell high! *Research Affiliates*.

Arnott, R. D., Hsu, J., Kalesnik, V., & Tindall, P. (2013). The surprising alpha from Malkiel's monkey and upside-down strategies. *The Journal of Portfolio Management, 39*(4), 91–105.

Arnott, R. D., Hsu, J. C., Li, F., & Shepherd, S. D. (2010). Valuation-indifferent weighting for bonds. *Journal of Portfolio Management, 36*(3), 117–130.

Asness, C. S., Frazzini, A., & Pedersen, L. H. (2017). *Quality minus junk*. AQR Capital Management, Working Paper, June 5.

Asness, C. S., Liew, J. M., & Ross, S. (1997). Parallels between the cross-sectional predictability of stock and country returns. *Journal of Portfolio Management, 23*, 79–87.

Asness, C. S., Moskowitz, T., & Pedersen, L. H. (2013). Value and momentum everywhere. *Journal of Finance, 68*(3), 929–985.

Baltas, A.-N., & Kosowski, R. (2013). *Momentum strategies in futures markets and trend following funds*. Research Collection BNP Paribas Hedge Fund Centre.

Banz, R. W. (1981). The relationship between return and market value of common stocks. *Journal of Financial Economics, 9*(1), 3–18.

Basu, D., & Miffre, J. (2013). Capturing the risk premium of commodity futures: The role of hedging pressure. *Journal of Banking & Finance, 37*(7), 2652–2664.

Basu, S. (1977). Investment performance of common stocks in relation to their price-earnings ratios: A test of the efficient market hypothesis. *Journal of Finance, 32*(3), 663–682.

Beck, N., & Kalesnik, V. (2014). Busting the myth about size. *Research Affiliates*, December.

Bender, J., & Samanta, R. (2017). Quality assurance: Demystifying the quality factor in equities and bonds. *The Journal of Portfolio Management, 43*(5), 88–98.

Bender, J., & Wang, T. (2016). Can the whole be more than the sum of the parts? Bottom-up versus top-down multifactor portfolio construction. *The Journal of Portfolio, Management, 42*(5), 39–50.

Brandes, C. H. (2004). *Value investing today* (3rd ed.). McGraw-Hill.

Brennan, M. J. (1993). *Agency and asset pricing*. Working Paper, UCLA: Finance. Retrieved from https://escholarship.org/uc/item/53k014sd

Brooke, P. G., Docherty, P., Psaros, J., & Seamer, M. (2018). Internal governance does matter to equity returns but much more so during 'flights to quality. *Journal of Applied Corporate Finance, 30*(1), 39–52.

Carvalho, R. L., Dugnolle, P., Xiao, L., & Moulin, P. (2014). Low-risk anomalies in global fixed income: Evidence from major broad markets. *The Journal of Fixed Income, 23*(4), 51–70.

Chow, T. C., Kose, E., & Li, F. (2016). The impact of constraints on minimum-variance portfolios. *Financial Analysts Journal, 72*(2).

Cooper, M. J., Gulen, H., & Schill, M. J. (2008). Asset growth and the cross-section of stock returns. *Journal of Finance, 63*(4), 1609–1651.

Correia, M., Richardson, S., & Tuna, I. (2012). Value investing in credit markets. *Review of Accounting Studies, 17*(3), 572–609.

Cowles, A., 3rd., & Jones, H. E. (1937). Some a posteriori probabilities in stock market action. *Econometrica, 5*, 289–294.

De Bondt, W. F. M., & Thaler, R. H. (1987). Further evidence on investor overreaction and stock market seasonality. *Journal of Finance, 42*(3), 557–581.

Fama, E., & French, K. (1992). The cross-section of expected stock returns. *Journal of Finance, 47*(2), 427–465.

Fama, E., & French, K. (1998). Value versus growth: The international evidence. *Journal of Finance, 53*(6), 1975–1999.

Fama, E., & French, K. (2014). A five-factor asset pricing model. *Journal of Financial Economics, 116*(1), 1–22.

Fischhoff, B., Slovic, P., & Lichtenstein, S. (1977). Knowing with certainty: The appropriateness of extreme confidence. *Journal of Experimental Psychology: Human Perception and Performance, 3*(4), 552–564.

Fisher, L. (2006). Yield elasticity: A new, objective measure of interest-rate risk. *Journal of Applied Finance, 16*, 161–173.

Foye, J., & Mramor, D. (2016). *A new perspective on the international evidence concerning the book-price effect*. Working Paper, University of Ljubljana.

Frazzini, A., Kabiller, D., & Pedersen, L. H. (2018). Buffett's alpha. *Financial Analysts Journal, 74*(4), 35–55.

Frazzini, A., & Pedersen, L. H. (2014). Betting against Beta. *Journal of Financial Economics, 111*(1), 1–25.

Frehen, R., Goetzmann, W. N., & Rouwenhorst, G. K. (2013). New evidence on the first financial bubble. *Journal of Financial Economics, 108*(3), 585–607.

Gartley, H. M. (1935). *Profits in the stock market*. Lambert Gann Publishing Company.

Geman, H., & Nguyen, V. N. (2005). Soybean inventory and forward curve dynamics. *Management Science, 51*(7), 1076–1091.

George, T. J., & Hwang, C.-Y. (2010). A resolution of the distress risk and leverage puzzles in the cross section of stock returns. *Journal of Financial Economics, 96*, 56–79.

Gompers, P., Ishii, J., & Metrick, A. (2003). Corporate governance and equity prices. *Quarterly Journal of Economics., 118*(1), 107–156.

Graham, B. (1949). *The intelligent investor*. Harper & Brothers, 1973.

Graham, B., & Dodd, D. (1934). *Security analysis*. McGraw-Hill.

Greenblatt, J. (2010). *Little book that beats the market*. John Wiley & Sons.

Hafzalla, N., Lundholm, R., & Van Winkle, E. (2011). Percent accruals. *The Accounting Review, 86*(1), 209–236.

Hamdan, R., Pavlowsky, F., Roncalli, T., & Zheng, B. (2016). *A primer on alternative risk premia*. SSRN Working Paper.

Harvey, C. R., Liu, Y., & Zhu, H. (2015). ... and the cross-section of expected returns. *Review of Financial Studies, 29*(1), 5–68.

Hasanhodzic, J., & Lo, A. W. (2007). Can hedge-fund returns be replicated?: The linear case. *Journal of Investment Management, 5*(2), 5–45.

Haugen, R. A., & Heins, J. A. (1972). *On the evidence supporting the existence of risk premiums in the capital market*. Working Paper, unpublished. Available at SSRN.

Hong, H., & Stein, J. C. (1999). A unified theory of underreaction, momentum trading and overreaction in asset markets. *Journal of Finance, 54*(6), 2143–2184.

Houweling, P., & Zundert, J. (2017). Factor investing in the corporate bond market. *Financial Analysts Journal, 73*(2), 100–115.

Hsu, J., Kalesnik, V., & Kose, E. (2019). *What is quality? Forthcoming in Financial Analysts Journal*. SSNR Working Paper.

Huang, D., Jiang, F., Tu, J., & Zhou, G. (2015). Investor sentiment aligned: A powerful predictor of stock returns. *Review of Financial Studies, 28*(3), 791–837.

Jacobs, B. I., & Levy, K. N. (1988). Calendar anomalies: Abnormal returns at calendar turning points. *Financial Analysts Journal, 44*(6), 28–39.

Jegadeesh, N., & Titman, S. (1993). Returns to buying winners and selling losers: Implications for stock market efficiency. *Journal of Finance, 48*(1), 65–91.

Jostova, G., Nikolova, S., Philipov, A., & Stahel, C. W. (2013). Momentum in corporate bond returns. *Review of Financial Studies, 26*(7), 1649–1693.

Kahneman, D., & Tversky, A. (1972). Subjective probability: A judgment of representativeness. *Cognitive Psychology., 3*(3), 430–454.

Kahneman, D., & Tversky, A. (1974). Judgment under uncertainty: Heuristics and biases. *Science, 185*(4157), 1124–1131.

Kahneman, D., & Tversky, A. (1979). The prospect theory: An analysis of decision under risk. *Econometrica, 47*(2), 263–291.

Kalesnik, V., & Kose, E. (2014). The moneyball of quality investing. *Research Affiliates*.

Kalesnik, V., & Linnainmaa, J. (2018). Ignored risks of factor investing. *Research Affiliates*, White Paper.

Karceski, J. (2002). Returns-chasing behavior, mutual funds, and beta's death. *Journal of Financial and Quantitative, Analysis, 37*(4), 559–594.

Keynes, J. M. (1930). *A treatise on money*. Macmillan.

King, D., & Zaher, F. (2017). *Can including fallen angels enhance returns?* Market Insight, Legal & General Investment Management.

Koijen, R. S. J., Moskowitz, T. J., Pedersen, L. H., & Vrugt, E. B. (2016). *Carry*. Chicago Booth Research Paper No. 15–20.

Li, Z., Zhang, J., & Crossen, C. (2012). A model-based approach to constructing corporate bond portfolios. *The Journal of Fixed Income, 22*(2), 57–71.

Lin, H., Wang, J., & Wu, C. (2011). Liquidity risk and expected corporate bond returns. *Journal of Financial Economics, 99*(3), 628–650.

Maeso, J.-M., & Martellini, L. (2017). Factor investing and risk allocation: From traditional to alternative risk premia harvesting. *Journal of Alternative Investing, 20*(1), 27–42.

Malmendier, U., & Tate, G. (2008). Who makes acquisitions? CEO overconfidence and the market's reaction. *Journal of Financial Economics, 89*(1), 20–43.

Martellini, L., & Milhau, V. (2015). *Factor investing: A welfare improving new investment paradigm or yet another marketing Fad?* EDHEC Working Paper.

McLean, D., & Pontiff, J. (2014). Does academic research destroy stock return predictability? *Journal of Finance, 71*(1), 5–32.

Miller, E. M. (1977). Risk, uncertainty, and divergence of opinion. *Journal of Finance, 32*(4), 1151–1168.

Nickerson, R. (1998). Confirmation bias: A ubiquitous phenomenon in many guises. *Review of General Psychology, 2*, 175–220.

Novy-Marx, R. (2013). The other side of value: The gross profitability premium. *Journal of Financial Economics, 108*(1), 1–28.

Oberoi, R., Rao, A., Mrig, L., & Subramanian, A. (2016). *One size does not fit all: Understanding factor investing*. MSCI Research Insight.

Ohlson, J. A. (1980). Financial ratios and the probabilistic prediction of bankruptcy. *Journal of Accounting Research, 18*(1), 109–131.

Oppenheimer, H. R. (1984). A test of ben Graham's stock selection criteria. *Financial Analysts Journal, 40*(5), 68–74.

Papaioannou, M. G., Park, J., Pihlman, J., & Hoorn, H. D. (2013). *Procyclical behavior of institutional investors during the recent financial crisis: Causes, impacts, and challenges*. IMF Working Paper (WP/13/193).

Penman, S., Richardson, S., & Tuna, I. (2007). The book-to-price effect in stock returns: Accounting for leverage. *Journal of Accounting Research, 45*, 427–467.

Pindyk, R. S. (2001). The dynamics of commodity spot and futures markets: A primer. *The Energy Journal, 22*(3), 1–29.

Piotroski, J. (2000). Value investing: The use of historical financial statement information to separate winners from losers. *Journal of Accounting Research, 38*, 1–41.

Piotroski, J. D., & So, E. C. (2012). Identifying expectation errors in value/glamour strategies: A fundamental analysis approach. *Review of Financial Studies, 25*(9), 2841–2875.

Pouget, S., Sauvagnat, J., & Villeneuve, S. (2017). A mind is a terrible thing to change: Confirmation bias in financial markets. *Review of Financial Studies, 30*(6), 2066–2109.

Ritter, J. R. (1988). The buying and selling behavior of individual investors at the turn of the year. *Journal of Finance, 43*(3), 701–717.

Roll, R. (1992). A mean/variance analysis of tracking error. *The Journal of Portfolio Management, 18*(4), 13–22.

Rosenberg, B., Reid, K., & Lanstein, R. (1985). Persuasive evidence of market inefficiency. *Journal of Portfolio Management, 11*, 9–16.

Ross, S. (1976). The arbitrage theory of capital asset pricing. *Journal of Economic Theory, 13*(3), 341–360.

Rouwenhorst, K. G. (1998). International momentum strategies. *Journal of Finance, 53*(1), 267–284.

Rouwenhorst, K. G. (1999). Local returns factors and turnover in emerging stock markets. *Journal of Finance, 54*(4), 1439–1464.

Rowley, J., Kahler, J. R., & Schlanger, T. (2016). *Impact assessment: Explaining the differences in funds', securities lending returns*. Valley Forge, PA: The Vanguard Group.

Senchack, A. J., & Martin, J. D. (1987). The relative performance of the PSR and PER strategies. *Financial Analysts Journal, 43*, 46–56.

Sharpe, W. F. (1992). Asset allocation: Management style and performance measurement. *The Journal of Portfolio Management, 18*(2), 7–19.

Siegel, J. (2002). *Stocks for the long run*. McGraw-Hill.

Sloan, R. G. (1996). Do stock prices fully reflect information in accruals and cash flows about future earnings? *The Accounting Review, 71*(3), 289–315.

Wei Ge. (2018). The Curious Case of the Mid-Cap Premium. *The Journal of Index Investing, 8*(4), 22–30.

Index[1]

A

Absolute momentum, 121
Accounting-based approach, 192, 195
Accruals/accrual screen, 40, 80, 87–89, 94, 96, 98
Active investment/active manager, 5, 9, 18, 19, 41, 42, 98, 115, 137–139, 144, 147, 173, 180, 181, 215
Alpha, 16, 41, 100, 144n3, 147, 208, 210, 232, 233
Alternative beta, 1, 205, 207
Alternatively-weighted/alternatively-weighting, 15, 18, 34, 36, 67, 175, 182, 185, 203
Alternative risk premia (ARP), 6, 22, 171, 179, 205–234
Altman/Altman Z-score, 86, 192, 193
Anchoring bias, 145, 146
AQR Capital Management, 92, 140
ARP, *see* Alternative risk premia
Asset allocation, 26, 43, 101, 114–115, 152, 165, 178, 179, 209, 210, 229, 230

Asset and liability management, 5, 18, 52, 109, 110, 209, 210, 231
Asset approach, 56
Asset pricing theory, 135–136
Assets under management (AUM), 3, 10, 13–15, 21, 22, 42, 78
AUM, *see* Assets under management
Availability bias, 94

B

Backtests, 4, 20, 21, 45, 68, 155, 158, 169
Backwardation, 216–218, 226
Bank of America-Merrill Lynch, 25
Bankruptcy/bankruptcies, 86, 97, 148, 193
Behavioural
 biases, 70, 78, 107, 120, 127, 142, 205, 206
 drivers, 4, 70–71, 94, 107–109, 127–130, 141, 142, 145–146, 199

---

[1] Note: Page numbers followed by 'n' refer to notes.

© The Author(s) 2019
F. Zaher, *Index Fund Management*, https://doi.org/10.1007/978-3-030-19400-0

241

Benchmark/benchmarking, 10, 13, 16, 19, 28, 34, 37, 38, 43, 65, 70, 71, 77, 81, 92, 101, 109, 110, 131, 137, 146, 173–175, 182, 184, 191, 193, 194, 197, 203, 208, 232
Beta, 1, 9, 14, 16, 19, 20, 67, 100, 102–104, 107, 110, 130, 131, 141, 153, 154, 158, 193, 205, 207, 210, 212
Bogle, John, 12
Bond carry premium, 219–220
Bond index/bond indices, *see* Fixed income indices
Bond market, 23, 25, 42, 174, 176–179, 188–191, 199, 201, 203, 220, 221
Book-to-market, *see* Price-to-book
Bottom-up approach, 155, 157–159
Buffett, Warren, 49, 55, 58, 72, 95, 136
Business cycle, 77, 163, 164, 176, 177, 224
Buybacks, 37, 80, 93

C

Capacity, 1, 21, 23, 42–43, 65, 146, 147, 182, 216, 233
CAPE, *see* Cyclically adjusted price-earnings
Capital Asset Pricing Model (CAPM), 99
Capital structure, 81, 90, 91, 174, 192
CAPM, *see* Capital Asset Pricing Model
Carry premia/carry trade/carry trades, 207, 212–222, 229
Cash flow, 14, 38, 39, 57, 81, 82, 87, 88, 91, 93, 94, 98, 106, 175, 193
Cash management, 39, 40
CDS, *see* Credit Default Swap
CDX, 221
Central banks, 5, 29, 128, 162, 178, 205
Commodities value premium, 224–226
Commodity carry premium, 216–219

Commodity indices, 24, 26, 27, 32
Commodity Trading Advisor (CTA), 124, 207, 210, 227, 228, 231, 233
Conduct risk, 39
Confirmation bias, 127, 129–130
Contango, 217, 218, 226
Contrarian, 50, 51, 162, 164
Convenience yield, 218, 226
Corporate actions, 36–39, 146
Corporate governance, 39, 41, 77, 78, 80, 88–90
Cost approach, 56
Counterparty risk, 39
Covenants, 176
CRB Index, *see* Thomson Reuters
Credit cycle, 175–178
Credit Default Swap (CDS), 187, 221, 228
Credit risk, 86, 175, 178, 181, 187, 191, 192, 196, 197, 201, 203, 206
Crisis/crises, 88, 95, 99, 111, 113, 128, 155, 182, 185, 205, 208, 215
Cross-sectional momentum, 121–123, 130, 132, 228
Crowding risk, 23, 40–42
CTA, *see* Commodity Trade Advisor
Currency carry premium, 213–216
Currency value premium, 222–224
Cyclically adjusted price-earnings, 69

D

Data mine/data mining, 3, 45, 67, 146, 181, 212
Debt-to-equity ratio, 58, 91
Debt-weighted, 174, 175, 183, 184, 186, 187, 191, 193, 196, 212
Deutsche Bank, 27, 207, 226
Deutsche Bank Commodity Momentum, 228
Distance to default, 194–195

Diversification/diversify, 4, 16, 18, 19, 21, 33, 35, 41, 43, 67–69, 72, 87, 99, 132, 138, 147, 148, 152–156, 162, 164, 209, 219, 232, 233
Dividend, 14, 39, 40, 55, 58, 61, 64, 84, 92, 93, 106, 141, 174, 193, 221
Dot-com boom, 53, 54, 65, 78, 108, 111, 142, 215
Dow Jones Industrial Average, 12, 34, 37, 163
Downside volatility, 103, 105, 106
Drawdown, 21, 41, 79, 95n6, 100, 102, 132, 135, 139, 141, 148, 149, 152, 169, 194, 233
DTS, see Duration-Times-Spread
Dual-momentum, 125
Duration risk, 175, 189, 220
Duration-Times-Spread (DTS), 201
Duration-Times-Yield (DTY), 190, 201
Dynamic factor allocation, 162, 165

E

Earning-per-share, 59, 61n5
Economic growth, 93, 140, 151, 153, 184, 185, 188, 226
Economic recession, 67, 73
Economic value, see Intrinsic value
Efficient market, 9, 47, 48, 99, 117, 136, 191, 213
EM, see Emerging markets
Emerging markets (EM), 11, 33, 79, 100, 112, 135, 142, 178, 184, 185, 187, 188, 195, 201, 204, 214, 215, 219
Endowment funds, 128
Enron, 78
Enterprise Value-to-EBITDA ratio, 57
Enterprise Value-to-Sales ratio, 57
Environmental, Social and Governance (ESG), 15, 15n1, 34, 35

Equal Risk Contribution, 35
Equal weighting, 33–34, 67, 80, 85n2, 138, 189, 215, 229
Equitisation, 40
Equity factor investing
 high-quality, 77–98
 low risk, 99–115
 momentum, 117–133
 size, 135–149
 value, 47–75
Equity issuance screen, 80
Equity multi-factor investing, 151–169
ESG, see Environmental, Social and Governance
ETF/ETFs, see Exchange Traded Fund
Euro debt crisis, 99, 114, 164, 174, 181, 186
Exchange Traded Fund (ETFs), 3, 7, 13–15, 36, 40, 48, 49, 78, 99, 101, 105, 115, 120, 152, 209, 231

F

Factor attribution, 166
Factor cycles/factor dynamics, 162–164
Factor premium, 16, 22, 43, 48, 70–72, 78, 98, 99, 101, 107–110, 113, 127, 137, 139, 149, 161, 167, 178, 191, 218
Factor sensitivities, 162–164
Factor timing/factor allocation, 152, 153, 162, 164, 165
Factor zoo, 20
Fair value spread (FVS), 196, 197, 202
Fallen angel, 197–199
Fama, E., 10, 48, 49, 53, 60–62, 83, 117, 135, 138, 151, 180, 191
Familiarity bias, 145
Fiscal policy, 185
Fixed income benchmarks, 173
Fixed income indices, 13, 32, 36
Fixed income style investing, 180

Free-float, 28, 30, 33, 137
French, K., 48, 53, 60–62, 83, 138, 139, 151, 167n1, 180, 191, 213
FTSE, 40, 93, 106, 137, 138, 146, 160, 166
FTSE 100, 23, 37
FTSE-Russell, 14, 15, 126, 143
Fundamental investing/fundamental weighting, 32, 47

G
GDP growth, 20, 153, 182, 187
Generally Accepted Accounting Principles (GAAP), 98
Global financial crisis, 1, 3, 10, 64, 70, 78, 95n6, 125, 162, 164, 178, 209, 215
Global Quality Income Index, 92
Goldman Sachs, 23, 26, 27, 32
Government bond indices, 29
Government bond style factors, 181–191
Graham, Benjamin, 9, 48, 49, 54, 56–60, 63, 64n7, 78, 90, 92, 98
Greenblatt, J., 92, 136
Gross margin, 91
Gross profit, 32, 82, 83, 98
Growth investing/growth stocks, 18, 34, 49, 51–54, 71, 72, 92, 121, 163, 222

H
Hedge fund/hedge funds, 41, 51, 205, 207, 208, 215, 231–233
Herding, 127–129
High beta, 100, 102, 107, 110, 130, 131, 153, 212
High yield (HY), 178, 192–194, 196, 197, 199–201, 204, 206, 221, 229
Holding period, 50, 79, 80, 122
HY, *see* High yield

I
Idiosyncratic risk, 72, 73
IG, *see* Investment Grade
Illiquidity risk, 141
Implementation, 5, 10, 12, 13, 38, 39, 41, 43, 104, 110, 132, 147, 149, 155, 179, 181, 188, 202, 206–209, 211, 221, 229, 232, 233
Income approach, 55, 56
Income statement, 81, 83
Index architecture/index construction, 5, 7, 22–26, 28, 30, 35, 43, 86, 110, 148
Index fund management, 3, 7, 37, 43
Index replication, 4, 43
Initial Price Offering (IPO)/public equity offerings, 28, 84
Institutional Shareholder Services, 89
Interest coverage ratio, 86
International Financial Reporting Standards (IFRS), 98
International Monetary Fund, 128
Intrinsic value, 47, 49, 54–57, 59, 74
Investment Grade (IG), 24–26, 32, 178, 191–193, 196–201, 204, 206, 221, 229
Investment horizon, 69, 71, 79, 101, 122, 206
Investment screen, 80, 83–85
Investment trust, 12, 14
IPO, *see* Initial Price Offering/public equity offerings
iTraxx, 221

J
January effect, 141–144

L
Large-cap, 135–147, 149
Lehman Brothers, 125

Index

Leverage/leverage screen, 62, 65, 80, 83, 85–87, 91–93, 110, 168, 194, 200, 205, 206, 211, 216, 222, 232
Life insurers, 128
Liquidity, 6, 11, 21, 27, 29, 30, 33, 35, 36, 39, 42, 43, 90, 128, 142, 147, 148, 179, 180, 191, 202, 203, 221
Long-Term Capital Management (LTCM), 215, 233
Long-term Debt-to-Assets ratio, 91
Lookback period, 122–125, 131, 132, 228
Lottery demand theory, 107
Low asset growth, 78, 80, 85, 93, 96
Low beta, 20, 100, 102, 110, 130, 131, 154
Low investment, *see* Low asset growth
Low risk factor for equities, *see* Equity factor investing
Low volatility factor, 99–102, 105–107, 110–115, 178, 190–191, 201
Low volatility factor for corporate bonds, 201
Low volatility factor for government bonds, 190–191

M

M&A, *see* Mergers and acquisitions
Macro managers, 210, 213
Macroeconomic risk, 141
Market approach, 56
Market-based approach, 192, 194–196
Market capitalisation, 11, 12, 16, 18–20, 27, 28, 32, 33, 36, 37, 41–43, 48, 49, 54, 57, 57n1, 60–65, 67, 69, 72, 79, 80, 84, 85, 89, 93n5, 95, 95n6, 96, 99–103, 105, 106, 111–113, 120, 124, 130, 131, 136–140, 144–147, 151, 154, 159, 163, 200, 212, 222, 229
Market cycle/market cycles, 24, 73, 115, 153, 162–164, 230
Market neutral, 11, 205n2, 219, 220, 222, 226, 228, 229, 232
Market risk, 10, 16, 20, 78, 141, 176, 197, 205, 209, 226, 228
Market structure/market structures, 4, 71–72, 74, 94, 109–110, 130–131, 133, 142, 175, 176, 191, 199, 205, 232, 233
Market timing, 166, 179, 210, 212
Market volatility, 51, 95, 128, 148, 164, 180, 193, 201, 208, 222
Markowitz, Harry, 16, 35
Maximum Sharpe ratio, 35
Mean-reversion, 50, 69, 121, 222–226
Mega-cap, 137, 145
Mergers and acquisitions (M&A), 37, 94
Micro-cap, 137, 140, 145, 147
Mid-cap, 135, 137–143, 145, 147–149
Minimum variance/minimum volatility, 100, 104, 106
Modern finance theory, *see* Modern Portfolio Theory
Modern Portfolio Theory, 2, 16, 78
Modularity, 27–28
Momentum factor for corporate bonds, 199–200
Momentum factor for equities, *see* Equity factor investing
Momentum factor for government bonds, 189
Moody's, 148, 185, 194, 196, 197n2
Morgan Stanley, 92, 207
Morningstar, 3, 14, 15
MSCI, 41, 67, 79, 83, 92, 94, 105, 106, 125, 126, 137, 138, 140, 147, 160
Multi-asset, 125, 171, 205–234
Multi-factor, 115, 139, 151, 152, 154–158, 160, 162, 164–169, 173, 202, 204, 229
Multi-factor approach, 78, 151, 152, 159
Municipal bonds, 178

Mutual fund/mutual funds, 7, 14, 41, 59, 99, 101, 105, 107, 117, 128, 133, 167n1, 207

N

Nano-cap, 137, 145
NBER, 140, 177
Net income (NI), 57n1, 82, 90, 91
New debt offering, 38
Nikkei 225, 34
Nominal GDP-weighted index, 183
Norwegian Government Pension Fund (NGPF), 10, 11

O

Off the run, 179, 180
On the run, 180
Operating cash flow (OCF), 57, 82, 91, 98
Operating efficiency, 90, 91
Operating Profit-to-Book Value (OP/BV), 83, 84
Optimisation, 34–35, 103, 104, 106, 126, 158, 193, 229
Over the counter (OTC), 36, 203
Overconfidence/overconfidence bias, 94, 101, 107, 108, 130
Overcrowding, 1, 21, 40

P

P/B, *see* Price-to-book
P/E, *see* Price-to-Earning/Price-to-Earning ratio
Pension funds, 12, 42, 128, 207
Piotroski, J. D., 90, 92
Portfolio fit, 28, 29, 210
Pre-trade analysis, 39
Price-to-book (P/B), 48, 54, 60–62, 60n4, 67–69, 74, 79, 92, 168, 188, 222

Price-to-Book Value ratio, 57, 60
Price-to-Cash Flow ratio, 57
Price-to-earning/Price-to-Earning ratio (P/E), 48, 57–59, 62–64, 73, 79, 188, 222
Price-to-Sales/Price-to-Sales ratio (P/S), 57, 64–65
Price weighting, 33, 34
Private placement, 28
Profitability
    premium, 81–82
    screen, 80–84, 93
P/S, *see* Price-to-Sales/Price-to-Sales ratio (P/S)
Public debt offerings, 84
Purchasing power parity (PPP), 222, 223, 224n7

Q

Quality factor for corporate bonds, 192–195
Quality factor for equities, *see* Equity factor investing
Quality factor for government bonds, 185–187

R

Rank approach/rank-based, 103, 104, 125
Rebalance/rebalancing, 21, 26, 32, 36, 38, 39, 42, 43, 79, 85n2, 106, 122–126, 131, 132, 139, 143, 146, 147, 155, 215, 228
Recency bias, 70
Reconstitution, 36
Relative strength, 119
Replication, 37–40, 43
Representativeness, 26–27, 70, 108, 127, 129–130
Representativeness bias, 70, 107, 130

Index

Research Affiliates (RAFI), 14, 67, 95, 106, 160, 164, 187, 193, 194
Retail investor, 72, 99, 101, 132
Return on assets (ROA), 82, 91, 98
Return-on-Invested-Capital (ROIC), 82, 92
Risk-adjusted return/risk-adjusted returns, 67, 70, 99, 110, 135, 173, 218
Risk-based explanations, 93, 94, 141–142
Risk budget, 101, 229, 230
Risk factors, 1, 18, 30, 62, 99, 100, 102–106, 126, 190, 206, 207, 214, 218, 229
Risk premium/risk premia, 6, 16, 21, 22, 27, 33, 97, 130, 171, 175, 176, 179, 191, 205–234
Risk-weighting, 229
ROIC, *see* Return-on-Invested-Capital
Roll yield, 216–218
Rules-based, 1, 5, 18, 21, 23, 24, 56, 65, 69, 70, 74, 80, 86, 102, 119, 121–125, 143, 185, 197, 207, 211, 215, 217, 220, 222, 226–229, 232
Russell, 67, 137, 138, 140, 144

S

S&P, 90, 126, 137, 185
S&P 500, 13, 16, 23, 24, 37, 40, 58–60, 105, 111
Scientific beta, 67, 158, 160
Seasonal effect, 131
Securities lending, 39–40
Semi-variance, 105, 106
Shiller, Robert, 69, 213
Size factor for equities, *see* Equity factor investing
Size factor for government bonds, 182–185
Size factor in corporate bonds, 200–201
Size factor/size premium, 42, 45, 78, 135–149, 182, 184, 200, 201
Small-cap, 11, 42, 135–149
Solactive, 67, 106, 112, 115, 197n2
South Sea Company, 118, 119
Sovereign wealth funds, 128, 207
Stock-picking, 37, 109
Storage costs, 218
Style analysis, 165–168, 167n1
Systematic risk, 141, 205
System Open Market Account Holdings, 29

T

Term premium/term spread premium, 179, 206
Thomson Reuters, 23
Tilt approach/tilting/titling approach, 15, 34–35, 104, 186, 193, 226
Time-series momentum, 121, 123–125, 132, 227, 228
Top-down approach, 155–156, 158, 159
Tracking error, 38, 39, 43, 101, 106, 110, 144, 159, 187, 191, 193
Tradability, 36
Trading volume, 142
Transaction costs, 11, 38, 42, 47, 105, 112, 124, 132, 202
Transparency/transparent, 3, 12, 19, 23–25, 35, 37, 88, 103, 104, 144–145, 148, 155, 158, 160, 168, 181, 203, 206, 207, 209–212, 231, 232
Trend-following, 121, 207, 210, 212, 227–229
Turnover, 32, 33, 36, 38, 61n5, 69, 79, 91, 105, 106, 112, 123, 124, 126, 132, 139, 146, 147, 152, 155, 158, 162, 165, 189, 199

U
Uncovered interest rate parity, 214

V
Value ARP strategies, 222–227
Value factor for corporate bonds, 196–199
Value factor for government bonds, 188–189
Value factor investing for equities, *see* Equity factor investing
Value trap, 72–74, 197
Volatility index, 99, 105, 106, 111–113

W
Weighting methods, 31, 32
Worldcom, 78, 196

9783030193997

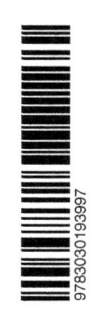